HIGHER AND HIGHER:
MAKING JEWISH PRAYER PART OF US

Steven M. Brown

Edited by Stephen Garfinkel

United Synagogue of Conservative Judaism
Department of Youth Activities

UNITED SYNAGOGUE OF CONSERVATIVE JUDAISM

DEPARTMENT OF YOUTH ACTIVITIES

Jules A. Gutin DIRECTOR
Karen L. Stein ASSISTANT DIRECTOR
Aviva Tilles PROJECTS COORDINATOR
Rena Aplebaum PROGRAM COORDINATOR
Adam Kofinas MEETINGS MANAGER
Matthew Halpern COMMUNICATIONS COORDINATOR
Itzik Yanai CENTRAL SHALIACH
David Keren DIRECTOR, ISRAEL PROGRAMS
Yitzchak Jacobsen DIRECTOR, ISRAEL OFFICE
Yossi Garr DIRECTOR, NATIV

INTERNATIONAL YOUTH COMMISSION

Bob Sunshine, CHAIR

UNITED SYNAGOGUE OF CONSERVATIVE JUDAISM

Dr. Ray Goldstein, INTERNATIONAL PRESIDENT
Rabbi Jerome M. Epstein, EXECUTIVE VICE-PRESIDENT
Dr. Marilyn Lishnoff Wind, VICE PRESIDENT FOR YOUTH SERVICES AND EDUCATION

A publication of the International Youth Commission
United Synagogue of Conservative Judaism
155 Fifth Avenue, New York, New York 10010
http://www.uscj.org/usy

8th Printing, 2007

Printed and bound in the United States of America
Cover and Book design by Hy Nitka
Illustrations by Hedy Klein

Library of Congress Catalog Card Number: 80-54158
Copyright 1980 United Synagogue Youth

Dedication

To SHELLY AND DORY,
the ongoing fulfillment
of my prayers

The author wishes to add special thanks to Cantor Charles Davidson; Rabbi Seymour Rosenbloom, for his excellent collection of source material; to Rabbi Stephen Garfinkel, whose sensitivity, warmth, and prodding made this all possible; and to my dear secretary, Mrs. Evelyn Swarttz, who typed so much from my dictaphone.

ACKNOWLEDGEMENTS

The editor expresses appreciation to the following publishers who have kindly granted permission to reprint selections under their copyrights:

BEHRMAN HOUSE, INC. PUBLISHERS, New York: *When a Jew Prays*, Seymour Rossel, 1973.

BOARD OF JEWISH EDUCATION, UNITED SYNAGOGUE OF AMERICA, Philadelphia: *Idea Cookbook*, Howard Wasserman, Ellen Z. Charry, Diane King, Jerome Ruderman, eds., 1976.

THE BURNING BUSH PRESS, New York: *Justice and Mercy*, Max Arzt, 1963. Reprinted by permission.

Excerpted with permission of Farrar, Straus & Giroux, Inc. from *Man is Not Alone* by Abraham Joshua Heschel, Copyright © 1951 by Abraham Joshua Heschel.

PHILIPP FELDHEIM, PUBLISHER, New York: *The World of Prayer*, Elie Munk, 1954.

HART PUBLISHING COMPANY, INC., New York:
Personalizing Education: Values Clarification and Beyond, Leland W. Howe and Mary M. Howe, 1975.
Values Clarification, Sidney B. Simon, Leland W. Howe, and Howard Kirschenbaum, 1975.

From *How Does a Poem Mean?* by John Ciardi. Copyright © 1959 by John Ciardi. Reprinted by permission of Houghton Mifflin Company.

THE JEWISH PUBLICATION SOCIETY OF AMERICA, Philadelphia:
Jewish Worship, Abraham Millgram, 1971.
Rembrandt, The Bible and The Jews, Franz Landsberger, 1946.

LEADERS TRAINING FELLOWSHIP OF THE JEWISH THEOLOGICAL SEMINARY OF AMERICA, New York: *Keva and Kavanah in Jewish Prayer*, n.d.

MELTON RESEARCH CENTER, New York: *The Teaching of the Traditional Liturgy*, Burt Jacobsen, 1971.

NATIONAL RAMAH COMMISSION OF THE JEWISH THEOLOGICAL SEMINARY OF AMERICA, New York: *T'fillah: Considerations for Dialogue with Ramah Counselors*, Seymour Rosenbloom, 1972.

Reprinted by permission of THE RABBINICAL ASSEMBLY and THE JEWISH THEOLOGICAL SEMINARY OF AMERICA, New York: *Conservative Judaism*, Vol. XXIII, No. 1 (Fall, 1968).

Reprinted by permission of THE RABBINICAL ASSEMBLY and THE UNITED SYNAGOGUE OF AMERICA, New York: *Sabbath and Festival Prayer Book*, 1946.

Reprinted by permission of Schocken Books Inc., from *Franz Rosenzweig: His Life and Thoughts*, presented by Nahum N. Glatzer. Copyright © 1953 by Schocken Books Inc.

CHARLES SCRIBNER'S SONS, PUBLISHERS, New York: *Man's Quest for God*, Abraham Joshua Heschel, 1954.

SHENGOLD PUBLISHERS, New York: *The Graphic History of the Jewish People*, Pinchas Wollman-Tsamir, 1963.

UNION OF AMERICAN HEBREW CONGREGATIONS, New York: *Bechol Levavcha: With All Your Heart*, Harvey J. Fields, 1977.

THOMAS YOSELOFF, INC., Cranbury, New Jersey: *The Service of the Heart*, Evelyn Garfiel, 1958.

Hebrew transliteration in this volume uses the following system:

ḥ ח (ḥet)
ch כ (chav)

However, transliterations appearing in quotations retain the spellings of the original source.

"He who repeats something in the name of him who said it brings deliverance to the world..." (Pirkay Avot 6:6)

Table of Contents

Editor's Preface

One volume cannot be sufficient to deal with all aspects of prayer. It is hoped, however, that this source book will provide a basis for future reading and the impetus for readers to desire further study. It is based on the premise that "a little done with intention and understanding is better than much done without intention" *(Tur Shulḥan Aruch 1).*

United Synagogue Youth is proud to have Dr. Steven Brown as author of this book, someone qualified to combine the best of formal and informal Jewish educational methods. The original manuscript has benefited from field testing and the reactions of individuals who have given a great deal of time and effort. We are extremely grateful to these readers for their guidance:

Rabbi Jerome M. Epstein
Rabbi Joel Epstein
Rabbi Paul Freedman
Barbara Friedman
Dr. Neil Gillman
Dr. Eli Grad
Jules Gutin
Rabbi Jules Harlow

Dr. Avraham Holtz
Rabbi Barry Dov Lerner
Rabbi Clifford Miller
Rabbi Yaakov Rosenberg
Eric Sherby
Ḥazzan David Tillman
Rabbi Benjamin Z. Kreitman

In addition, we thank Rabbi Joel Epstein, Dr. Joel Roth, and Yaffa Schlisserman for unlimited conceptual advice and technical assistance. We also wish to thank Lori Jacobs and Susan Michael for typing and retyping the manuscript from pages which were nearly impossible to decipher. I am also personally indebted to my family, Robin and Arielle, for working around my very disruptive schedule.

A few comments about using this publication are in order:

1. The source book cannot be understood without using a Siddur. Most of the prayer references and analyses will be clear only by examining the prayer texts being discussed.

2. Statements of practice or custom are generalizations. Often there are variations among synagogues or communities which must be determined, in each instance, by checking with the rabbi, the local religious authority. The book is not designed as a guide to practice, but rather as a framework to practice with understanding.

3. Hebrew transliterations are phonetic, although certain standard spellings have been retained for clarity or within quotations. Hebrew words are *italicized* the first time they appear, or as deemed necessary by context. Hebrew words and brief phrases, and quotations from the Siddur and *Mishnah Torah* have been vocalized.

Finally, a word about the title of our source book and the values it incorporates. *L'ayla L'ayla,* an Aramaic phrase, originates in the Targum (Deuteronomy 28:43), a translation of the Torah designed to facilitate understanding by as many people as possible. In the prayer book, the phrase appears in the Kaddish recited--in Ashkenazic communities--during the Ten Days of Repentance. Of interest is that it is based on the wording of the Kaddish recited daily, but modified for the special time of year. This is typical of Jewish prayer; basic structures used every day are modified for Shabbat, holidays, and special occasions. Thus, the outline of the service allows for familiarity and regularity without monotony.

The meaning of L'ayla L'ayla, "Higher and Higher," represents the approach we take -- a gradual, step-by-step increase in our understanding and commitment. We hope, therefore, that this book will enable you to participate in Jewish worship with increasing devotion, לְעֵלָּא לְעֵלָּא .

S.G.

SECTION I
WHAT IS JEWISH PRAYER?

CHAPTER I   WHY PEOPLE PRAY
Introduction

For the Jewish people praying is as normal as breathing. The heart and soul of our people are expressed in our worship as recorded in the *Siddur*, the "prayer book." The Hebrew word for prayer is usually תְּפִלָּה (*t'fillah*), and the activity of praying is לְהִתְפַּלֵּל (*l'hitpallel*), a verb which comes from the root פלל, meaning "to assess." In its reflexive form (l'hitpallel) means "to seek consideration, to pray, to plead, even to intercede."[1] For the Jew, prayer is a way of relating to ourselves, our fellows, and to God. Through prayer we consider who we are, and what we should become. We turn to prayer for personal comfort, strength, fellowship, self-expression, self-assessment, and identity.

Many years before any written Siddur, our tradition understood the basic human emotions involved in the desire to pray and relate to God. Even in the Bible, long before the familiar institutions of prayer developed as we now know them, we read of Ḥannah, who--praying that she might give birth to a child--declared,

וָאֶשְׁפֹּךְ אֶת־נַפְשִׁי לִפְנֵי ה'.

"I pour my soul to the Lord" (I Samuel 1:15).

Prayer is both a means of serving God and a way of relating to and understanding God. It stems from a need we all have to go beyond ourselves and become part of something greater, more infinite.

In the following pages we shall investigate a wide range of topics concerning the why's, how's and meanings of Jewish worship patterns. We'll look into the history, structure, poetry and purpose of our liturgy.* At the same time we will try to enable you, the reader, to develop your own personal understandings and responses to our prayer tradition. Becoming comfortable with the complexities of t'fillah is a long and involved process, not easily mastered in one convention, course, or summer encampment. It is a life-long process which is pursued in small steps. So don't be overwhelmed by the amount of material, but, rather, begin to consider what initial small steps you can take towards climbing *higher and higher* on the ladder of making Jewish prayer more a part of yourself.

The very act of studying prayer is a *mitzvah* ("commandment"); prayer study is in itself a form of worship. Therefore, throughout this source book we have included sections called עִיּוּנֵי תְּפִלָּה ("prayer analyses"), which are designed to help you better grasp the literal meanings, poetic implications, ethical consequences, and personal adaptability of the particular t'fillah being studied. The source book is organized topically rather than in the order of our worship services in order to give you an opportunity to confront a wide range of issues and problems that are fundamental to prayer. Accordingly, before we actually study individual prayer texts, their overall structures, and inter-relationships, we will first deal with such issues as why people pray and why they don't; the discipline of prayer; prayer as a process of self-analysis and ethical consciousness raising; the role of prayer in relating the individual to the community; prayer as a mechanism for highlighting our awareness of the wonder of life.

In Chapter 2 of this first section we shall concern ourselves with the languages of prayer: poetry, music, body language, God and faith talk. Only after dealing with these issues will we be prepared to begin a systematic structural analysis of the liturgy itself, in Sections II and III. **

We are aware, of course, that in North America today, language is not held in high esteem, words are cheap, and religious forms in general are not in vogue. Thus, for many people the whole subject of institutionalized worship presents tremendous problems and frustrations. Even if we have fairly positive experiences in a peer group context (such as in USY or Camp Ramah), when left to our own devices, or upon returning as individuals to our own synagogues, the questions of

---

*Liturgy means the collections of words, prayers, songs, music, gestures and organizational patterns which make up our prayer traditions.

**Whenever we study a prayer we shall look at its background (consisting of origin, history, specific customs, etc.); concepts (basic ideas, values, and philosophies extrapolated from the text); and "analyses," as explained above.

3

"why pray?" or "what does prayer do for me?" remain serious problems. This source book is an attempt to help you grow in your understanding of and commitment to the magnificent and special gift the Jewish people has bequeathed us in our Siddur and in our tradition of עֲבוֹדָה שֶׁבַּלֵב -- our service to God with our hearts, minds, and actions.

Why Pray?

The questions of why one should pray, or why one should pray regularly, or why one should pray Jewishly are the key questions underlying the writing of this volume. It is our hope that by the time you finish this course of study you will understand not only why Jews pray, but also why it is important for you personally to participate in this great Jewish institution which has held our people together for thousands of years. There are various reasons people pray, many of them personal, some of them communal. Many are represented in the list below. Check off in the "yes" or "no" column reasons which seem valid for you personally, or which you can see being applicable to your own situation at some time in your life.

REASONS FOR PRAYING

Yes	No	
———	———	1. *Need to express innermost feelings:* People need to show gratitude, humility, excitement, wonder, awe, amazement, appreciation, and thankfulness for being alive.
———	———	2. *Fulfillment of desires:* People have needs and desires and often turn to God (through prayer) to help them achieve those desires or help them in times of trouble or distress.
———	———	3. *Relationship with God:* Through prayer, people try to clarify and establish a personal, loving, and intimate relationship with the Power behind the universe. Prayer can enable an individual to feel a partnership with God in completing the work of creation.
———	———	4. *Fear:* People have basic fears, problems, and guilt feelings and turn to prayer to enunciate and clarify them.
———	———	5. *Identification:* Prayer enables the Jew to identify with past, present, and future members of the Jewish people, as well as with a particular community or peer group engaged in prayer activity and ritual.
———	———	6. *Ethical responsibility:* Prayer gives people the opportunity to evaluate themselves and their society by assessing the needs of others and evaluating their own values in the light of the values expressed in the prayers.
———	———	7. *Study:* The act of Torah study itself is considered a form of Jewish worship and is included within prescribed prayer rituals. It is vitally important in enriching one's intellectual abilities and adding to knowledge about living good lives.
———	———	8. *To shape experience:* The act of prayer can significantly change a given event. Saying a blessing at the appropriate time raises the experience to a higher and more spiritual level. Both the experience and the individual are enriched by a prayerful act.

_____ _____ 9. *Self-discipline:* Regulating one's life around prayerful activity makes one sensitive, on a daily basis, to the wonders, mysteries, and challenges of living.

_____ _____ 10. *Joy of language and words:* Many people enjoy the beauty and power of well-written poetry. Prayer is written, for the most part, in the language of poetry and many enjoy this type of emotional and intellectual experience.

_____ _____ 11. *Mitzvah:* People engage in traditional prayer activities because they feel commanded by God to do so.

Now that you have checked off the reasons for praying which seem appropriate to you, it is only fair to look at pressures and problems which prevent people from participating enthusiastically in a prayer experience. In the list below, indicate those issues which seem to be most bothersome to you personally.

REASONS FOR NOT PRAYING

Yes   No

_____ _____ 1. God really doesn't listen (or maybe His answers always are "No").

_____ _____ 2. I'm quite happy the way I am.

_____ _____ 3. It takes too much time.

_____ _____ 4. I don't understand the Hebrew language.

_____ _____ 5. I don't believe in God (or at least I'm not sure I do).

_____ _____ 6. It's boring.

_____ _____ 7. I'm angry with the way God has messed up the world.

_____ _____ 8. Why should He listen to me with everybody else to worry about?

_____ _____ 9. I don't like my synagogue (or its rabbi or cantor).

_____ _____ 10. I don't know enough about prayer to be comfortable.

_____ _____ 11. It's just not what I'm interested in.

_____ _____ 12. I'm afraid of what it might do to me (e.g., make me more religious, perhaps).

_____ _____ 13. None of my friends are interested in the synagogue or prayer.

_____ _____ 14. It's old fashioned.

_____ _____ 15. I like to be spontaneous, not told what to say.

————	————	16. I was turned off by Hebrew school.
————	————	17. The prayers don't seem to meet my needs.

Now, for each "yes" that you have checked off above, ask yourself the following questions:

1. Is this a real reason for not praying or a convenient excuse?

2. Do I really believe this is a problem, or am I just afraid that if I give prayer a real chance it might become important to me?

3. Do I believe this myself or is it what most of my friends seem to believe?

4. What could I do to change this particular negative feeling?

5. What would be the first steps I could take if I really wanted to change this particular negative reaction to prayer?

EXERCISE I

We have begun to discuss all kinds of reasons and purposes for praying. Below is an exercise which is designed to make you think about those issues in your life that could become part of your prayer experience. For each item, determine two values you hold and list the source of each value in your upbringing (e.g., school, parents, Judaism, friends, etc.).

Discuss with others in your group or answer the following questions in writing:

1. What is one thing you would change in the world? in your town? your school? your neighborhood?

2. What is one thing you hope your own children will not have to go through?

3. What is one thing about which you have changed your mind recently?

4. Who is one person you know whom you would like to be like?

5. How did you handle a recent disagreement?

6. What issue would you have Ralph Nader work on next? Why?

7. What is one issue on which you have not yet formed a definite opinion?

8. What is something in the news that really disturbs you lately?

9. What do you want to be doing in 20 years from now?

10. How much time do you spend worrying about warfare?

11. What one quality do you want in a friend?

12. What is something you really want to learn how to do before you die?

13. What do you feel most guilty about?

Based on Sidney B. Simon, Leland W. Howe and Howard Kirschenbaum, *Values Clarification* (New York: Hart Publishing Co., Inc., 1972), 131.

Now let us look at some of the various aspects of prayer which may make it more important to you.

1. Prayer As Self-Discipline

If you play a musical instrument or participate intensively in a sport, or dance, or engage in some other artistic pursuit you are aware of how many hours of practice, drudgery, tedium, exercising, workouts, or rough sketches are necessary before you can achieve any measure of expertise or even enjoyment. For a pianist to perform in Carnegie Hall and produce a truly aesthetic experience, he must have practiced for hours on end. For an athlete to achieve greatness in a sports event, he or she must have given hours and hours of some kind of boring and even upsetting practice, often foregoing many everyday pleasures. Anything which is worthwhile doing in life and which gives us a rewarding experience takes effort, time, patience, continuity and devotion. How often have we heard Jews come into the synagogue on Rosh Hashanah and Yom Kippur, or to a Bar or Bat Mitzvah service as guests of the family, and praise or criticize the rabbi or cantor depending on whether they were given a "religious experience"? Obtaining a religious experience must be worked on as hard as any of the sports or skills we try to master in the other areas of life. Prayer is as much an art as it is a skill. Prayer demands as much time and attention (and often drudgery and tedium) in order to achieve a moment of high religious inspiration as any other worthwhile endeavor. Too often we believe that every time we pray we must feel something important or be changed in some manner. Even if we are discouraged when we have a bad work out day in a sport, do we quit? Do we give up playing the piano if we didn't quite get the nuance of the piece we are striving to perfect? Obviously not! Yet, when it comes to the art of prayer, many people feel that each experience has to be a climactic one. Nothing can be further from the truth. As we will see in the section on "Keva-Kavanah" (fixed form -- intention, feeling), our Rabbis also understood that daily repetitive prayer helps prepare the way for possible peak experiences. There are very few religious peaks in our life; most of the time we're either in the valleys or on a plateau. To have any chance at all of achieving great spiritual experiences we must put in the time, effort, and devotion which will make those experiences possible. Each time we pray, we add to our own personal repertoire of experiences in prayer. Those of you who might have attended USY Israel Pilgrimage, USY on Wheels, or Camp Ramah, or have celebrated some important family event which included a religious service, realize that you build up a personal history of prayer. Then, suddenly, one day in your own synagogue when you close your eyes and remember where you prayed that same t'fillah previously you are transported into a beautiful and personalized religious experience. Disciplining oneself to pray regularly is the only way to achieve that magnificent experience of emotionally fulfilling prayer. Dr. Abraham Heschel related the following story about a small Jewish town off the beaten path to make a similar point:

> ...it had all the necessary municipal institutions: a bath-house, a cemetery, a hospital, and law court; as well as all sorts of craftsmen--tailors, shoemakers, carpenters, and masons. One trade, however, was lacking: there was no watchmaker. In the course of years many of the clocks became so annoyingly inaccurate that their owners just decided to let them run down, and ignore them altogether. There were others, however, who maintained that as long as the clocks ran, they should not be abandoned. So they wound their clocks day after day though they knew that they were not accurate. One day the news spread through the town that a watchmaker had arrived, and everyone rushed to him with their clocks. But the only ones he could repair were those that had been kept running--the abandoned clocks had grown too rusty![2]

And so it is with prayer, too.

The following exercises are designed to help you confront your own feelings and establish some goals in making Jewish prayer a more important and regular part of your life. For Jews, the holiest possession we have besides certain essential ritual objects (e.g., Torah, tefillin, mezuzah) is *time*. The way we use time can enrich and enoble our lives, or waste and diminish them. As Jews we sanctify time and make it special by setting aside occasions in time--daily prayer, Shabbat, holidays--as a means of highlighting the precious gift of life. Regular worship, on a routine basis helps sensitize us to our most important possession--our time on this earth. In the next few pages, at the beginning of your study of Jewish worship, you will look at some of these issues and set some personal prayer goals. We suggest that after you complete your work in this source book, you go back to this section to reexamine your goals and positions.

EXERCISE I
TEACH US TO NUMBER OUR DAYS

Psalm 90 says that we have approximately 70 years to live (and with extraordinary strength, 80 years). Draw a time line beginning with your birth and put in various important events in your life. Extend the line through your future, as far as you can. Along this line, list the years of events and activities which you think or hope will occur in your life, e.g., marriage, graduations, birth of children, becoming a grandparent, achievements in the business or professional world, contributions you might make to society. Take a look at your projected life time line and see how you are numbering your days.

Birth Date _____

EXERCISE 2

In numbering our days sometimes we look at the long distant future and don't pay particular attention to how we live each individual day. Write a short outline of a diary of two weeks in your life and the times you spend with your closest companion or friend. List all the occasions you have been together and what you have done. Use dates, times and a brief word or two to list the activity. Now after you have completed listing, imagine that your friend is no longer with you--that the person has either moved away or died. Think about the void that would be left in your life and add these thoughts to the way you are spending your time with people. Perhaps the importance of "numbering each of our days," making them worthwhile, will be reemphasized for you.

EXERCISE 3

We hope to help you begin the process of making t'fillah a regular part of your life. Since every activity has to start some place, it often becomes easier to begin something new by thinking about just which steps to take first. Indeed, it may be overwhelming to think of yourself as being someone who feels comfortable in the synagogue or handling the Siddur. Often, looking at the final product is so threatening that it inhibits the first steps. In the exercise below, list the first steps in each of the areas mentioned, along with the possible goal date of taking those steps to get you started on the road of regular, personal commitment to t'fillah. (While you should look over the exercise now to understand the approach being taken, you will better be able to complete it after studying the major sections of this sourcebook.)

	What I'd like to learn to do, or be able to do better in t'fillah	Beginning Date	First steps I will take in the process.
What times will I devote to t'fillah?			
Which t'fillot will I start with?			
Which t'fillot will I learn how to translate word for word?			
Which music will I learn first?			
How often will I wear tallit or t'fillin?			
When and how often will I pray in a minyan?			
Which prayers will I respond to in a creative way?			
Which times of day will I devote to prayer?			
Which prayers do I want to learn the history of?			
Which prayer rules do I want to learn first?			
How can I modify my schedule to make it more possible to begin to pray regularly?			
What should I read first to help me understand prayer better?			
Whom should I turn to for questions and advice?			
How do I prevent frustration and laziness?			
What ethical considerations will I deal with in prayer?			
What personal dreams will I consider in prayer?			

EXERCISE 4

Below appear two circles called "The Pie of Life." In the first circle divide up the pie representing the 24 hour day into the number of hours you spend on such things as sleep, school, a job, chores, socializing with friends, homework, being alone, being with family, eating, miscellaneous other pastimes, Jewish activities. Section your pie and list in each section the activity it represents. Having completed the previous exercises on trying to establish t'fillah as a regular part of your daily existence, section the pie of life which represents an ideal towards which you might strive, integrating t'fillah and other Jewish activities with your current daily routine. You might decide to shorten or expand various other activities in your life, shown by drawing a smaller or larger piece of the pie to represent them. Compare the two circles and see whether or not you have been influenced by the previous reading and exercises.

Based on Simon, *Values Clarification*, p. 229.

CURRENT DAY   IDEAL DAY

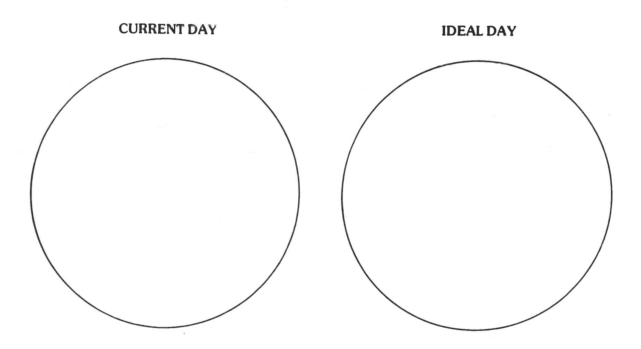

EXERCISE 5

Below are continua on certain issues dealing with personal prayer. Determine where you stand on each issue. Then, compare your place on each continuum with other students' views; reflect on your choice and choices of others.

1. How often do you feel you should spend time in prayer?

_____
never   three times a week   every day

2. Approximately how long a period should each of your prayer experiences last?
   (Consider for weekday and Shabbat.)

_____
30 seconds   20 minutes   1 hour

3. How much of a given service do you think you should recite?

_____
as little as I like   minimum legal   every prayer in that service

4. What percentage of the t'fillot should you recite in Hebrew?

_____
0%   50%   100%

5. How willing are you to discipline yourself to some regular daily prayer?

_____
unwilling   somewhat willing   extremely willing

6. Are you a person of habit or whim?

_____
whim: I do things   can get used to something   creature of habit;
when I feel like   if I make effort   easily get into routines

7. What percentage of your waking hours do you spend doing things you like to do?

_____
0%   50%   100%

8. What percentage of your waking hours to you spend doing things you must do?

_____
0%   50%   100%

9. How much more effort are you willing to expend to make (daily/ Shabbat) prayer more a part
   of your life?

_____
very little effort   moderate amount   a great deal of effort

2. Prayer as Self-Analysis and Ethical Consciousness Raising

One of the basic goals of Jewish worship is to force us on a regular, daily basis to confront ourselves honestly: asking ourselves who we are, what's important to us, how we relate to others, and what are our goals in life. In fact, within our tradition there is an opinion that one of the highest forms of prayer is silence--giving us the opportunity to contemplate the answers to the above questions. Daily prayer, which reflects and embodies the values and insights of our tradition, is the mechanism by which this self-confrontation is helped to take place.

Despite our possible problems of faith in God, the questions of personal commitment to various religious behaviors, it is important to understand how Jewish prayer provides an opportunity for looking at the kind of human beings we are and what, in the light of our tradition, we ought to become. One of the tasks of prayer, then, is to push us from where we are (emotionally, intellectually, interpersonally) to where we ought to be. But this self-analytical process is more than "getting in touch with yourself" and much more than a philosophy of "am I doing my own thing?" The self-analysis involved in prayer is more than self-expression or catharsis; it is much more complex and important. It is a process of comparing ourselves to the values, standards, and demands laid down by 3,000 years of our tradition. As someone often centered on the present, you may feel that a tradition has no claim on your own ideals and beliefs. But, just by reading this book you have already made somewhat of a choice to investigate Jewish tradition as a possible source of influence on your own life. Hopefully, you will see it has much to offer, and also that your feelings and attitudes may help shape our future as a people.

The following exercises are designed to make you sensitive to your own values as a way of preparing you for an investigation of the values and ideals found in the Siddur.

EXERCISE 1

Which values do you feel are most important in your own life? Rank them from the most important to the least important, using "1" for the value you feel most important.

_____	Wealth	_____	Success
_____	Equality	_____	Peace
_____	Family	_____	Justice
_____	Progress	_____	The Jewish People
_____	Jewish Tradition	_____	Beauty
_____	Freedom	_____	Wisdom
_____	Love	_____	Power
_____	The People of Israel	_____	Happiness
_____	Health	_____	(other values:)

Now look through a Siddur and see if you can find examples of these values in various prayers. Work on your own or with another participant in the group.

_____

Based on Leland W. Howe and Mary M. Howe, *Personalizing Education: Values Clarification and Beyond* (New York: Hart Publishing Co., Inc., 1975), 238-239.

EXERCISE 2

Which personal character traits do you consider most important for yourself or for those people you love or consider good friends? Put a "1" in front of the character trait you esteem most highly and number the others in descending order.

_____ Honesty

_____ Playfulness

_____ Self-confidence

_____ Order

_____ Being Aggressive

_____ Courage

_____ Cooperation

_____ Being competitive

_____ Creativity

_____ Loyalty

_____ Responsibility

_____ Caring

_____ Independence

_____ Spontaneity

_____ Friendliness

_____ Flexibility

_____ Open-mindedness

_____ Being self-sacrificing

_____ (other traits:)

Based on Howe and Howe, *Personalizing Education*, 239-240.

Now look through a Siddur and see if you can find sentences or whole prayers which refer to the particular traits you esteem most highly in yourself or in others.

EXERCISE 3

The act of praying is to help make us sensitive to an ethical and moral life style. Many of us bring to the prayer book our own opinions and feelings about what is right and what is wrong, based on the lives we lead in general society. Judaism, when it is successful, is often subversive of the general society, asking us to act not necessarily as everyone else does, but according to a standard set down in our tradition. As a way of checking what your personal views are and whether or not they might be changed by understanding the Siddur, do the following exercise. Begin it now at the beginning of your study of t'fillah, and then come back to the second half of the chart after you have completed this course of study to see whether your ideas have changed. Do be aware that prayer is not always meant to be a "result-producing" activity.

Instructions

Place an X in the column (A, B, or C) which best expresses your attitude on each of the topics listed in the "Item" column. After studying the Siddur complete the remaining columns. See if you can find a place in the Siddur which deals with, or relates to the "Item" (Column D). Then put an X in the appropriate column (E, F, or G) to see if your views have changed.

BEFORE YOUR STUDY OF SIDDUR

Item I feel this is:	A. Morally wrong	B. Morally right	C. Not a moral issue
1. Using an addictive drug			
2. Smoking pot			
3. Destroying public property			
4. Destroying private property (one's own; parent's; other's)			
5. Shoplifting			
6. Gossip			
7. Slander			
8. Telling lies to protect friends			
9. Telling lies to protect your own interests			
10. Destructive exploitation of animals			
11. Air and water pollution			
12. Racial prejudice			
13. Religious prejudice			
14. Disliking someone because of looks			
15. Assimilation			
16. Intermarriage			
17. Inter-dating			
18. Pre-marital sexual relationships			
19. Extra-marital sexual relationships			
20. Pushing pot or heroin			
21. Cheating			
22. Israel's territorial integrity			

AFTER YOUR STUDY OF SIDDUR

D. Place in Siddur	E. Morally wrong	F. Morally right	G. Not a moral issue

3. Prayer as the Link Between Individuals and Community

As anyone experienced in Jewish prayer knows, praying with others in community is basic to our entire prayer structure. Though an individual is permitted to pray alone if he or she can't participate with a *minyan* (quorum of 10) the preferred situation is communal prayer. Many people see this as a tension between the right of a person to relate privately and personally to God and involving oneself in a community of people supporting one another. cantor Max Wolhberg, Professor in Ḥazzanut at the Jewish Theological Seminary of America and one of the most respected Ḥazzanim in the country, has written,

> Jewish liturgy has two salient qualities: it is congregation-oriented and it has to be chanted in an agreeable manner.
>
> Although in the absence of an alternative one is permitted to pray privately, synagogue attendance and participation in communal worship is mandatory. Indeed, we are warned not even to dwell in a place that is without a synagogue. Furthermore, we are exhorted that a community without regular worship arouses the ire of the Almighty.
>
> The Talmud *(Berachot 7b-8a)* records a revealing dialogue between Rabbi Isaac and Rabbi Naḥman.

Why, asked the former, does the master not attend synagogue prayer? I cannot, the latter replied. Then, continued Rabbi Isaac, why not collect a *minyan* at home? That, maintained Rabbi Naḥman, would involve me in too much trouble. Then, persisted Rabbi Isaac, why not ask the ḥazzan to inform you of the exact time of the congregational service, so that you may synchronize your prayers with theirs? But look, asked Rabbi Naḥman, why all this fuss? Because replied Rabbi Isaac, Rabbi Yoḥanan quoted Rabbi Simeon ben Yoḥai (on Psalms 69:14 , "But as for me, let my prayer be unto Thee, O Lord, in an acceptable time") as teaching: *What time may be considered acceptable? When a congregation is at prayer.*[3]

אמר ליה רבי יצחק לרב נחמן: מאי טעמא לא אתי מר
לבי כנישתא לצלויי? אמר ליה: לא יכילנא. אמר ליה:
לכנפי למר עשרה וליצלי! אמר ליה: טריחא לי מילתא!
ולימא ליה מר לשלוחא דציבורא בעידנא דמצלי
ציבורא, ליתי ולודעיה למר! אמר ליה: מאי כולי האי?
אמר ליה: דאמר ר' יוחנן משום ר' שמעון בר יוחי: מאי
דכתיב "ואני תפלתי לך ה' עת רצון" (תה' סט, יד).
אימתי עת רצון? בשעה שהציבור מתפללין!

Maimonides (a 12th century Jewish philosopher and law codifier, known as *Rambam*) stressed the importance of communal prayer as an obligation of members of the community towards one another:

Prayer of the congregation is always heard (by God). Even if there are sinners among them, the Holy One, blessed be He, does not reject the prayer of the congregation. Therefore, a person should associate himself with the congregation, and not recite his prayers by himself anytime he is able to pray with the congregation. One should always attend synagogue, morning and evening, since one's prayers are not heard at all times except in the synagogue. Whoever has a synagogue in his town and does not worship there with the congregation is called a bad neighbor.

תְּפִלַּת הַצִּבּוּר נִשְׁמַעַת תָּמִיד, וַאֲפִלּוּ הָיוּ בָהֶם חוֹטְאִים
אֵין הַקָּדוֹשׁ־בָּרוּךְ־הוּא מוֹאֵס בִּתְפִלָּתָם שֶׁל רַבִּים. לְפִיכָךְ
צָרִיךְ אָדָם לְשַׁתֵּף עַצְמוֹ עִם הַצִּבּוּר, וְלֹא יִתְפַּלֵּל יְחִידִי
כָּל־זְמַן שֶׁיָּכוֹל לְהִתְפַּלֵּל עִם הַצִּבּוּר. וּלְעוֹלָם יַשְׁכִּים אָדָם
וְיַעֲרִיב לְבֵית־הַכְּנֶסֶת, שֶׁאֵין תְּפִלָּתוֹ נִשְׁמַעַת בְּכָל־עֵת
אֶלָּא בְּבֵית־הַכְּנֶסֶת. וְכָל מִי שֶׁיֶּשׁ־לוֹ בֵּית־הַכְּנֶסֶת בְּעִירוֹ
וְאֵינוֹ מִתְפַּלֵּל בּוֹ עִם הַצִּבּוּר, נִקְרָא: שָׁכֵן רָע.

Rambam, *Hilchot T'fillah ("Laws" of Prayer)*, 8:1

18

People need each other's support in moments of joy, sorrow, guilt, and frustration. Have you ever performed solo, and later in a group? Which was less pressured? Why? The following statement shows that the Rabbis felt all Israel must support one another by formulating prayers in the first person plural ("we," "our") rather than the first person singular ("I," "my"):

Rabbi Yaakov said in Rav Ḥisda's name: Whoever goes on a journey must recite *T'fillat HaDerech* (the prayer for traveling). What is it? "May it be Your will, O Lord my God, to lead me in safety and direct my steps in safety... Blessed are You, O Lord, who listens to prayer." Abaye said, "One should always associate with the congregation. How should he recite it? 'May it be Your will, O Lord our God, to lead us in safety and direct our steps in safety...'"

ואמר רבי יעקב אמר רב חסדה: כל היוצא לדרך צריך להתפלל תפילת הדרך. מאי תפילת הדרך? "יהי רצון מלפניך ה' אלהי שתוליכני לשלום ותצעידני לשלום ... בא"י שומע תפילה." אמר אביי: לעולם לישתף איניש נפשיה בהדי ציבורא! היכי נימא? "יהי רצון מלפניך ה' אלהינו שתוליכנו לשלום וכו'."

B'rachot 29b-30a

Even though you as an individual might not have a need at a given moment to ask God for a particular blessing (for instance, health, peace, knowledge) you are nevertheless required to make the request as a means of supporting a fellow community member who may be in need. This is one way of sensitizing you to the needs, conditions, and desires of others. An important example of this concept is *Al Ḥayt*, (the "Confessional," "For the sins *we* have committed...") said on Yom Kippur by the entire congregation together, in the plural.

Though community prayer is paramount, our Rabbis were very sensitive to the individual's need while participating in communal prayer.

Sometimes a compromise was established between the needs of the individual and the need to participate with the community, for instance, in sanctifying God's name during prayers such as the *Kaddish*, or *K'dushah*, which require congregational responses. Thus, in the case of someone (who has presumably come to services late, and is) reciting the Amidah silently, we are taught,

One does not stop (to respond with the congregation) for Kaddish or K'dushah. Rather one should remain silent and pay attention to what the *Shaliaḥ Tzibbur* (person leading the congregational prayer) says, and be *as if* he were responding. After completing the blessings of the *Amidah*, but (even) before reciting the paragraph "O Lord, guard my tongue...," One may respond to K'dushah, Kaddish, or *Barechu*.

אינו פוסק לא לקדיש ולא לקדושה, אלא ישתוק ויכוין למה שאומר השליח צבור ויהא כעונה ... אחר שסיים י"ח ברכות קודם "אלהי נצור," יכול לענות קדושה וקדיש וברכו.

Shulḥan Aruch Oraḥ Ḥayyim 104:7-8

Yet another example of this compromise between individual's prayer needs and responsibility to the community involves sensitivity to group needs and respect for other people's time:

הַמִּתְפַּלֵּל עִם הַצִּבּוּר — לֹא יַאֲרִיךְ בִּתְפִלָּתוֹ יוֹתֵר מִדַּאי: אֲבָל בֵּינוֹ לְבֵין עַצְמוֹ — הָרְשׁוּת בְּיָדוֹ.
Someone praying with the congregation should not lengthen his prayer too much (i.e., take too much time). But when someone prays alone, he may do so.

Rambam, Hilchot T'fillah 6:2

But what constitutes a community in Judaism? In connection with prayer a community (or congregation) is the minyan (which literally means "counting"). In one derivation, the rabbinic tradition found support for the idea that God is to be approached in a minyan, and that the number of ten adults was needed to constitute the minyan by reference to a verse in Psalms (82:1):

אֱלֹהִים נִצָּב בַּעֲדַת־אֵל
God stands in the holy congregation...

19

In particular the word עֵדָה , congregation, is connected with the story of the ten spies sent by Moses to spy out the land. The spies were also referred to as an עֵדָה . So, it was reasoned, a "congregation of God" must consist of ten. Although in ancient times in Palestine fewer than ten was acceptable, in Babylonia, ten participants were required, and that practice has come down to us today. A minyan is required to recite certain parts of the service (which are discussed elsewhere in the source book): Kaddish, Barechu, K'dushah, and the public Torah reading.[4]

The individual's private aspirations and needs are also given an important place in our tradition. We shall see in our discussion on "fixed versus spontaneous" prayer just how forcefully our greatest rabbis and teachers argued for individual creativity within our prayer tradition. There are many תְּפִלּוֹת רְשׁוּת , optional prayers, throughout the liturgy. Some are communal; others are individual. Over the centuries people have written special meditations and reflections. Other additions are prepatory prayers to be recited before the performance of a particular mitzvah such as putting on *tallit* and *t'fillin,* before taking the *lulav* and *etrog,* upon lighting the Shabbat candles, or upon visiting the Western Wall or Rachel's Tomb. As we shall soon see, one's prayer was especially enriched with personal devotions added to the accepted ritual formats. Many personal prayers were written in the first person singular to express the authors' own aspirations. But it must be understood that all of these literary creations were clothed in the framework of Jewish ideas, history, idioms, *halachah*, and customs. One requirement in writing our own prayers today and continuing this ancient tradition of individual liturgical creativity is to check whether our creative efforts are consistent with our tradition, or at least attempt to grapple with it honestly.

The Siddur has always been the focus of tremendous personal creativity. Interestingly, part of that creativity was stifled more than anything else by the invention of the printing press in 1440. Once prayers were available in print, and widely disseminated, they took on a special standing and sanctity of their own regardless of their origin or universality of use. What had been an oral tradition and very open to creative change became more rigid once reduced to the printed form.

These issues are quite important for people who enjoy mobilizing creative energy and talents to write prayers, compose new music, and even develop new rituals for the liturgy. Throughout this source book you will be challenged to respond creatively to the t'fillah experience. You will be asked to interpret prayers, and express their ideas and concepts in your own forms. However, it is important to realize that not "anything goes" even if it's original and full of "you." We ask you to be authentically Jewish in your creative responses, looking to the values, norms, and aspirations of our past and people as resources from which to draw. The following checklist is a way for you to measure or judge the Jewish authenticity of your creative efforts in prayer.

CHECKLIST FOR CREATIVE PRAYER COMPOSITION

When you write a new t'fillah, or compose a song, dance, story, or prayer interpretation, see how many of the following questions can be answered positively.

—— Does your prayer creation contain Jewish values?

—— Does your prayer go beyond self-centered needs and include others?

—— Is your language appropriate for confronting concerns and questions of ultimate importance?

—— Does your creation go beyond "human-centeredness" to something greater? to God?

—— Would it be meaningful to anyone else besides you?

—— Does it reflect an ethical approach to life?

—— Does it refer directly or indirectly to any Jewish sources (e.g., quotes from the Talmud, the Bible, Codes of Law, other prayers)?

—— Is it well written (grammar, syntax, language)?

—— Do the poetic images stand up to the overall theme of the prayer upon close inspection?

—— Did you make a conscious choice to use rhyme or meter?

—— Would your prayer creation be meaningful to someone living in a different time or place?

—— Would it be meaningful 1,000 years from now?

—— Can you honestly say you will be able to read (perform, sing, see) it over and over again?

Obviously, not every prayer creation has to meet *all* of these evaluative criteria and there may be criteria to be added if you do want something you develop to be valuable to yourself and to others. However, over a period of time, it will have to meet many of these standards.

LINKAGE TO TRADITION THROUGH COMMUNITY

Another extremely important aspect of communal prayer involves the linkage it provides between the Jewish generations past, present, and future. If you understand the development of our liturgy and its responses to life, you are in immediate touch with all the generations of Jews who came before us. We don't stand alone in the world; rather we can turn to generations of our people before us for help and guidance, sharing their experience in meeting life's joys, frustrations, and triumphs. Learning to empathize with the writer of a prayer, written at a particular time and place in response to a particular feeling, makes Jewish history live for us. As part of the Passover Haggadah we recite   בְּכָל דּוֹר וָדוֹר חַיָּב אָדָם לִרְאוֹת אֶת עַצְמוֹ כְּאִלּוּ הוּא יָצָא מִמִּצְרַיִם

"In every generation each person must view himself as if he, personally, has come out of Egypt." This idea of reliving the past and linking ourselves with those who have preceded us can give us a sense of roots, of belonging, of feeling a part of something bigger than our individual selves. The sensational popularity of Alex Haley's *Roots* -- or in a very different way, Gerald Green's *Holocaust* -- among all segments of the American population gives eloquent testimony to this basic need in us all to know who we are and from where we come. Interestingly, we sometimes need television docu-dramas to remind us of our spiritual treasures, although they are constantly available to us in the siddur.

Similarly, the impetus for communal prayer provides a link among Jews throughout the world who relate to the same words, can feel comfortable with the same basic religious services and rituals, and who reflect common values and understandings of what is important in life.

Some teenagers do not include as personal priorities these notions of being linked with the past and building on it or finding experiences in common with other human beings around the world. But, for most people in their high school years, community (in the form of peer groups, close friends, youth groups, sports teams, or school-related organizations) is of crucial importance. You might understand, therefore, why organizations like USY, Camp Ramah, or LTF, by creating a strong sense of community, can do so much in helping to make Jewish values important.

The following activity may give you a more tangible sense of who you are in relation to the Jewish people.

EXERCISE 1

TREE OF LIFE

The Torah has been compared to a tree of life, deeply rooted, giving strength, support, and shelter to our people. This symbol might be extended to each of us individually. We may interpret our own Jewishness through the symbol of a tree. The strength of its supporting root structure will determine its longevity. The sweetness of its fruit might determine its beauty, worth, and desirability to others. Try the following representation.

On a large piece of newsprint or a ditto sheet draw a giant tree and call it a "me" tree. On the roots write, draw symbols, or paste pictures of your Jewish roots: things that have to do with your Jewish education, your Jewish upbringing, your feelings and identification with things Jewish, trips to Israel, camping experiences, anything which goes into making your Jewish self. In the branches draw symbols, paste pictures, or simply write your Jewish accomplishments: skills you have developed, experiences that you have undergone (*Brit Milah*; naming; Bar/Bat Mitzvah, etc.), papers you have written on Jewish topics, Hebrew language speaking achievements, Jewish artistic productions, etc. Place these trees around the room to give all the participants a sense of who you are and how much you have all produced together Jewishly.

Adapted from Howe and Howe, *Personalizing Education*, 97.

4. Prayer as a Response to the Wonder of Being Alive

Perhaps the real secret of being able to pray is in retaining an almost childish sense of wonder and awe at the incredible fact of "merely" being alive. Anyone who has seen the wonder on a baby's face when she sees an airplane, a dog, or a butterfly knows what this reaction to life includes. All of us, at one time or another, have felt an overpowering feeling of amazement while witnessing a striking natural phenomenon or when hearing a great work of music, or when feeling the mysterious power of love. We all have felt the need to express this overwhelming sense of beauty and gratefulness in some tangible manner--through words, gestures, music, art or dance. At its heart, prayer is the human response to the archetypical experiences common to all people. Prayer is the way a culture puts into touchable, hearable, seeable form its deepest sense of morality and concepts of beauty.

However, our experience of the awe and wonder of living is often clouded by everyday life experiences and tempered by our modern world views.

Λ person often loses his power of appreciation because he comes in contact with the same things time after time; the world becomes stale because we take things for granted.

We often come to believe that the world is ours because we can understand, control and even destroy the phenomena of nature and society by our minds and wills .... But while the basic patterns of life do indeed recur over and over, the concrete life of man in the community is too dynamic to fall completely into the grasp of predictability and understanding....

Discovering the depths of another person, falling in love, the joy at the marriage ceremony, the birth of a first child, watching the child grow, change and develop, (as a parent or as a teacher) a first summer trip to Israel, a discovery in a science lab -- in each of these instances we may experience again something of the excitement and wonder of our childhood where our routine concerns for security, predictability, the control of the world about us are for a time broken by a greater hunger within us -- to experience the joy, the spontaneity and wonder which opens our senses to a fresh appreciation of an individual event.

It is unfortunate that ... these kinds of experiences are often lived through joyously and then their impact is forgotten as we return to our humdrum ordered worlds. The ordered world demands continuity but there is something in these moments of wonder which eludes continuity; thus it is the ordered world which takes precedence in our lives and the world of wonder becomes a part-time outlet for pent-up emotional hunger.... Even our worship services themselves, which should ideally give us forms through which we can again recover an uncommon understanding of existence, often become routine....

"Wonder or radical amazement," as Dr. Heschel tells us "is the chief characteristic of the religious man's attitude toward history and nature. One attitude is alien to his spirit: taking things for granted, regarding events as a natural course of things...." Wonder is born in curiosity. The human imagination is touched off by some novel occurance which seems mysterious; the mind races in to fill the vacuum, to give meaning to the mystery.

Through empirical analysis of available data, scientists can often trace the causal relations that brought about the marvel and yet, for the sensitive scientist, the mystery remains.[5]

Albert Einstein, a most sensitive scientist, summed up this view, when he said, "The most beautiful and most profound emotion one can experience is the sensation of the mystical. It is the source of all true science."[6]

23

One of the main problems for the modern person steeped in the world of technology and scientific method is to understand that religion and science both respond to the wonderous, miraculous mysteries of life. *Science wants to know what is; religion seeks to go beyond and asks why things are and what they ought to be.*

Ultimately, the profound difference in the ways science and religion respond to the world are reflected in the way each system of perception asks and answers the questions it poses. They respond in different languages of expression. Whereas science uses the language of analysis (mathematics, hypothesis, proof), religion uses the language of poetry.

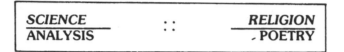

SCIENCE   :: RELIGION
ANALYSIS   :: POETRY

Both are valid methods of expressing truths, though we could make a strong case that while scientific analysis leads to continually changing truths (e.g., latest theories on quantum mechanics, origins of the universe, structure of the atom) religion's poetic responses to the mysteries of life have been more enduring. Ultimately all science is also based on faith, but scientists call their beliefs axioms, unprovable assumptions on which they base their theories. Sometimes these axioms turn out to be wrong!

My own teacher, Dr. Avraham Holtz, taught me the fundamental principle of how the religious human being reacts to the wonder of life. It has been summed up by Dr. Heschel:

To intercept[a] the allusions[b] that are submerged in perceptabilities, the interstitial[c] values that never rise to the surface, the indefinable dimension of all existence, is the venture of true poetry. This is why poetry is to religion what analysis is to science, and it is certainly no accident that the Bible was not written *more geometrico*[d] but in the language of the poets.[7]

a. to grasp, understand
b. passing references, metaphors
c. situated between the elements of a structure or part

d. language of geometry or mathematics

Thus, in difficult and highly poetic terms, Heschel says that poetry "reads between the lines" of life. True poetry captures the most essential and important feelings, emotions, values, and sensitivities evoked by living.

This search for understanding the mystery behind reality has led many people in our times to drugs. In an attempt to rise above the mundane, repetitive experiences of everyday living and to get closer to others and "in touch" with themselves, many people have tried drugs as a shortcut. However, feeling the joyous emotions of life at its richest is not an invention of the twentieth century culture. The entire thrust of Jewish tradition, and prayer in particular, is to help us experience life to the fullest, using our own mental, emotional, communal, spiritual, and interpersonal resources. Prayer can be an important aid in helping experience the mysteries of reality.

To heighten your sensitivity to these issues try the following exercise:

EXERCISE 1

Now that you have read and discussed some things about the concepts of awe and wonder in the Siddur and in religion in general, respond to the following incomplete sentences:

I wonder if ...

I wonder about ...

I wonder why ...

I wonder how ...

I wonder whether ...

I wonder when ...

Based on Simon, *Values Clarification,* 166.

5. Prayer as Torah Study

An integral part of daily Jewish life and prayer is study. The origin of making study part of the worship experience goes all the way back to Ezra, a Babylonian Jew who returned to Israel in the mid-fifth century B.C.E. When he came back to Jerusalem he was upset to find that the Jewish community was greatly disorganized. The Bible tells us that he fasted and prayed in order to rectify this situation. As a community leader he began a number of reforms which climaxed in his assembling the entire people to whom he read the Torah; (Nehemiah 8). This act of reading and teaching the Torah to the entire people was a revolutionary one in ancient times. In those days, the priests of any culture or religion were the ones who guarded the sacred words of their tradition among themselves. Judaism changed this ancient tradition by making the Torah available to all the people. Ezra also began the tradition of reading the Torah on Mondays and Thursdays, which were market days, when people gathered and could then be taught Torah. Others followed Ezra's lead and by using sermons and lessons taught Torah in the synagogue. To this day we follow Ezra's custom of reading Torah on Shabbat, holidays, fast days and Mondays and Thursdays as a part of the liturgy. We recite a Haftorah (portion of the Prophets) on Shabbat, holidays, and fast days, as a result of later developments.

In addition, many passages from the Torah and from rabbinic literature are incorporated into the Siddur to give the Jew daily experiences in study. The opportunity for daily Torah study is an important part of Jewish religious practice.

The beginning of the morning service (*shaharit*) includes a *b'rachah* (blessing) over the study of Torah and continues with the beautiful prayer *Veha'arev-na*, asking that we be capable of internalizing the teachings of Torah and communicating them to our descendants. The prayer was written by the *Amora'im* -- talmudic sages from the period of 220-500 C.E. -- Rabbi Yohanan and Sh'muel. We pray to learn Torah לִשְׁמָה , for its own sake; study itself is a mitzvah and a form of worshipping God. Then we recite the b'rachah also used when we have a Torah aliyah, *Asher Bahar Banu*, praising God for choosing us, giving us the Torah. (This b'rachah was written by Rabbi Hamnuna in the fourth century C.E.) It is the Torah which gives shape and meaning to our lives and so we start off the morning (even before saying the rest of the daily prayers) by studying from that source of life. Immediately following the Torah study benedictions are selections from each of the three "branches" of Jewish literature: the Bible (the Kohen's Blessing, Numbers 6:24-26); the Mishnah *(Aylu D'varim,* based on Peah 1:1) and the Gemara *(Aylu D'varim She'adam,* Shabbat 127a). We show our love and appreciation for God's gift by immediately using it!

Text study was one way of worshipping God, even when the texts describe worship rituals no longer performed (such as sacrifices). Thus, in some Siddurim, following the *Birchot Hashahar* section we find quotations from the Torah about sacrifices, recalling our earliest form of worshipping God. The Rabbis considered studying these passages a vicarious means of offering the sacrifices. They preceded them with the story of the *Akedah*, The Binding of Isaac (Genesis 22), as a way of recalling the devotion with which Abraham was willing to serve his God.

There are numerous other passages of study throughout the Siddur. Some Siddurim include the well-known tractate from the Mishnah, *Pirkay Avot, Ethics* (or *Chapters) of the Fathers,* which is studied on Shabbat afternoons between Pesah and Shavuot (or Rosh Hashanah). Another passage for study found in some prayer books as part of the Friday evening service is *Bameh Madlikin.* This passage from the Talmud *(Masechet Shabbat)* deals with the various laws of Shabbat preparation. (It may have been added to the service so that late-comers would not have to finish their prayers alone and walk home in the dark unaccompanied. However, a Sephardic custom is to recite this passage before the beginning of the *Ma'ariv* service so that the people who might have forgotten something in preparation for Shabbat will be reminded and still be able to attend it!)

All these forms of Torah study are clearly one way and one aspect of worshipping God.

EXERCISE 1

1. Read through the passage Aylu D'varim in the Shaḥarit service and give a priority order to those mitzvot which are most important to you. Which ones would you be willing to commit yourself to in the next week? month? year? Then list the first steps you'll have to take to begin practicing or enriching your practice of your preferred mitzvot. Traditionally there is no hierarchy of mitzvot, but given our limited time this exercise can help us determine starting points. (Note that the mitzvot are listed by short descriptions which do not adequately describe or translate each mitzvah.)

Mitzvah		*Priority #*	*First Steps*
Leaving corners of field to the poor	פֵּאָה		
Bringing first fruits to the Temple	בִּכּוּרִים		
Appearing in Jerusalem on Festivals with pilgrimage offering	רְאָיוֹן		
Practice of good deeds	גְּמִילוּת חֲסָדִים		
Honoring father and mother	כִּבּוּד אָב וָאֵם		
Regular times of attendance at the House of Study	הַשְׁכָּמַת בֵּית הַמִּדְרָשׁ		
Hospitality	הַכְנָסַת אוֹרְחִים		
Visiting the sick	בִּקּוּר חוֹלִים		
Giving a dowry to the bride	הַכְנָסַת כַּלָּה		
Burying the dead	הַלְוָיַת הַמֵּת		
Devotion in Prayer	עִיּוּן תְּפִלָּה		
Causing peace	הֲבָאַת שָׁלוֹם		
Torah Study	תַּלְמוּד תּוֹרָה		

CHAPTER 2 : THE LANGUAGES OF PRAYER
Introduction

In the previous chapter we looked at the underlying motivations of prayerful activities. In this chapter we shall study the processes involved in translating those needs, emotions, desires, frustrations, goals, and hopes into concrete actions. As noted already, we live in a society where words are not taken too seriously, even though the heart of our people's method of communication is the written and spoken word. Words, in the form of poetry, are the chief means of expression of the religious human being. It should be noted, however, that by poetry we mean much more than rhymed words written in meter. By poetry we signify all of the symbolic, aesthetic, thoughtful modes of expression used by human beings to represent our most profound beliefs, ideals, and emotions in a tangible and lasting manner. So poetry can include written language, music, body language, visual representations, ritualized touch, taste and smell activities -- all of which enrich and ennoble us. We now turn to a look at the various "languages" of prayer central to Jewish worship.

1. The Language of the Written Word: Poetry

One of the most important aspects involved in understanding Jewish prayer lies in an appreciation of the nature of poetry and how it works. All too frequently, many of us have had poor experiences in studying poetry in our secular educations. The few of us who have ever written poetry know how difficult it can be, and those of us who enjoy reading poetry regularly realize the particular sensitivity required for its appreciation. We are living in a society which has come to suspect words. We are taught not to believe what we read in the papers, or what we hear on television. We live in a society where words are cheap, no longer with the power and force they held in the past. We use a lot of speech, but don't use it carefully and don't value the power or beauty of the words. This is particularly important when we look at Judaism and see that the basic method of communication in our tradition is the written word. Our Torah, commentaries upon it, our Siddur and even the decorations in many synagogues are based on the written word. In a society where words are no longer taken as seriously as they once were, it may be difficult for us to pray, because prayer really involves using words and understanding how they work with one another and how we can make them work in our own lives. Perhaps, one of the overriding purposes of this entire manual is to give you an understanding of how words work together to create mood, focus our attention on values, and lift our spirits in making us better. In the pages which follow we shall attempt to teach you a bit of how words work in the Siddur. Through some explanations and some exercises we hope to make you sensitive to the magnificence of words in motion, so you can look to the Siddur with more affection, knowledge, and participation.

Obviously, one of the most difficult issues for North American youth looking at the Siddur is the problem of the Hebrew language. Even when we are successful in learning a bit of conversational Hebrew we realize that there is a long distance between that knowledge and an ability to understand and appreciate the Hebrew in the Siddur. Secondly, the translations of many Siddurium are stilted and archaic. So we are put off, and ignorance does not always lead to concern. However, it is impossible to appreciate Jewish prayer completely and to understand what it is trying to tell us unless we seek to understand Hebrew. The Hebrew poet Hayyim Nahman Bialik once compared reading a language in translation to kissing a bride through her veil. (It's just not the same!) To prove to you that language, and particularly Hebrew, conveys certain images and meanings by the very nature of its world of discourse, try the following exercise.

EXERCISE 1

A number of words are listed below. As you read each English word, write down your first reaction to it. Do not feel restrained. Write what you think and do not feel uncomfortable if the association you make might not fit in with the other purposes of this book.

1. Messiah
2. Savior
3. Our Father who art in Heaven
4. Redeemer
5. Sin

6. Adoration
7. Halleluyah
8. King of kings
9. Resurrection
10. Nigh draws the hour of the redeemer's birth

Don't be surprised if many of the initial responses you give have some Christian overtones, for the English language is the language of Western Christianity. All of the words in the list above are taken from translations of Hebrew phrases in the Siddur. The list of the original Hebrew phrases follows:

1. מָשִׁיחַ
2. מוֹשִׁיעַ
3. אָבִינוּ שֶׁבַּשָּׁמַיִם
4. גּוֹאֵל
5. חֵטְא

6. עָלֵינוּ
7. הַלְלוּיָהּ
8. מֶלֶךְ (מַלְכֵי) הַמְּלָכִים
9. תְּחִיַּת הַמֵּתִים
10. קָרְבָה אֶל נַפְשִׁי גְאָלָהּ

The connotations of the Hebrew words often differ from the English words. Hopefully, as you begin to study the Siddur in greater depth you will see that the Hebrew radiates a unique set of meanings. In other words, English is not the language of the Jewish people; it is a language steeped in Christian thought and belief, and often communicates Christian values and ideas. That is why an understanding of Hebrew makes a vast difference in one's appreciation of the prayer book. This does not mean we should ignore the Siddur if we don't understand Hebrew, but that we will approach it from a different perspective.

Let us now turn to a look at how poetry works and show some examples of it in operation in the Siddur. Remember that most of our t'fillot (with a few exceptions, such as some passages taken from the Torah or rabbinic material) are written in poetry. The rules of Hebrew poetry differ from English poetry, but the fundamentals of what makes poetry work are very much the same no matter what the language. A well known author and scholar, John Ciardi, wrote a magnificent book entitled, *How Does a Poem Mean?*[8] Even from the title you should detect an interesting approach. Most people look at a poem trying to find out what it's talking about or what it means. They don't really get to the heart of the matter, which is *how* does that poem convey its meaning. The difference between journalism, for instance, and poetry is that *in its form* the poem conveys its content. The same is true for art in general. There is a very famous painting by Rembrandt, reproduced below. It shows Moses holding the tablets of the law above his head, waiting to break them as he views the golden calf. If you look at the geometric forms in this picture, you will see that Moses could be outlined as an upright pillar, with the outline of his arms holding the tablets of the law encased in a diamond shape leaning to one side. Look at the diagram below.

 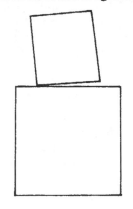

From Franz Landsberger, *Rembrandt, The Bible, and The Jews.*

The diamond is at the brink of falling and shattering into a million pieces. Likewise, the narrative of the painting, the story of the painting, is saying that Moses is waiting to throw the tablets down and break them into pieces, thus ending the new civilization, the new law, the new way of life he is bringing to the people. The picture is one of impending doom and disaster. Were a modern painter or sculptor to reproduce the feeling of this painting, he might not show Moses holding the tablets at all, but might just portray the pillar with the diamond tilting to one side. We know that in geometry one of the most stable forms is the triangle. If you've ever seen the *Mona Lisa* and outlined its geometrical form, you would see that she fits very neatly into a beautiful stable triangle. This is the secret of great art, which works also in music and literature: *form mirrors content.* So it's not enough to ask *what* something means, but the secret of art is *how* it means. How are the words arranged? What does the arrangement of the words produce? Why is one word chosen and not another word? Why are the words in the order they are in? What is left out, and why? All of these things are what makes the difference between good poetry and bad, between just writing a note to someone and writing a lasting piece of literature. The reason poetry may seem so boring is that instead of spending time on how poems mean we tend to spend too much time on what they mean, paying lip service to concepts and terms such as metaphors and similes without paying attention to the art which has been created.

Fundamentally, a poem or a prayer was caused by an experience. Some memorable experience caused someone to sit down and write a reaction to something felt, believed, or desired. So one of the fundamental tasks in looking at any t'fillah-poem must be to try to understand what the incident or occurence was which caused its creation. It is the purpose of poetry to capture the experience of one human being and make it available to many others.

Many of you may wonder how someone can take a paragraph of poetry or prayer and draw from it all kinds of meanings and implications that you don't seem to see yourself. This can be a very intimidating experience, for you feel unknowledgeable, assuming you'll never attain that sophistication. We would like to prove that this is not necessarily true. You can hang your own life experiences on the hooks of prayers--once you understand how they work--because they are written in poetry. "Learning to experience poetry is not a radically different process from learning any other kind of play. The way to develop a poetic sense is by using it. And one of the real joys of the play-impulse is in the sudden discovery that one is getting better at it than he had thought he would be."9

To understand t'fillah as poetry we must understand how symbols work.

> For a symbol is like a rock dropped into a pool: it sends out ripples in all directions, and the ripples are in motion. Who can say where the last ripple disappears? One may have a sense that he at least knows approximately the center point of all those ripples, the point at which the stone struck the water. Yet even then he has trouble marking it precisely. How does one make a mark on water? ... But the ripples continue to move and the light to change on the water and the longer one watches the more changes he sees. And such shifting-and-being-at-the-same-instance is of the very sparkle and life of poetry. Of poetry and of life itself. For the poem is a dynamic and living thing. One experiences it as one experiences life -- one is never done with it: every time he looks he sees something new, and it changes even as he watches10

Thus words, when chosen carefully by a poet or the writer of a prayer (a *payyetan*, in Hebrew) look different to different people and continue to evoke new impressions. Such is the case when the poet takes different words and mingles them together, throws them into the pond of experience. Each word radiates its own meaning and has that meaning changed and amplified by the other meanings radiating from other pebbles or words in the same pond of experience. This makes t'fillah lasting. Not all of us are poets. Not all of us are able to find the right words at the right moment to express our feelings when we want to. This ability to relate our own thoughts and expressions to the symbols handed down to us by others is at the heart of the prayer experience. To paraphrase Ciardi, a prayer is not something simply printed on the page; a prayer is an event that happens when a prayer writer and a reader meet inside the form in such a way that the reader makes real for himself those connections between things that the writer saw for himself and the things the reader feels for himself. By using intellect, imagination, and memory you can attach yourself to the same experience and gain from it.

Many symbols become so potent and so forceful over time that they take on centrality and convey an entire concept or constellation of ideas. In our tradition words such as *tzedakah, mitzvah, talmud Torah, or malchut shamayim* mean much more than their specific or even poetic meanings. Dr. Max Kadushin has called them value-concepts, which interact with each other and with the experience of the reader.11 They stand for whole systems of behavior and approach to life, taking on a special sanctity of their own. To put it another way,

> It seems clear that not only in poetry but in history itself--which is to say in the very motion of men's lives--symbols acquire emotional expansion and intensity in the process of being sustained over a period of time. As the flag became associated with more and more of the nation's struggles and triumphs, it tended to become less and less evidently the predetermined legislative code it was at birth, and increasing the symbol of a much broader emotional force. That emotional force, moreover, became so powerful that in many ways the flag tended to lose its character as a symbol and to become a living force in itself.12

So many words which once represented a particular idea or notion have become much greater in their importance to us, much more content-laden and behavior-oriented.

Words convey much more than a specific meaning. When we need to look for a specific meaning of a word we can go to a dictionary, but there are other ways in which words communicate to us. It is this understanding that helps us appreciate the power of t'fillah. Borrowing Ciardi's schema of poetry, we can understand how words work in prayer:

1. *A word is a feeling.* **Many of you will hear the word "examination" or "S.A.T. score" and get an immediate reaction. No one translated it, no one defined it, but yet you respond with a very strong emotional reaction. The same is true for many words in the prayer book:**

a. Who chooses His people Israel in love   הַבּוֹחֵר בְּעַמּוֹ יִשְׂרָאֵל בְּאַהֲבָה

b. Jerusalem   יְרוּשָׁלַיִם

c. The Holy Shabbat   שַׁבָּת קוֹדֶשׁ

d. Remember *(Yizkor)*   יִזְכּוֹר

e. All vows *(Kol Nidray)*   כָּל נִדְרֵי

2. *A word involves the whole body.* **Though words may stand for thoughts or ideas, they must be produced by our bodies in order to exist--by saying them, reading them, or writing them. There is a physical action involved which requires muscles and breath; thus the sound of a word can help convey meaning.**

a.   שְׁמַע יִשְׂרָאֵל ה' אֱלֹהֵינוּ ה' אֶחָד.
There is a custom of holding the last syllable of *eh-ḥad*. Among other reasons, this lends finality and emphasis to the statement.

b. "So that you will remember"   לְמַעַן תִּזְכְּרוּ
(from the third paragraph of the Shema). It is customary to pronounce this *l'ma'an tiZk'ru*, emphasizing the "z" so the word is not confused with *tiSk'ru* (that you will make money...) or *tiSg'ru* (that you will close...).

c.   אָמַר אוֹיֵב אֶרְדֹּף אַשִּׂיג אֲחַלֵּק שָׁלָל תִּמְלָאֵמוֹ נַפְשִׁי.
The enemy said, "I will pursue, I will overtake, I will divide the spoil." Especially when pronounced correctly, this verse enables us to hear and feel the horses' hoof beats.

3. *A word is history.* **In our tradition, individual words and prayers carry with them centuries of Jewish history and cannot be separated from all that has gone before them.**

יִתְגַּדַּל וְיִתְקַדַּשׁ שְׁמֵהּ רַבָּא.

Yitgadal v'yitkadash sh'may rabbah...
These words remind us of personal and communal losses, and faith in God.

4. *A word is a picture.* **Many words trigger a mental image which is just as real and immediate as a Polaroid picture. When you look at the picture behind the word you can very often see what that word really stands for and how it is different from synonyms or other words which are like it.**

a.   בָּרוּךְ אַתָּה ה' בּוֹנֶה יְרוּשָׁלָיִם.
"Blessed are You, O Lord, who rebuilds Jerusalem." (We can see the city of gold and copper.)

b.   אִלּוּ פִינוּ מָלֵא שִׁירָה כַּיָּם וּלְשׁוֹנֵנוּ רִנָּה כַּהֲמוֹן גַּלָּיו.
"If our mouths were filled with song as the sea and if our tongues with singing as its many waves..." (We can picture the vast oceans and how powerless we are by comparison.)

33

After looking at individual words we realize that sometimes we use words separately, but most often we use them in phrases. The phrase is really what is central to the use of words in prayer and poetry. This tendency of words to form together is a basic process in all language. For the Jew, the example *par excellence* of this idea is the Shema: שְׁמַע יִשְׂרָאֵל ה׳ אֱלֹהֵינוּ ה׳ אֶחָד.
Each word in the Shema conveys its own separate ripples of meaning, but taken together they form a powerful, irreducible, and memorable phrase which has become central to everything Jewish. Later in this book we will analyze the phrase in more detail, but it best exemplifies the idea of words working together in phrases modifying each other. Words work together to create an overall impression. The choices for combining words with one another can be evaluated according to the following criteria:[13]

1. *A sense of the whole language stirring.* The sense that the whole language, the whole culture, is stirring when certain words are dropped, so to speak, into the pond is at the heart of many t'fillot and many good poems. When the ḥazzan recites the Kiddush for *Erev Shabbat,* the majesty and power of those words and the notion of how many other times in our liturgy similar words occur all come rising to the surface. One gets the feeling of the entire Jewish people and its language rising to praise and glorify God.

2. *Correct language and diction.* Not every word is always appropriate. Not every style of word is always appropriate for any poet or any prayer. Our Rabbis often wanted the prayer book to stress God's merciful nature as opposed to His role as a stern Judge. Thus, the listing in the Siddur of God's attributes (found in the Torah service for holidays) pictures God as forgiving. However, the listing is taken from the Bible (Exodus 34:7), which states that God will not forgive. The Siddur usage omitted the final two Hebrew words in order to change the tone of the statement. So the diction, the style of wording, became very important to the message that the prayer wanted to convey.

3. *A context for making choices.* Every t'fillah is conceived by a particular poet who has a particular experience he or she wishes to express. At each point in the poem, the poet must select the next word or idea or image. That process of choosing is at the heart of the creative process, but it also sets up a pattern of ideas and values. The b'rachah following Barechu speaks of God as "creator of light and maker of everything." A poetic paragraph follows the b'rachah. The paragraph recited on weekdays is based on the theme of light. Another poet who wrote a prayer based on the same brachah chose the word "everything" as his basis, and that poem is recited on Shabbat. In other words, there are choices and there are different paths which various t'fillah poets have taken. This can lead you to your own creative responses to the prayer book and to prayer in general.

4. *Active language of good poetry.* Most t'fillot discuss the actions of either man or God. The most powerful prayers describe the actions of God. If you look at the second blessing of the Amidah -- G'vurot -- you will see how many of the words are active words describing God as acting in history and in human affairs. Many t'fillot revolve around words of action and those same words "rippling" in their meanings should be influencing our actions as well.

Moreover, the Hebrew in most t'fillot is in the present tense. Most grammarians say that Hebrew does not really have tenses like Latin, or German, or French, but that Latin grammar was imposed upon Hebrew for teaching purposes. Hebrew basically has actions which have been completed, which are in process, or which will occur. Thus, what we refer to as the past tense in Hebrew really is speaking about an action which is already completed. The present tense in Hebrew is really a state of being. (You may notice there are only four forms in the "present tense" of Hebrew: masculine and feminine, singular and plural; whereas, in the past and future "tenses" there are many more forms.) Thus, when we refer to God's actions in the prayer book in the present tense, we are talking about a process which is currently going on, not one which has been completed. Therefore, reading a line like פּוֹתֵחַ אֶת יָדֶךָ וּמַשְׂבִּיעַ לְכָל חַי רָצוֹן.

"You open your hand and satisfy every living thing with favor" (from Ashray), we might first react by saying "It isn't true; there are many people in the world who have not been satisfied by God's helpfulness." But looking at the grammatical construction of the line, we see that we are talking about an ongoing process. God is involved in that process, though it is not yet completed. Mankind, too, has a role: we are partners with God in creation. God did not finish the creation in the beginning. He left part of it undone so that man could become His partner. So our prayers are written in the present voice as a way of saying to us that the processes are ongoing, not yet completed. They are as much hope as they are fulfillment; they are as much our responsibility as they are our request.

Now try your hand at some exercises which highlight some of the poetic concepts just discussed.

EXERCISE 1

Find other examples in the Siddur of the way words work alone and in combination with others. (One place to start is in one of the many Psalms contained in the liturgy.) Use the categories outlined below.

1. A word is a feeling:

2. A word involves the whole body:

3. A word is history:

4. A word is a picture:

5. The whole language stirring:

6. Correct language and diction:

7. Context for making choices:

8. Active language:

EXERCISE 2

Symbols

In order to understand better the force and power of symbols design a flag for yourself or a coat of arms for your family name. On it place such values as things you like to do, words or phrases that are important to you, an important day in your life, colors you like, an important Jewish object or ritual, career goals, etc. After completing your flag or coat of arms, show it to a few friends without telling them who did it. See what the others think you stand for as reflected in the symbol. This may show you about the way symbols work, that they contain ambiguities, and that people can interpret different things from the same symbol.

EXERCISE 3

To help you understand better how poetry and prayer work, try the following exercise. Often poets choose a symbol or metaphor to help them show us their true feelings and sensitivities. Think of an animal that best expresses something about your own personality. Try to conceive of yourself as becoming that animal and ask yourself the following questions:

1. What do I like best about this animal?

2. How am I most like this animal?

3. How would I like to be more like this animal?

You might even want to role play your role as this animal.

Variation:

Select a famous person, flower, or building. What do you like best about your selection? How are you most like your selection? How would you like to be more like it? Discuss your choices and how they symbolize you. Discuss why a symbol can sometimes be particularly helpful to enable you to understand who you are and what you want. Relate this to various symbols of God in the prayer book such as God the Creator, Judge, Father, Protector, Freer of captives, etc. Consider the fine line between symbols and attributes of God (such as God the Merciful One) to see which approach you find more beneficial.

EXERCISE 4

Below is a list of values. Think of (or find) a concrete object that represents each of the values. Write the reason you chose that object to represent the value. You may do this as individuals or in a group. This activity may help you appreciate one aspect of poetry, and its role in the Siddur.

VALUE	OBJECT	REASON YOU CHOSE IT
1. Beauty		
2. Love		
3. Friendship		
4. Truth		
5. Peace		
6. God		
7. Israel		
8. Torah		
9. Repentance		
10. Thanksgiving		
11. Creation		
12. Revelation		
13. Redemption		
14. Equality		
15. The Jewish People		

2. The Languages of Structured and Spontaneous Prayer

One of the most hotly debated issues in both rabbinic and modern times regarding prayer is whether, and to what degree, prayer should be structured or spontaneous. Many people today who find the t'fillah experience to be a difficult one claim it is because they are unable to say words written by someone else in some other time as their own. Yet, we are not the first nor will we be the last generation to feel this way. As a matter of fact when our liturgy was first being organized, our greatest Rabbis debated whether t'fillot were to be required and structured or personal and private. As our tradition and liturgy began to grow from its earliest sources in the Temple to the t'fillot which developed in the *Beit Kenesset* (synagogue), the Rabbis continued their debate. As you can see, our tradition opted for a prescribed, structured prayer system. But within that system the Rabbis gave us wide opportunity and latitude for spontaneous, personal prayer. Moreover, they felt that we had to work very hard at making even the prayer of another as if it were our own. They developed many kinds of mechanisms to enable people to do that. Listed below are some sources showing the Rabbis' attitudes on fixed prayers (קֶבַע , *keva*) versus spontaneous prayers, (those with כַּוָּנָה , *kavanah*, "intention"). The notion of kavanah applies to spontaneous personal prayer as well as to reciting fixed, written prayers with deep emotion, feeling, and concentration. Franz Rosenzweig has summarized the relationship between fixed and spontaneous prayer.

> The difference between prescribed prayer and spontaneous prayer is that the latter is born out of the needs of the moment, while the former teaches him who prays to seek a need he might otherwise not feel.[14]

The ultimate goal of the prayer experience for the Jew is to start from the fixed prayers of our tradition and attempt to relate to them with as much kavanah as possible, so that complete empathy will take place between ourselves and the printed word.

First, let us look at some background sources urging the establishment of institutionalized prayer as well as ongoing devotion and spontaneity. The need for institutionalized prayer was summarized by Rambam, whose view is explained by Seymour Rosenbloom:

> There seem to be two motives described in this passage *(Hilchot T'fillah 1:4)*, distinct but related. One is the result of human differences. Some men have greater facility than others with language and expression...
>
> The other motive for institutionalization of prayer texts is the product of a crisis in the Jewish community precipitated by the Babylonian exile. The Rambam concentrates on a problem of language. Dispersed among alien cultures, knowledge of Hebrew, he postulates, was lost. The older generation did not use it regularly; the younger generation knew it only haltingly. Just as Americanization meant the demise of Yiddish as a spoken language for the children of East European immigrants, the fate of Hebrew under "Babylonization" was similar. Jews could no longer speak a good Hebrew sentence, much less compose their own Hebrew prayers.
>
> One is tempted to speculate, however, that the Rambam did not consider this the real problem, but only symbolic of it. Nowhere does he specify that the mitzvah of prayer can be fulfilled only in Hebrew. Perhaps the real problem is not one of language but of ideas. The result of being in a foreign culture is not only the adoption of the host culture's language. Jews--especially the return from Babylonia Jews--would naturally begin to assimilate Babylonian ideas which have no foundation in Judaism and which may be antithetical to the Jewish world view.[15]

Even much earlier, talmudic Rabbis spoke about the need for fixed, detailed, prescribed liturgical forms. An incident is recorded about Rabbi Yoḥanan and Rabbi Yonatan:

They entered a town and found a ḥazzan who recited, "The great, powerful, awesome, mighty, courageous God," and they silenced him. They said, "You are not permitted to add to the phrasing which the Sages have established for blessings."

עליון לחד אתר ואשכחון לחזנא דאמר: האל הגדול הגבור והנורא האביר והאמיץ ושיתקו אתו. אמרו לו: אין לך רשות להוסיף על מטבע שטבעו חכמים בברכות.

Yerushalmi B'rachot 9:12d

Some Sages did not feel the need for specific wording for b'rachot. Others agreed there was to be a fixed form, but disagreed about specific content:

If someone sees a loaf of bread and says, "What a fine loaf that is; blessed is God (HaMakom, the 'Omnipresent') who created it," he has fulfilled his obligation. Or if he sees a fig and says, "What a fine fig this is; blessed is God who created it," he has fulfilled his obligation. This is Rabbi Meir's view. But Rabbi Yose says, "Whoever changes the phrasing which the sages determined for b'rachot has not fulfilled his obligation . . . Rav said, "Any blessing which does not mention God's name is not a b'rachah." But Rabbi Yoḥanan said, "Any blessing that does not mention God's kingship is not a b'rachah."

ראה פת ואמר: כמה נאה פת זו, ברוך המקום שבראה — יצא; ראה תאנה ואמר: כמה נאה תאנה זו, ברוך המקום שבראה — יצא, דברי ר' מאיר; ר' יוסי אומר: כל המשנה ממטבע שטבעו חכמים בברכות לא יצא ידי חובתו . . . אמר רב: כל ברכה שאין בה הזכרת השם אינה ברכה, ורבי יוחנן אמר: כל ברכה שאין בה מלכות אינה ברכה.

B'rachot 40b

In some portions of the liturgy, they even prescribed the inclusion of various concepts or ideas:

One reading the Shema in the morning (service) must mention the exodus from Egypt as part of *Emet V'yatziv* (following the Shema). Rabbi (Yehuda HaNasi) says, "One must mention God's kingship in it." Others say, "One must mention the parting of the Red Sea and the plague of the killing of the first born sons." Rabbi Yehoshua ben Levi says, "One must include them all, and must say, 'Rock of Israel and his Redeemer.'"

הקורא את שמע בבוקר צריך להזכיר יציאת מצרים באמת ויציב; רבי אומר: צריך להזכיר בה מלכות; אחרים אומרים: צריך להזכיר בה קריעת ים סוף ומכת בכורים; ר' יהושע בן לוי אומר: צריך להזכיר את כולן וצריך לומר "צור ישראל וגואלו."

Yerushalmi B'rachot 1:3d

Of course, most of the above sentiments did become binding on our people. However, at the same time our Rabbis were careful to stress the need for personal spontaneity and enthusiasm in prayers. The two extremes were bridged succinctly, as expressed by Rabbi Shimon:

Be careful, when reciting the Shema and Amidah. And when you pray, do not make your prayer rigid, but rather compassionate and pleading before God.

רַבִּי שִׁמְעוֹן אוֹמֵר: הֱוֵי זָהִיר בְּקְרִיאַת שְׁמַע וּבִתְפִלָּה וּכְשֶׁאַתָּה מִתְפַּלֵּל אַל־תַּעַשׂ תְּפִלָּתְךָ קֶבַע, אֶלָּא רַחֲמִים וְתַחֲנוּנִים לִפְנֵי הַמָּקוֹם.

Pirkay Avot 2:18

The Rabbis even resorted to hyperbole to stress the need for devotion in prayer:

"Bless the Lord." Resh Lakish said: Whoever responds, "Amen" with all his strength, the gates of Paradise are opened for him, as it is said, "Open the gates and the righteous nation which keeps faithfulness will enter." Don't read "which keeps faithfulness" but (based on a play on words in Hebrew) "which say 'Amen.'"

"בְּרְכוּ ה' " . . . אמר ריש לקיש: כל העונה "אמן" בכל כוחו פותחין לו שערי גן עדן, שנאמר "פתחו שערים ויבא גוי צדיק שמר אמנים." (יש' כו, ב) – אל תיקרי "שמר אמנים" אלא "שאומרים אמן."

Shabbat 119b

They asked us to pray with the emotion we would feel if we were actually standing in the presence of a king:

One who is praying must feel in his heart the meaning of the words on his lips, and consider that the Shechinah (God's Presence) is opposite him, and put aside all thoughts which distress him, until his thoughts and intentions are clear in his prayer. He must give consideration; if he were speaking to a human king he would organize his words and give them proper attention so he would not make mistakes. How much more so before the King of kings of kings, the Holy One, blessed be He, who explores all thoughts.

המתפלל צריך שיכוין בלבו פירוש המלות שמוציא בשפתיו, ויחשוב כאילו שכינה כנגדו, ויסיר כל המחשבות הטורדות אותו עד שתשאר מחשבתו וכוונתו זכה בתפלתו. ויחשוב, כאילו היה מדבר לפני מלך בשר ודם היה מסדר דבריו ומכוין בהם יפה לבל יכשול. קל וחומר לפני מלך מלכי המלכים, הקדוש ברוך הוא שהוא חוקר כל המחשבות.

Shulḥan Aruch, Oraḥ Ḥayyim 98

They even went so far as to suggest that if understanding Hebrew were a barrier to deep devotion and concentration, one could use any language which one understood:

These may be said in any language...recitation of the Shema, the Amidah, and Birkat HaMazon (Grace after Meals) ...

אֵלּוּ נֶאֱמָרִין בְּכָל לָשׁוֹן: . . . קְרִיאַת שְׁמַע, וּתְפִלָּה, וּבִרְכַּת הַמָּזוֹן . . .

Sotah 7:1

Commenting on this concept (specifically commenting on the Shema), Rambam cautions that,

One reciting in any language must be careful of mistakes in that language, and must be as precise in that language as he would be if reciting it in Hebrew.

וְהַקּוֹרֵא בְּכָל־לָשׁוֹן – צָרִיךְ לְהִזָּהֵר מִדִּבְרֵי שִׁבּוּשׁ שֶׁבְּאוֹתָהּ הַלָּשׁוֹן, וּמְדַקְדֵּק בְּאוֹתָהּ הַלָּשׁוֹן, כְּמוֹ שֶׁמְּדַקְדֵּק אִם קְרָאָהּ בִּלְשׁוֹן הַקֹּדֶשׁ.

Rambam, Hilchot K'riyat Shema 2:10

We are encouraged, even required, to add our own prayers of special personal need and importance in the Amidah:

...If someone wants to add to each of the intermediate blessings (on the same topic as the b'rachah) he may do so. How? If he is concerned about someone sick, he seeks compassion for him in the blessing for the sick, according to his own eloquence. If he needs sustenance, he adds supplication and request in the blessing for a prosperous year. It is done in this manner in every b'rachah. If he wants to ask for all his needs in the blessing, "...who listens to prayer," he may ask.

וְכֵן אִם רָצָה לְהוֹסִיף בְּכָל־בְּרָכָה וּבְרָכָה מִן־הָאֶמְצָעִיּוֹת מֵעֵין הַבְּרָכָה – מוֹסִיף. כֵּיצַד? הָיָה לוֹ חוֹלֶה – מְבַקֵּשׁ עָלָיו רַחֲמִים בְּבִרְכַּת חוֹלִים כְּפִי צַחוּת לְשׁוֹנוֹ; הָיָה צָרִיךְ לְפַרְנָסָה – מוֹסִיף תְּחִנָּה וּבַקָּשָׁה בְּבִרְכַּת הַשָּׁנִים. וְעַל־דֶּרֶךְ זֶה בְּכָל־אַחַת מֵהֶן. וְאִם רָצָה לִשְׁאוֹל כָּל־צְרָכָיו בְּשׁוֹמֵעַ תְּפִלָּה – שׁוֹאֵל.

Rambam, Hilchot T'fillah 6:2-3

In other words, we are to follow carefully a fixed routine of institutionalized prayer, while approaching it with love, devotion, and a continued sense of renewal and spontaneity. Maimonides goes on to express this dual approach:

These services (three daily) may not be lessened, but one may add to them. If a person wants to pray all day, he may do so. The prayers which he adds are like a free-will offering. Therefore, one must make an appropriate thought (as if it were) new in each of the intermediate blessings. If one makes the addition in even one blessing it is sufficient, making it known that the prayer is voluntary and not (just) obligatory. As to the first three and last three blessings (of the Amidah), one must neither add to them nor lessen them, and should not change anything in them.

תְּפִלּוֹת אֵלּוּ – אֵין פּוֹחֲתִין מֵהֶן, אֲבָל מוֹסִיפִין עֲלֵיהֶן:
אִם רָצָה אָדָם לְהִתְפַּלֵּל כָּל־הַיּוֹם כֻּלּוֹ – הָרְשׁוּת בְּיָדוֹ.
וְכָל־אוֹתָן הַתְּפִלּוֹת שֶׁיּוֹסִיף – כְּמוֹ מַקְרִיב נְדָבוֹת. לְפִיכָךְ
צָרִיךְ שֶׁיְּחַדֵּשׁ דָּבָר בְּכָל־בְּרָכָה וּבְרָכָה מִן־הָאֶמְצָעִיּוֹת
מֵעֵין הַבְּרָכוֹת. וְאִם חִדֵּשׁ אֲפִלּוּ בִּבְרָכָה אַחַת – דַּיּוֹ, כְּדֵי
לְהוֹדִיעַ שֶׁהִיא נְדָבָה וְלֹא חוֹבָה. וְשָׁלֹשׁ רִאשׁוֹנוֹת וְשָׁלֹשׁ
אַחֲרוֹנוֹת – לְעוֹלָם אֵין מוֹסִיפִין בָּהֶן, וְלֹא פּוֹחֲתִין מֵהֶן,
וְאֵין מְשַׁנִּין בָּהֶן דָּבָר.

Rambam, *Hilchot T'fillah 1:9*

In our own time, Abraham J. Heschel reinvestigated the need for t'fillot keva and kavanah, calling them "Prayers of Empathy" and "Prayers of Expression." The prayer of empathy helps us pray by providing us with a starting point of established words. When carefully considered, such prayers can elicit sensitive, emotional and prayerful reactions from us. By trying to empathize with the experience contained in a fixed prayer we can enrich ourselves and trigger deep emotions. We try to recreate the experience of another human being, as it were, without ever having known that person. In addition, since we are not all eloquent enough to express our deepest and most important feelings in words of dignity and power, the prayer of empathy gives us the words and helps us express ourselves. The prayer of empathy also broadens our own range and knowledge of experience: none of us can have been everywhere and done everything, and we rely on the collective experience of our people to expand and enrich our lives. This type of prayer requires concentrated attention to the words and their meanings, thus changing established prayer into a personal, creative experience. The prayer of expression, on the other hand, occurs as a reaction to some experience we have undergone which causes us to utter our own words or perform our own gestures of feeling. Personal prayers responding to our most personally felt needs and desires fit into this category. Many of the fixed prayers (i.e., prayers of empathy) in the Siddur started as personal, private devotions (i.e., prayers of expression). Ultimately we must keep both kinds of prayer in proper balance in order to achieve a full, meaningful prayer experience.

Now look at the arguments listed below for fixed and spontaneous prayer. Decide which of those arguments seem valid to you and which arguments are weak. See if you can come up with the ways of counteracting arguments against fixed prayer and see if there are problems with any of the arguments for spontaneous prayer.

The following selection is from Harvey J. Fields, *Bechol Levavcha: With All Your Heart* (New York: Union of America Hebrew Congregations, 1977).

ARGUMENTS FOR FIXED PRAYER

1.

We are a congregation, and, in order for us to feel a sense of unity with one another, we need to use the same words. The more we share, the closer we will feel.

2.

If we wait until we feel like composing a prayer, we might never pray or we might lose the ability to pray. Prayer demands the discipline of regular practice and the same words if we are to be successful at it.

3.

Not all of us are great poets or writers. It is silly not to make use of the outstanding poetry and prayers of our tradition that have been tested by time and many generations. They can express our feelings better than we ourselves can.

4.

When we use prayers composed by Jews throughout our history, we identify ourselves with the traditions and generations of our people. When we pray with the same prayers used by Jews throughout the world, we feel at one with our people no matter where they are. Fixed prayer insures the unity of the Jewish people.

5.

Often when an individual composes a prayer, it is self-centered and expresses only his own selfish concerns. Fixed Jewish prayer is concerned with the welfare of the community and has been carefully written so as to avoid selfish, fleeting needs.

6.

The rabbis teach us that a person should not be hasty to utter a word before God. That temptation is eliminated by fixed prayer. Spontaneous prayer is often hastily and carelessly composed. Prayer ought to be written with concentration by individuals possessing great skill. Fixed prayer fulfills this requirement.

7.

Spontaneous prayer causes confusion among the worshipers. The talmudic sage, Rabbi Zeira, once said: "Every time I added new words to my prayers, I became confused and lost my place." Such confusion takes away from the beauty and meaning of the prayer experience. A fixed order of worship solves this problem.

8.

Beautiful prayers, like great poetry, never lose their meaning through repetition. The more we read them with open minds and hearts, the more meanings we can discover. The cure for dull prayer experiences is in us, not in the creation of new prayers.

OTHER:

ARGUMENTS FOR SPONTANEOUS PRAYER

1.

While the fixed prayers may be beautiful, after you have said them over and over again, they become dull, repetitive, and lose their meaning. The rabbis recognized this and, in the Mishnah, they tell us: "Do not let your prayers be a matter of fixed routine but rather heartfelt expressions."

2.

Spontaneous prayer allows us to express our feelings, hopes, and concerns. If we are bound by a fixed text, we are prevented from making our worship as personally meaningful as it should be. The Bratzlaver Rebbe, a leading teacher of Chasidism, once said to his students: "You must feel your words of prayer in all your bones, in all your limbs, and in all your nerves." When we use our own prayers we feel deeply about that for which we are praying.

3.

We are not machines and we can't be programed to be in the same mood as everyone else at the same time. Spontaneous prayer allows us the freedom to express our true feelings in the moment we pray.

4.

We should not forget that the fixed prayers of tradition were once spontaneous expressions of individuals and their communities. Throughout Jewish history, Jews have been composing new prayers and adding them to the prayer book. We need to continue that creative process for it has helped keep Jewish prayer meaningful, and even added to the survival of Judaism.

5.

In every generation our people has faced new problems and challenges. These should be expressed in our prayers. Obviously, if we are bound to a fixed text or style of prayer, we cannot include contemporary issues or forms in our worship.

OTHER:

EXERCISE 1

Now that we have studied some of the issues involved in fixed versus spontaneous prayer, try the following exercise to see where you stand on the problems and tensions involved.

Below is a continuum line with one end being keva and the other end kavanah. If you place yourself at the keva end, you are saying that you believe only in a fixed routine type of prayer that is prescribed in every detail. Placing yourself at the other end means that you are opposed to fixed prayer and believe in a totally spontaneous, self-initiated prayer experience. Mark the spot on the line you feel best represents your position, and consider the elements which place you in that position.

Keva   Kavanah

(fixed prayer)   (spontaneous prayer)

EXERCISE 2

The book of Psalms occupies an important place in our liturgy. Our Rabbis developed an ingenious Midrash on prayer from the way many psalms begin:

"To David, a psalm" -- (psalms that start this way) teach God's Presence rested on David and only afterward did he write the psalm. "A psalm, to David" -- teaches us that David wrote the psalm and only afterward did the Divine Presence rest on him.

"לדוד מזמור" — מלמד ששרתה עליו שכינה ואחר כך אמר שירה.

"מזמור לדוד" — מלמד שאמר שירה ואחר כך שרתה עליו שכינה.

Pesaḥim 117b

The two orders in which the opening words appear recall the two basic types of prayer experiences. The first is like the prayer which flows first from emotions and is then expressed in words; the latter is comparable to prayer in which by empathizing with the words, emotions are generated. Can you relate similar experiences in your own prayer history, in which you went from experience to the need for prayer, and first praying to heightened awareness and enriched experience? (You may first want to consider the fixed versus spontaneous tensions you have experienced in other endeavors such as sports, music, or dance.)

3 The Language of Music

Most religious traditions have realized that man must go beyond mere words in expressing himself at moments of deepest emotion. Music is perhaps the most abstract and expressive language known to human beings. Music has been defined as sound which has been organized. Through the system of its organization, music conveys mood and motion by its orchestrational form. Music helps us when words are insufficient; it helps us renew the meaning of words said again and again by filling them with new dynamism and movement.

The following article was written by my dear friend, teacher, and colleague, Ḥazzan Charles Davidson, Cantor of Congregation Adath Jeshurun in Elkins Park, Pennsylvania, and Instructor of Nusaḥ at the Cantors Institute of the Jewish Theological Seminary of America.

THE MUSIC OF THE SYNAGOGUE: A Brief Overview

For most of us, the words "Jewish Heritage" mean our common history, sacred texts, holidays and rituals. The average Jew is usually unaware that the rich and unique history of Jewish music parallels and embellishes the totality of Jewish experience.

The very beginnings of Jewish music are rooted in the mists of our pre-history. While we don't know what the sounds were like, we do know that our biblical ancestors sang and played instruments. There are many accounts in the Bible of songs of joy and triumph, songs of sadness and despair, occasions of prayer and prophecy, all sung or chanted or accompanied by instruments. What we do not know are the actual musical sounds of those performances.

We have a clear picture of the patterns of sacrifice and prayer used in the days of the First Temple, when all was accompanied by music on a grand scale. King David had even established special music schools to train singers and musicians for the Temple service. The kings of other countries would request the use of Jewish musicians for their own courts, such was their reputation. We even know from the headings of various Psalms, some of the instruments used; music specialists and archaeologists can even reconstruct a general pattern of sound from the descriptions given. We can deduce, for example, that the minimum number of instruments used was twelve, from references in Psalm 150.

After the destruction of the First Temple and the return from the Babylonian exile in the mid-fifth century B.C.E., Ezra the Scribe reinstated the service in the Second Temple. We know that certain early prayers were sung. They included *Ahavah Rabbah*, blessings of the Amidah, *Sim Shalom*, and *Hallel*. The musical service was introduced by a signal from a large pipe organ (called a *hydralis*), followed by trumpet and cymbals. The people would sing *Amen, Halleluyah, Hoshanah*, and other responses. All in all, it must have been a magnificent and splendid sight.

As explained previously, Ezra also instituted the public reading of Torah on market days, Mondays and Thursdays. The Torah was chanted in a loud and strong voice so that all could hear. This cantillation of the Torah--trope--is shown by musical notation which serves grammatical and exegetical functions, *ta'amay hamikra* or *ta'amay n'ginah*. They put down in a final form an oral tradition that had been maintained for centuries. The Ashkenazim today have six systems of cantillation, each reflective of the texts and time of chanting. For example, on Tishah B'av the tunes are sad and doleful; on Purim the trope resembles a speedy narrative; the readings of the Yamim Nora'im are quite majestic, and so on.

These biblical cantillations and the tunes of the Temple service--with the exception of the knowledge of making and playing the Temple instruments--were carried away to the Diaspora. (Today, some of our oldest Jewish communities such as those of Yemen and Cochin, India, still have the remnants of Temple psalmody in their musical tradition, as do, incidentally, the Catholic, Byzantine and Armenian Churches.)

The synagogue which developed in the Diaspora utilized a simple form of prayer chant for weekdays and Shabbat that had, in fact, some basis in the biblical cantillations.

These prayer chants have come down to us today and are known as *nusha'ot*. There are, according to most Jewish musicologists, three main modes: *Ahavah Rabbah, Magen Avot,* and *Adonai Malach.* The chanting of the service varies according to the day, time of day and often from one t'fillah to another. This system of *nusha'ot* was more widely adhered to in the past than in recent years, according to the knowledge of the Jewish community and their familiarity with tradition. Too often, in recent years, relatively trite and simplistic tunes have become the vehicle for our elevated texts, mostly because of a lack of understanding and of taste for the meaning of the texts.

With the rise of special *piyyutim*, an ornate form of religious poetry beginning in the 7th century and written under the influence of Arabic meter, the leader of the synagogue service was required to become more musical. The singing of the special tunes to which the piyyutim were set made great demands on the leader. This prepared the way for the professional hazzan.

In addition to the modes, there are many prayers which have their special melodies. Some of these tunes are called *Mee-Seenai* ("from Sinai") because we don't know their origin. While there is not always agreement on the number of such melodies, we do know that such tunes have interchangeable phrases within their own melody and that these phrases can be arranged with other texts as the skill of the hazzan may dictate.

Out of this enormous mass of local and general customs and musical influences, Temple melodies, biblical cantillations, *Mee-Seenai* tunes, nusha'ot and other influences, two main bodies of Jewish music and prayer have evolved: The Ashkenazic and Sephardic.* They exhibit some similarities and many differences and add to the richness of our Jewish musical heritage.

---

*Ashkenazic refers, now, to Jews of Western (and Northern) Europe and Russia, and their descendants. Sephardic Jews are those who trace their ancestry to Greece, North Africa, and parts of the Middle East, originating in Spain.

The Relationship Between Various Nusaḥ Traditions

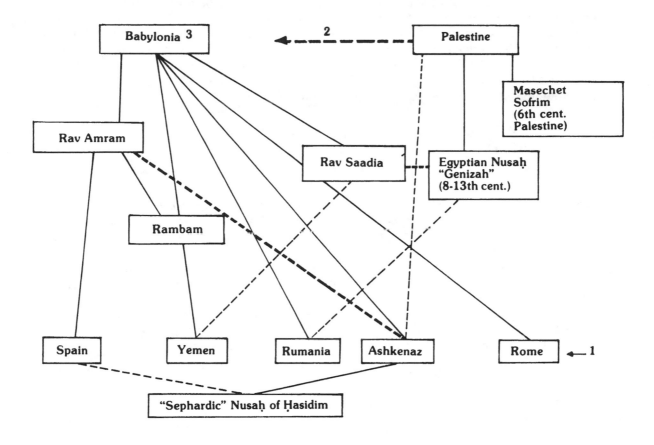

——————— Clear line of origin and influence; clear roots[4]
▬ ▬ ▬ ▬ ▬ Clear influence
— — — — — Marginal influence

Notes:
1. All these rituals had the same Amidah, unlike rituals influenced by Palestine.
2. In talmudic times there was not one, unified nusaḥ.
3. Though there was some Palestinian influence on the Babylonian nusaḥ, the reverse is not true.
4. The lines of influence are seen mainly in the non-obligatory prayers (such as piyyutim, meditations, etc.).

Based on Yosef Heinemann, *T'fillot Yisrael V'toldotayhen.*[16]

The Ḥazzan and Congregational Prayer

There are two partners which make up the musical aspects of the worship service: the congregation and the שְׁלִיחַ צִבּוּר (*shaliaḥ tzibbur,* "representative of the congregation.") Traditionally, this person, who stood and led the prayer service was simply one who was knowledgeable in the prayers, nusaḥ and rituals. In the Middle Ages, the profession of hazzan, cantor, came to dominate synagogue music. Our references here, however, are to the non-professional Jewish prayer leader. Even in the Temple there were antiphonal (responsive) and congregational chants and songs. Today the dialogue between the shaliaḥ tzibbur and congregation goes on in such responses as

אָמֵן, הַלְלוּיָהּ, בָּרוּךְ הוּא וּבָרוּךְ שְׁמוֹ, בָּרוּךְ הוּא

(Amen, Halleluyah, Blessed is He and Blessed is His name, Blessed is He.) The cantor invites our participation with such phrases as

וְאִמְרוּ . . .‏, בָּרְכוּ אֶת ה' הַמְבֹרָךְ, כֻּלָּם כְּאֶחָד עוֹנִים.

(and say...; Praise the Lord who is to be praised; they all answer in unison...). Our service is paced by the "messenger of the congregation" introducing and concluding each prayer. (Incidently, in Yemenite and some Sephardic rituals the ḥazzan chants everything aloud, often joined by the entire congregation.)

Since our musical tradition has grown up around the format of a shaliaḥ tzibbur leading a congregation, it is important to understand what kind of person that "representative" was ideally to be:

The shaliaḥ tzibbur must be of good character. What is good character? That the person is free of sins and does not have a bad reputation (even in his youth), is humble, acceptable to the people, possessing a pleasant voice, and accustomed to chanting biblical selections.

שליח צבור צריך שיהיה הגון. ואיזהו הגון שיהא ריקן מעבירות ושלא יצא עליו שם רע אפילו בילדתו ושיהיה עניו ומרוצה לעם ויש לו נעימה וקולו ערב ורגיל לקרות תורה, נביאים וכתובים.

Shulḥan Aruch, Oraḥ Ḥayyim 53:4

One who stammers (or has indistinct pronounciation) ... or one who cannot pronounce the letters (or words) correctly, should not be appointed as shaliaḥ tzibbur.

וְכֵן הָעִלֵּג, כְּגוֹן: מִי שֶׁקּוֹרֵא לְאָלֶ״ף עַיִ״ן, אוֹ לְעַיִ״ן אָלֶ״ף, וְכָל מִי שֶׁאֵינוֹ יָכוֹל לְהוֹצִיא אֶת הָאוֹתִיּוֹת כְּתִקּוּנָן — אֵין מְמַנִּין אוֹתוֹ שְׁלִיחַ צִבּוּר.

Rambam, Hilchot T'fillah 8:12

Therefore, simply wanting to lead the congregation is not enough; there are many elements which go into being an adequate shaliaḥ tzibbur.

Below is a checklist against which you can measure your readiness to be a shaliaḥ tzibbur and see where you have to develop your present skills or attitudes.

Attributes of the Good Shaliaḥ Tzibbur

_____ Pronounces all Hebrew words correctly, with proper accent.

_____ Seeks to sing melodies which correctly accent Hebrew words, or reshapes cadence of melody to accent words correctly.

_____ Knows the correct nusaḥ (musical motif) of the particular prayer service and is familiar with special changes which occur within the service (e.g., change of mode from *P'sukay D'zimrah* to new mode at *Yishtabaḥ* in morning; reversion to weekday nusaḥ for beginning of repetition of Amidah during Shabbat Minḥah etc.).

_____ Is thoroughly familiar with order of service, or page changes, so as not to hesitate or seem confused.

_____ Introduces each prayer in a strong voice, fades down but is still audible by congregation, rising in volume at closing passage.

_____ Listens to the pace of the congregation to gauge when to conclude a prayer.

_____ Sets pace and tone of service; chooses melodies which are aesthetic and in keeping with nusaḥ; doesn't overburden congregation with too many arias or solos.

_____ Leads congregational singing with dominant voice, setting the pace.

_____ Senses proper musical key which is comfortable for congregation.

_____ Gives congregation time to finish prayers recited silently.

_____ Senses rhythm of service, knowing where to add a melody or continue straight chanting.

_____ Is properly attired (depending on custom of congregation; but too skimpy clothes are never appropriate).

_____ Takes role as shaliaḥ tzibbur seriously and seeks to pray with kavanah.

_____ Senses that it is a privilege to be honored by the congregation in being asked to serve as its shaliaḥ tzibbur.

EXERCISE 1

Many different Jewish communities have evolved their own particular nusaḥ of prayer. Many of them have different customs and even variations among prayers. Often when a traveler is visiting a place like Israel he may be invited to the home of a Yemenite, Moroccan, or Italian Jew and faced with customs quite different from his own. For example, this author was faced with the invitation to partake in a big bowl of popcorn when he spent Pesaḥ with a Yemenite family. Yemenites eat corn on Pesaḥ, but Ashkenazic Jews do not. So, there was a question as to what to do.

List some of the varying customs you've seen or experienced in different synagogues. Examples may include standing for the Shema or kaddish, abridgement of certain parts of the service, or use of choir and organ. Discuss how you should behave when confronted by a custom you're not used to. Should you join in? Sit quietly? Try to have the congregation change? Other?

Consider the dictate of our tradition, אַל תִּפְרוֹשׁ מִן הַצִּבּוּר "Don't separate yourself from the congregation" and the practice of observing מִנְהַג הַמָּקוֹם , "the custom of the place."

The height of false piety is to snicker at a practice which, though different from yours, is quite within our tradition -- but may be unfamiliar to you!

4. Body Language

Recently many books have been written discussing the ideas involved in body language. We all tell each other different things by the way we hold ourselves, the way we cross our legs, the way we cross our arms, the way we cock our heads. The language of our bodies is as powerful a communication vehicle as words themselves. Research shows 7% of our communication is in the meaning of our words, 38% in the way we say things, and 55% in non-verbal, body language. With our bodies we are also able to communicate strong emotions and feelings. We can communicate dislikes with a distortion of the face, love with a smile or a kiss, a shaking of the hand, or a salute. Through the ages human beings have found all kinds of ways to demonstrate physically their innermost hopes, beliefs, and concerns. We all know that bowing is practically a universal custom acknowledging respect or subordination. Some of you might also know that the origin of shaking hands may stem from medieval times when knights would hold out their right hand to show that they were unarmed and therefore, meeting in peace. Another way in which the body has been able to communicate values is through its adornment. In some cultures people paint their faces; in others they wear rings around their necks; in still others they wrap themselves in special garments which convey special meanings for special times.

The Jewish people, having lived in many places over a long period of time, has developed its own set of "body language" customs which have become central to our prayer experience. Often these customs help us to achieve greater kavanah in our prayers. They enable us to express physically what we are feeling or thinking. Performing many of these acts of body language in community helps us to identify with others and makes us feel part of a whole. At the same time if we look at the prayer experience as one of empathizing with the author of the prayer, the body language associated with the prayer helps us to understand the author's intent.

During every service (and especially on the high holidays) we look to God as King. In ancient times people were more used to kings, and the proper ways of relating to the king: bowing when coming into his presence; bowing without turning one's back on the king when leaving; bowing when making a request or offering praise. Those customs and rituals became a part of our prayer ritual since to a great extent God is conceived of as a king, and our entire prayer service is a kind of drama between His subjects, the people Israel, and His Majesty the King, God of Israel. It is sometimes difficult for us today to feel the awe of a subject coming into the presence of a king. Sometimes we feel that it might be necessary to create new types of body language, more appropriate to the society in which we live. Yet, when all is said and done there seem to certain basic ways of using our bodies to represent our most profound feelings. These seem to be well contained in our prayer rituals. What follows is a kind of survey of the body language of prayer. This is presented together in one section--rather than section by section with individual prayers-- so that you get a comprehensive view of the way we use our bodies to pray. As you read through this material look to see which particular body language customs you already perform and which you might want to incorporate into your own t'fillah experience. There are, of course, many variations among Jewish communities in certain customs, and there are different levels of importance to many of the customs.

Since Judaism embodies all of life and is concerned with every aspect of our daily existence, it is natural that the t'fillah body language experience begins as soon as the Jew awakens. In our physical actions we mirror our faith and values. Our physical hygiene is essential to the t'fillah experience and so a Jew may not approach prayer, or any religious activity, without having washed and groomed. Here are some sources of our early morning rituals of arising and preparing for prayer. Note that we do not even eat before we pray in the morning:

It is forbidden for someone to eat anything or to do any work after daybreak until he prays shaharit. And one should not visit a friend before shaharit or start out on a journey before praying.	אָסוּר לוֹ לְאָדָם שֶׁיִּטְעַם כְּלוּם, אוֹ שֶׁיַּעֲשֶׂה מְלָאכָה מֵאַחַר שֶׁיַּעֲלֶה עַמּוּד הַשַּׁחַר – עַד שֶׁיִּתְפַּלֵּל תְּפִלַּת שַׁחֲרִית; וְכֵן לֹא יַשְׁכִּים לְפֶתַח חֲבֵרוֹ לִשְׁאֹל בִּשְׁלוֹמוֹ קֹדֶם שֶׁיִּתְפַּלֵּל תְּפִלַּת שַׁחֲרִית; וְלֹא יֵצֵא בַדֶּרֶךְ קֹדֶם שֶׁיִּתְפַּלֵּל. Rambam, *Hilchot T'fillah 6:4*
It is permissible to eat before Musaf, that is, something like fruit or even more substantial food, but a full meal is forbidden.	מותר לטעום קודם תפלת המוספין דהיינו אכילת פירות ואפילו פת מועט אפילו טעימה שיש בה כדי לסעוד הלב אבל סעודה אסורה. Shulhan Aruch, *Orah Hayyim 286:3*
One who is thirsty or hungry is considered in the category of someone who is ill: if he is able to be attentive he should pray; if not, if he wants, he need not pray until he has had something to eat or drink.	הצמא והרעב הרי הם בכלל החולים: אם יש בו יכולת לכוין דעתו, יתפלל, ואם לאו, אם רצה אל יתפלל עד שיאכל וישתה. Shulhan Aruch, *Orah Hayyim 89:4*

(Often on Shabbat morning when the service may be long, some people partake in a light repast such as juice or tea and cookies to tide them over till the end of the service. Bread, however, is not eaten since that constitutes an "official" meal. Sometimes, in group situations such as summer camps, people break for breakfast after the Shaharit service and then reconvene for Musaf.) Also, before beginning to pray we recite the b'rachah over washing the hands and then the b'rachah which acknowledges our bodily functions (respiration, digestion, metabolism and excretion) and praises God who has created the human body. (These blessings appear in the Siddur at the beginning of the Shaharit service.)

> The Jew recognizes the wisdom of his Creator not with the sophistication of the scientist who scans the stupendous display of nature with a cold, detached objectivity. Instead he is brought to a sincere and humble admiration by the operations of the human body .... To him, these are miracles of Divine wisdom performed everyday within ourselves....
> Generally, this Bracha is recited only after the discharge of bodily functions. Still it is always to be said at this point of the daily service, as an offering of gratitude for our physical health. By also serving as the Bracha after excretion, it has the effect, so typical of the Jewish view of life, of bringing even the grossest physical act within the orbit of religion.[17]

A. Garments

Our desire to involve our physical selves in the t'fillah activity is reflected, also, in articles such as the *tallit, t'fillin,* and *kipah*.[18] We wrap ourselves in tallit and t'fillin, actions of body language, in which we are enveloped in objects of holiness and beauty. When putting on the tallit, the b'rachah recited is לְהִתְעַטֵּף בַּצִּיצָת , "to wrap oneself up in the *tzitzit* (fringes)." Some people put the tallit over their heads in an attempt to concentrate better, to block out, as it were, the outside world. (One other custom related to this notion of blocking out extraneous events in order to concentrate is associated with the Shema. Some people take a corner of the tallit, or just take their hand, and hold it over their eyes, while reciting the first line of the Shema.)

The third garment worn by the Jew, the kipah, is of uncertain origin. Part of its use developed from a desire of Jews to be different. As Christians began to take off hats in churches, Jews began to keep them on, as a sign of reverence to God. It has also been the custom for married women to cover their heads when lighting candles or in the synagogue, and some unmarried women now wear head coverings as well. Dress in general is an extremely important part of our body language messages. Jews are to dress appropriately for t'fillah:

How does one prepare his clothing? First, one prepares (adjusts) the clothing and then takes care of one's own appearance, as it is written, "Worship the Lord in the beauty of holiness" (Psalm 96:9). One does not stand praying (the Amidah) wearing a moneybelt, or with head uncovered, or barefoot (where it is customary not to stand before important people without shoes). One does not pray holding t'fillin in his hands or a Torah in his arms, since he would be preoccupied about (not dropping) them.

תִּקּוּן הַמַּלְבּוּשִׁים כֵּיצַד? מְתַקֵּן מַלְבּוּשָׁיו תְּחִלָּה וּמְצַיֵּן עַצְמוֹ וּמְהַדֵּר, שֶׁנֶּאֱמַר: הִשְׁתַּחֲווּ לַה' בְּהַדְרַת־קֹדֶשׁ (תהלים כט, ב). וְלֹא יַעֲמֹד בִּתְפִלָּה בַּאֲפֻנְדָּתוֹ, וְלֹא בְרֹאשׁ מְגֻלֶּה, וְלֹא בְרַגְלַיִם מְגֻלּוֹת אִם דֶּרֶךְ אַנְשֵׁי הַמָּקוֹם שֶׁלֹּא יַעַמְדוּ בִּפְנֵי הַגְּדוֹלִים אֶלָּא בְּבָתֵּי הָרַגְלָיִם. וּבְכָל־מָקוֹם לֹא יֶאֱחֹז תְּפִלִּין בְּיָדוֹ וְסֵפֶר תּוֹרָה בִּזְרוֹעוֹ וְיִתְפַּלֵּל – מִפְּנֵי שֶׁלִּבּוֹ טָרוּד בָּהֶם.

Rambam, *Hilchot Tfillah 5:5*

What "appropriate" dress is will vary depending on the situation, but one is always to look neat and clean. T'fillah is not a time for ostentation or sexual temptation, by means of clothing. (Refer to Section III in this source book on *Birchot Hashahar,* and particularly the b'rachah *malbush arumim* to confront this issue further.) Where dress is too casual, too informal, the prayer experience suffers as a result.

One other aspect of dress, the concept of *hiddur mitzvah* (literally, "embellishing a mitzvah") is to be noted. We seek to perform mitzvot in as beautiful a way as possible. So we create beautiful kiddush cups, Torah mantles, and other ritual objects. Likewise, it has become popular to weave, crochet, or needlepoint beautiful tallitot, tallit bags, or kippot. We further modify our clothing habits to help us in our prayer experience by performing special customs during the year. On Erev Yom Kippur, putting on the tallit before it is dark, we are able to symbolize the holiness and specialness of the occasion. At special times, such as the Yamim Nora'im, the Pesah Seder, or under the wedding canopy, it is a custom to wear a white "kittel" (gown), a symbol of purity and sanctity. (It is also this kittel in which some people are buried.) On fast days such as Yom Kippur and Tishah B'av it is the custom not to wear leather shoes. Leather was considered a sign of comfort and ostentation and, therefore, inappropriate apparel on a day of mourning or fasting. (By the way, the restriction is only for leather shoes; one may wear a leather belt.)

You may notice that the dress of many members of Hasidic sects is extremely different from ours. Out of a deep desire to retain their past and remain distinct from the secular culture, Hasisim often dress differently to emphasize their Jewishness. On Shabbat they don beautiful fur-covered hats and long caftans, wearing a special Shabbat belt which separates the upper spiritual part of the body from the lower more mundane part of the body. We may find the details of such customs inappropriate, but we can well understand that getting dressed up and wearing something special can make a time such as Shabbat or a holiday all the more special. So we wear something new, or a garment reserved especially for Shabbat or holidays, to help us feel the specialness of the day.

B. Standing

Standing is a sign of respect or of calling importance to a particular aspect of something we are doing. Accordingly, there are many times in the course of our prayer experiences when we stand to honor God the King, or to call attention to particularly important passages in the service. The prayer par excellence for standing is the Amidah (which literally means "standing"). So important is standing up straight, with heels together, that one is not to move his feet even the slightest amount while reciting the Amidah. (Often people stand close to a bench or chair, so that no one can walk in front of them and disturb them while they recite the Amidah.) Even when the hazzan recites the special *Alaynu* as part of the repetition of the Amidah on the High Holidays and bows down on the ground, he does not move his feet apart (and is often assisted back to a standing position).

What is the correct posture? When someone is standing and reciting the Amidah, his feet should be next to each other. He should cast his eyes down, as if looking at the ground, and direct his thoughts upward, as if standing in heaven. He rests his hands on his heart, right over left. He should stand like a servant before his master, in terror, awe and fear, and not rest his hands on his hips.	תִּקּוּן הַגּוּף כֵּיצַד? כְּשֶׁהוּא עוֹמֵד בִּתְפִלָּה צָרִיךְ לְכַוֵּן אֶת־רַגְלָיו זוֹ בְּצַד זוֹ; וְנוֹתֵן עֵינָיו לְמַטָּה, כְּאִלּוּ הוּא מַבִּיט לָאָרֶץ; וְיִהְיֶה לִבּוֹ פָּנוּי לְמַעְלָה, כְּאִלּוּ הוּא עוֹמֵד בַּשָּׁמַיִם; וּמַנִּיחַ יָדָיו עַל לִבּוֹ כְּפוּתִין הַיְמָנִית עַל הַשְּׂמָאלִית וְעוֹמֵד כְּעֶבֶד לִפְנֵי רַבּוֹ בְּאֵימָה בְּיִרְאָה וָפַחַד, וְלֹא יַנִּיחַ יָדָיו עַל חֲלָצָיו.

Rambam, *Hilchot T'fillot 5:4*

When reciting the Amidah individually, one may be seated upon concluding, but not in front of a fellow worshipper still in prayer. When the ḥazzan repeats the Amidah, we rise for the K'dushah (in most congregations, remaining seated for the first two b'rachot). Some congregations observe "duchanen" -- the custom whereby the kohanim bless the congregation with the three-part priestly blessing. Where that custom is observed, congregants rise, often bowing their heads or folding their tallitot around the young children, so they cannot see the kohanim standing at the front of the synagogue. (Among other reasons, this helps make the blessing as democratic as possible, lest anyone feel that the kohayn is not blessing him and favoring someone else, and so the kohayn will not be able to see whom he is blessing, directing his blessing toward one congregant rather than another.)

Not only *when* we stand, but the direction we face when praying is important.

We face towards the Temple; how? If one is outside of Israel, one prays facing towards Israel; in Israel, one faces Jerusalem; in Jerusalem, one faces toward the Temple (site). If one is in the Temple, he faces towards the Holy of Holies. A person who is blind, or one who cannot determine the proper direction, or one who is on a ship, directs his intention towards God's presence and prays.	נֹכַח הַמִּקְדָּשׁ כֵּיצַד? הָיָה עוֹמֵד בְּחוּצָה לָאָרֶץ – מַחֲזִיר פָּנָיו נֹכַח אֶרֶץ יִשְׂרָאֵל וּמִתְפַּלֵּל. הָיָה עוֹמֵד בָּאָרֶץ – מְכַוֵּן אֶת פָּנָיו כְּנֶגֶד יְרוּשָׁלָיִם. הָיָה עוֹמֵד בַּמִּקְדָּשׁ – מְכַוֵּן פָּנָיו כְּנֶגֶד בֵּית קֹדֶשׁ הַקֳּדָשִׁים. סוּמָא, וּמִי שֶׁלֹּא יָכוֹל לְכַוֵּן אֶת־הָרוּחוֹת, וְהַמְהַלֵּךְ בַּסְּפִינָה – יְכַוֵּן אֶת־לִבּוֹ כְּנֶגֶד הַשְּׁכִינָה וְיִתְפַּלֵּל.

Rambam, *Hilchot T'fillot 5:3*

What follows is a listing of places in the service we stand, and some of the underlying reasons. Be aware that customs vary among congregations in these rituals, as in most areas of observance.

We rise for the Birchot Hashaḥar, the morning blessings being seated at the word *koah*, before the final long b'rachah in the series. (It is customary in some communities to remain standing for the selections about sacrificies which follow.)

Mourners and those observing Yahrzeit rise if *Kaddish D'rabbanan* is recited at the end of the Birchot Hashaḥar section.

Once again we rise for *Baruch She'amar,* which begins the P'sukay D'zimrah section.

It is the custom to rise for the recitation of *Hodu*--Psalm 136, recited on Shabbat and festivals.

Again the congregation rises for the introduction to the Song of Moses which begins *vay'varech David;* the congregation is seated at the end of the Song of Moses.

All congregations rise for *Barechu*, the point in the service at which participants are asked to join together to praise God. Customs vary as to how much in advance of barechu to rise:

at Yishtabah shimcha, end of the P'sukay D'zimrah section;
at the Kaddish, the separation of the two segments of the service;
at Barechu itself.

One should follow the custom of his or her own community or the custom of the place in which one is praying.

In some congregations it is the custom to rise for the Shema since it is considered a pivotal part of the srvice. Respect is shown for it by rising. The difference of whether or not to rise for the Shema goes all the way back to a disagreement in the Talmud between Hillel and Shammai: Hillel felt that we should not separate the Shema from the two blessings preceding it, reciting the Shema in the same posture we recited the blessings. Shammai disagreed.

The congregation remains seated until it rises again in preparation for the Amidah, generally for the paragraph *Tzur Yisrael*. The Amidah is recited standing, as explained above.

When Hallel is recited (holidays and Rosh Hodesh) the congregation rises for it.

We stand for the Torah service, generally rising at the words *vay'hee bin'so'a*, just before the Torah is removed from the ark. The congregation remains standing until the Torah is finally placed on the reader's desk to be read. While the congregation stands reciting *V'zot HaTorah* (in some Sephardic congregations this is done prior to the Torah reading), the Torah is lifted after the reading, for all to see. At this point, some people raise a Siddur or corner of the tallit, holding it up towards the Torah, bringing the book or tzitzit to their lips to kiss, as a sign of love and respect.

We rise when we recite the blessing for the coming month, and for putting the Torah back into the Ark. Alaynu, at the end of the service, is also said standing at least through the lines in which we bend and bow, ending with the words *Hakadosh Baruch Hu*.

In some congregations on Shabbat morning *Shir HaKavod* is recited, and the ark is opened, while the congregation stands.

One other service in which we stand is Kabbalat Shabbat, on Friday evening. During that service we rise for Psalm 29 *(Mizmor L'David)* and then again for the last verse of the famous piyyut (liturgical poem) *L'chah Dodi*, in which we turn and face the entrance to the synagogue, bowing, as we welcome the Sabbath Bride.

In Ma'ariv on Friday evening it is the custom to rise for *V'sham'ru* and for *Magen Avot*, an abbreviated reader's Amidah repetition. We stand, as well, for *Vay'chulu*.

This long list of examples can be simplified to a degree for all services. As a generalization, the congregation stands for parts of the service requiring a minyan, times when the ark is open or the Torah is being carried, and, of course, for the Amidah. Other special occasions or parts of the service to be emphasized--recitation of Kiddush, blessing the children on Erev Shabbat, putting on or removing tallit and t'fillin, confessionals on the High Holidays--are also highlighted by our rising. So you can see that standing is an extremely important part of our prayer ritual. Not only does it call attention to certain prayers and separate sections of the service, but standing paces the service with ups and downs physically just as there are ups and downs emotionally and spiritually.

C. Bowing.

Bowing is a central part of the body language of our services. Bowing implies deference and respect. The service is punctuated by that physical action which serves as a kind of chorus to the verses of praise, thanksgiving, and prayer which we recite. Our physical genuflection (bending the knee and bowing) is a visible way of showing our reverence for something much greater than ourselves. At one time Jews used to prostrate themselves all the way to the ground, as a gesture of reverence. When this custom was taken over to a great extent by the non-Jewish world, Jews gave it up, retaining it only at certain times on the High Holidays when the hazzan (and in some congregations, many other worshipers) still bow all the way down, touching the forehead to the ground, recalling the service of the High Priest in the Temple. (This is done during the special recitation of Alaynu and during the *Avodah* service.)

There may be some confusion about how and when to bow; we hope the following explanation will help clarify things for you. Let us survey the bowing procedures in our regular services. Our "official" bow in the service comes with the barechu. The hazzan recites the word *barechu*, bowing only from the waist. Reciting the word *et*, he rises prepared to stand at attention for the word *Adonai*. The congregation then follows a similar procedure, bowing for the word *baruch*, and standing straight for God's name. This is the principle: the Jew stands straight when reciting *Adonai*, God's name.

As we begin the Amidah, we are coming into the presence of the King of kings. One does not just saunter in and casually begin addressing the King, but rather one comes to address God with dignity and honor. Therefore, the custom is to take three steps forward as if you are coming with reverence into the presence of the King. Since we are often stationed in a small aisle, we must take three steps backwards in order to take three steps forward.

Now, let me explain the procedure when one comes to the words בָּרוּךְ אַתָּה ה' in the Amidah: at the word *baruch* we bend the knees; at the word *attah* we bend the waist, straightening the knees; at the word *Adonai* we stand erect (since whenever a Jew hears God's name he stands erect, at attention). This procedure is outlined as follows:

When one bends the knee--it is at baruch (blessed); and when one straightens up--it is at God's name.

כשכורע – כורע בברוך, וכשזוקף – זוקף בשם.

Shulḥan Aruch, Oraḥ Ḥayyim 113:7

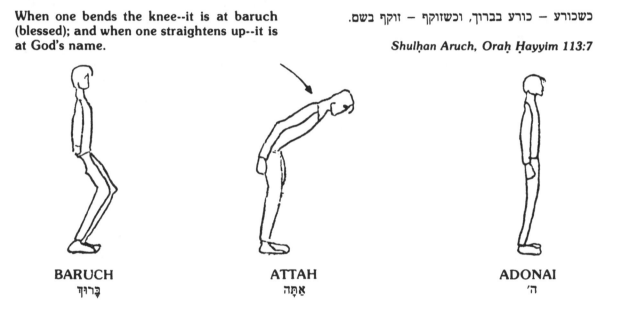

| BARUCH | ATTAH | ADONAI |
| בָּרוּךְ | אַתָּה | ה' |

In the Amidah we bow basically four times: the first b'rachah beginning the Avot passage and at the end of that passage (Magen Avraham); when we recite the prayer *Modim anahnu lach* (bowing only from the waist during the first three words); and at the end of that b'rachah, בָּרוּךְ אַתָּה ה' הַטּוֹב שִׁמְךָ . . .
The Shulḥan Aruch summarizes these places for bowing (*O.Ḥ. 113:1*):

These are the blessings at which we bow: Avot (the blessing "Ancestors"), beginning and end, and Hoda'ah (the blessing of "Thanksgiving"), beginning and end.

אלו ברכות ששוחין בהם: באבות – תחילה וסוף,
ובהודאה – תחילה וסוף.

At the end of the Amidah, when we come to the final phrase beginning with *oseh shalom bimromav*, we take three steps backwards and bow from the waist, and then come three steps forward as if gracefully taking leave of the royal Presence (*O.Ḥ. 123:1*):

One bows and takes three steps back with one bow. While still bowing, before standing up again and while saying "He who makes peace in His heavens," he turns toward the left; and when saying "May He grant us peace," turns toward the right; and afterward he bows forward, like a servant leaving his master.

כורע ופוסע שלושה פסיעות לאחריו בכריעה אחת, ואחר שפסע שלושה פסיעות בעודו כורע קודם שיזקוף כשיאמר עושה שלום במרומיו, הופך פניו לצד שמאלו, וכשיאמר הוא יעשה שלום עלינו – הופך פניו לצד ימינו, ואחר־כך ישתחוה כעבד הנפטר מרבו.

This stepping in and out at the beginning and end of the Amidah is a way of marking off this particular t'fillah time as being special, taking us out of the mundane world and letting us step in to a spiritual, enriched and uplifted world for a few moments. Since the same concluding phrase appears at the end of the Full Kaddish and the Mourner's Kaddish, the same procedure is followed.

Another "bowing type" custom found in the Amidah is associated with the K'dushah. When the reader or congregation reaches the words וְקָרָא זֶה אֶל זֶה "and they called one to the other," referring to the ministering angels, people bow to the left and right as if they are addressing and greeting peers, the angels. When reciting the words *Kadosh, Kadosh, Kadosh,* many people rise up on their tip toes as if to get closer to the holy Presence of God. One could question this custom, given the fact that Judaism believes that God is everywhere, and rising on one's tip toes to get closer to Him implies that God is above, somewhere. However, there are other interpretations of the custom, as well, and communities vary in many of these practices.

During the reader's repetition of the Amidah when the ḥazzan begins to repeat the prayer *Modim* (acknowledging and thanking God), it is customary for the congregation to bow in their seats, reciting another version of Modim. This is done since we can acknowledge God only for ourselves.

During the service for taking the Torah out of the ark, we also bow at the words *gadlu ladonai.* In some congregations, as the Torah is carried around, the congregants bow from the waist as a sign of respect.

The correct way of bowing for Alaynu is as follows. When we recite the word *va'anaḥnu* we are standing erect; at the word *kor'im* we bend the knees. As we say the word *u'mishtaḥavim* we bow deeply from the waist, remaining that way through the word *u'modim,* rising up straight and tall

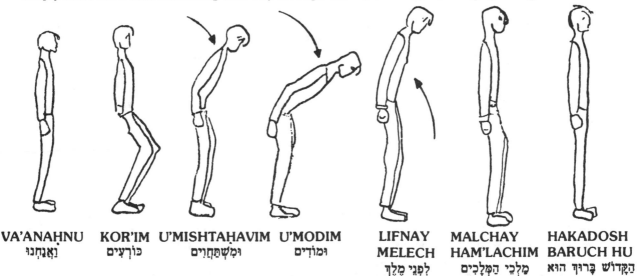

VA'ANAHNU	KOR'IM	U'MISHTAHAVIM	U'MODIM	LIFNAY MELECH	MALCHAY HAM'LACHIM	HAKADOSH BARUCH HU
וַאֲנַחְנוּ	כּוֹרְעִים	וּמִשְׁתַּחֲוִים	וּמוֹדִים	לִפְנֵי מֶלֶךְ	מַלְכֵי הַמְּלָכִים	הַקָּדוֹשׁ בָּרוּךְ הוּא

at the end of that word. There are various other examples of bowing. Thus, at the end of L'chah Dodi in the Kabbalat Shabbat service, we bow to welcome the Shabbat Queen. When the ḥazzan repeats the Amidah and recites Birkat Kohanim, the blessing used by the High Priest, he bows left, right, and forward as a way of directing the blessing to all members of the congregation. The many instances of bowing have a variety of meanings, depending upon the context and t'fillah. However, they all contribute to a sense of enriching our prayer.

D. Gestures of Affection and Confession.

Another area of body language which is extremely helpful in our prayer experience involves gestures which show our deepest affection for ritual items, and the fulfillment of mitzvot, or which represent our desire to become better people through repentance. During the course of the service we kiss a number of items at different times. When we recite Baruch She'amar it is a custom to gather and kiss two fringes, symbolically combining awe and love in our hearts simultaneously. Kissing the *tzitziyot* (fringes) of course, also occurs during the third paragraph of the Shema. The four fringes are gathered at the end of the blessing before the Shema ("...gather us in peace from the four corners of the earth...") As we recite the commandment to wear the fringes, we kiss them (at the words *tzitzit* and *emet*), as a reminder of what they represent, i.e., when we look at them we are to remember all of God's commandments. By kissing them we are forced not only to look at them, but to feel them and sense them and what they stand for on a much more personal basis. There is also a custom to kiss the t'fillin with the fringes during the first two paragraphs of the Shema, when reading the verses which command us to wear the t'fillin.

Many Jews, upon completing the Amidah, close the Siddur and kiss it, or do the same at the end of the service, as a sign of loving respect. Of course, it is a wide-spread custom to kiss a Siddur or Bible when we accidentally drop it, as a sign of our living respect for what the book is and what it contains. (It has been suggested by Dr. Yoḥanan Muffs that we might also read a selection from the book, showing it respect in the best way!) Still another gesture of affection is to kiss the Torah (either with a tzitzit, prayer book, or our hand) as it is carried around, as a sign of our love for the Torah and God's law. Also when we are called to the Torah, we take the tallit and touch it to the beginning and end of the text which is read for our aliyah, showing that we accept what is being read, making the aliyah really our own. In another gesture of respect, when the tallit and t'fillin are taken out and when they are put away, it is the custom to kiss them one at a time, again as a sign of parting and loving respect.

Another totally different gesture of respect is involved in taking the lulav and etrog on Sukkot. They are held together and waved in all direction (north, south, east, and west, up and down) to symbolize God's Presence throughout the entire universe and our praising that Presence wherever it is. This gesture is a very emotionally charged and powerful physical symbol of our desire to speak with God and relate to Him in very tangible terms.

On the other hand there are some gestures of confession in which we try to express our feelings of inadequacy and guilt, in concrete terms. When we reach the b'rachah in the Amidah which begins *s'laḥ lanu*, "Forgive us," we take our right hand and beat our chest over our heart. We do the same on Yom Kippur, during confessionals. This symbolic beating of the breast is a way of expressing our feelings of guilt, of having done wrong, and wishing devoutly to repent. A related custom is observed when we recite the penitential prayers *(taḥanun)* on some weekdays. It is the custom to bend forward, putting one's forehead on one's arm in a gesture of sorrow, and to ask for God's forgiveness. This is said to mirror the action of David when he was repenting for his sins.

E. All Senses.

We use our other senses in t'fillot, and their "body language" is extremely important, too. We taste the Matzah of Pesaḥ and the wine of Kiddush or *Havdalah*; we feel the heat and see the flame of the Havdalah candle; we smell the Havdalah spices and the etrog. In ancient times, a Shabbat lamp was lit as well as an incense lamp to give pleasant smells to the home over Shabbat and holidays. In terms of a "negative use" of our senses, however, on fast days we refrain from eating, diminishing the sense of taste.

Perhaps, the sense of all of the body languages can be summed up in one of the most unique gestures of prayer associated with Jewish tradition. For want of a better word we shall call it "shuckeling," a back and forth swaying motion which seems to summarize very adequately the desire of the Jew to achieve oneness with God. The rocking back and forth, the rhythmic swaying to the sound and the feeling of prayer, helps the Jew create a closer and more intimate relationship with his God. The poem *Nishmat* expresses it this way:

כָּל עַצְמוֹתַי תֹּאמַרְנָה ה' מִי כָמוֹךְ?

All my bones shall declare, "O Lord, who is like You?"

The ability to feel the words with one's entire body is what the prayerful act is aimed to achieve.

EXERCISE 1

To help you understand how various traditions of physical movements represented clear ways of expressing feelings, and how they evolved over time, try the following exercise.

Discuss how hair and clothing styles have changed in your own lifetime. What are your views towards these changes? Do you think that society accepts every change which comes along? Why, or why not? Are all changes for the better? Do you feel comfortable with the changes that occur?

Having considered these topics, now think about ways in which you could express spiritual or moral values through your physical self. What ways could you suggest to dramatize physically a basic belief or value that you hold dear?

Based on Howe, *Personalizing Education,* 146.

5. The Language of Faith: God Talk

Perhaps the greatest stumbling block for most people in making prayer part of their lives is the question of God. Many of us are very unsure of our beliefs, or we don't even know whether we believe in God. Others feel that because they have doubts, questions, frustrations, or even hostility in regard to God they can't sincerely involve themselves in prayer or in Jewish life to any great degree. Nothing could be more incorrect. Jews have always questioned God. Jews have always wondered about who, what, and how God is. Not to have doubts, not to question, is to be religiously dead. Grappling with these fundamental questions is a religious duty. It is the person who never deals with these questions who is in danger of writing himself or herself out of our tradition.

Not only do Jews ask questions about God; we even confront and argue with God. One classic instance of man's challenging God, can be found in the example of Abraham. Read Genesis 18-19, in which Abraham begs God not to destroy the cities of Sodom and Gomorrah. Abraham's challenge to God has been on the lips of Jews throughout our history: "Will not the Judge of all the earth deal justly?"

Let us now turn to this enormously important question of relating to and understanding God. Through a series of activities we hope to enable you to begin talking openly and honestly about your feelings and doubts, becoming more comfortable with "God Talk" in the process and perhaps more open to dealing with the possible roles of God in prayer. We won't try to answer your questions, but do hope to start you thinking.

Ultimately each person must make his or her own leap of faith regarding a belief in God. In the words of the prophet Ḥabbakuk (2:4),   צַדִּיק בֶּאֱמוּנָתוֹ יִחְיֶה.   , "the righteous lives by his faith." No one can prove or disprove matters of faith and belief--these are personal, real feelings to which each human being is entitled. Our attitudes concerning God can also develop, grow and change. This is healthy, productive and most certainly consistent with Jewish tradition.

61

EXERCISE 1
The Names of God

Since our relationship with God lies at the heart of prayer, the nature of our conceptions of God play a vital role in our willingness to pray and in our attempt to increase our participation in prayer. Often, we are not comfortable with the image of God in many prayers, or else we never think very seriously about the various images presented to us. Below is a long list of names, appellations, and descriptions of God found in our tradition. They are gathered from the Siddur, other Jewish literature, and the writings of theologians. The list is not complete, but is very comprehensive, (although other translations could have been used for many of the names). Find a quiet place and take from this list those names which describe God as you believe in Him (Her). Your list need not be long--just sincere. Share your preferences with others in the group. Then make a tally of the most-often selected designations. Ask yourself, or discuss, how your list compares with the most commonly referred to names in the Siddur. If your list is very different from what the Siddur contains, what does this mean? If your list is "close" to the Siddur, do you find yourself more comfortable with prayer than people whose lists are very different? Do you think you are free to deviate from 2,000 years of Jewish tradition when your list differs radically from the Siddur? Does that make the Siddur useless to you? Do you know better than many previous generations of Jews? Could you read a name for God in the Siddur and substitute for it one with which you're more comfortable? Should the Siddur shape you and your beliefs or should you change the siddur? Consider these questions and decide which names are most comfortable for you.

1. Adonai, "My Lord"

2. King

3. Lord

4. The True God

5. The Divinity

6. The Fear of Isaac

7. Mighty One of Jacob

8. El, The God of (The Patriot) Israel

9. Most High

10 Everlasting God

11. God Almighty

12. God of Vision

13. God of the Covenant

14. Everlasting King

15. Everlasting Rock

16. Ancient God

17. Everlasting Arms

18. Everlasting Life

19. YHWH, "He Causes to Be"

20. I am that I am

21. Lord of Hosts

22. Creator of Heaven and Earth

23. Holy One

24. Holy One of Israel

25. Shepherd of Israel

26. The Rock

27. King of Israel

28. The God of Truth

29. Former of All

30. Praiseworthy God

31. Guardian of Israel

32. Shield of Abraham

33. Rock of Israel

34. King over the king of kings

35. The Name	36. The Holy One, Praised be He
37. Heaven	38. Peace
39. I	40. Judge of the Earth
41. The Awesome One	42. My Rock
43. Eternal One of Israel	44. Ever-living God
45. Lover of His People Israel	46. The Ransomer
47. The Redeemer	48. The Guide
49. Our God, God of Our Ancestors	50. God of Abraham
51. God of Isaac	52. God of Jacob
53. The Mighty One	54. The Heroic One
55. Acquirer of All	56. The Living Lord
57. Rescuer	58. Reviver of the Dead
59. Father of Mercy	60. The Merciful One
61. The Merciful	62. The Holy God
63. The Place	64. The Might
65. The Faithful One	66. Lord of the Universe
67. He Who Spoke and the Universe Came Into Being	68. Our Father in Heaven
69. The Infinite	70. The Possessor of Will
71. Hosts	72. King of Compassion and Mercy
73. Rock of Our Lives	74. The Good One
75. He Who Is Merciful	76. Maker of Peace
77. "Thankworthy" God	78. The Holy King
79. Master of All	80 The Creator
81. He Who Caused His Name to Dwell in This House	82. Our Father, Our King
83. Our Shepherd	84. Mighty One of Israel
85. Our Healer	86. Mentor
87. The Living God of Majesty	88. Sovereign
89. The Compassionate One	90. The Patient One
91. The Bountiful One	92. The One Who is Forgiveness

93. The Generous One

94. The Eternal

95. Hidden of Hiddens

96. Ancient of Ancients

97. The First Cause

98. World-Soul

99. Absolute Spirit

100. Absolute Rest

101. The Power That Makes for Salvation

102. The Power That Makes for The Fulfillment of All Valid Ideals

103. Lord, Man of War

104. The Lord Who Hides His Face

After reading this list it should become obvious that in our tradition there are many images of God and no one need accept all of them. This allows, or encourages, a flexibility of belief which stems from the notion that in Judaism what one does in life is often more important than what one believes. We show our love and belief in God through our love and actions on behalf of humanity.

Based on Robert Blinder, "What's in a Name?" Genesis -- A Synagogue of Our Times, St. Louis, Missouri.

EXERCISE 2

Pretend God is the editor of the newspaper in your town. Write a "Letter to the Editor" expressing your ideas and opinions about any particular issue in God's "paper."

EXERCISE 3

Another problem many people face is a kind of loneliness in regard to their feelings and questions regarding faith and God. Too often we believe that because we have questions, we are, therefore, non-believers and write ourselves out of our religious tradition. Nothing could be further from the truth. Religious people of all times have had deep and fundamental questions. That's what being religiously alive is all about. The problem today is that we don't share our questions and doubts with each other. Be as honest as possible in answering the following questions. If you do this exercise with another person, after one person has been the "interviewer," switch roles.

Faith Interview:

1. If there is a God, how do you picture God?

2. Do you talk to God yourself?

3. Have you ever felt God talking to you, or have you ever felt God's presence?

4. What are some of your doubts about God?

5. If God is good, how can God permit evil in the world?

6. Do you know of any differences between the Jewish conceptions of God and Christian conceptions of God?

7. Is there anything that makes you angry about God?

8. Has God ever answered any of your prayers?

9. Why don't you think or talk about God more than you do?

10. Does God still function in the world as described in the Bible?

11. What is a miracle? Do you believe in miracles?

12. Do you believe in life after death? What form does it take?

13. Do you believe God punishes the sinners and rewards the righteous?

14. Do you think that the Jewish people has been chosen by God for something special?

15. If you were God, what would you do differently?

16. Do you pray to God more when you are sick and in trouble? Do you think more about God when someone you love is in trouble or in danger?

17. Do you thank God for the good things in your life as well as relating God to the bad things that happen?

EXERCISE 4   GODBELIEFS

From Howard Wasserman, Ellen Z. Charry, Diane King, Jerome Ruderman, eds., *Idea Cookbook* (Philadelphia: Board of Jewish Education, United Synagogue of America, 1976).

	Yes	No
1. I believe that God created the world and directs the happenings in it.	_____	_____
2. I believe that God has no power to interfere in the affairs of people.	_____	_____
3. I believe that the world came into being by accident.	_____	_____
4. I believe that God is aware of what I do.	_____	_____
5. I believe that God can answer prayer.	_____	_____
6. I believe that God punishes evil.	_____	_____
7. I believe that God intended us never to understand certain things about the world.	_____	_____
8. I believe that my concepts about God differ from the Torah's concept of God.	_____	_____
9. I believe that even if there were no people, God would still exist.	_____	_____
10. I believe that God decided what is good and what is evil.	_____	_____
11. I believe that God gets involved in human affairs when He wants to.	_____	_____
12. I believe that God rewards good.	_____	_____
13. I believe that God exists independently of, and outside of people.	_____	_____
14. I believe that prayer is an attempt to talk to God.	_____	_____
15. I believe that the Torah is the word of God.	_____	_____
16. I believe that God listens to prayer.	_____	_____
17. I believe that "God" is a term that people use to describe their best hopes for humanity.	_____	_____
18. I believe God exists only inside of people.	_____	_____
19. I believe that praying can benefit the person who prays, even if God doesn't listen.	_____	_____
20. I believe that "God" is an idea people use to describe those things beyond human understanding.	_____	_____
21. I believe prayer can have an effect on people's lives regardless of what they think about God.	_____	_____

What else do you believe about God?

6. The Language of Print

The following is excerpted from Abraham Millgram, *Jewish Worship* (Philadelphia: The Jewish Publication Society of America, 1971), 541-549.

In the year 1440 the printing press with movable type was invented by Johann Gutenberg. The invention seems rather simple to modern people. Nonetheless it was an event of historic proportions....

Prior to the invention of the printing press, education was a luxury available only to the elect. Books were scarce and expensive. Only a rich Jew could afford to own a manuscript *Siddur*.... Before the advent of printing it was not unusual for a synagogue to possess only one *Siddur*, for the reader. The precentor would recite most of the prayers aloud, and the worshippers either followed the reading in an undertone or just listened and responded at the appropriate places with the traditional Amen....

The printing press revolutionized the synagogue service as it did all cultural and spiritual activities. It was appropriately referred to by medieval Jewish writers as "a scribe with many quills." A single printing could produce thousands of volumes. The price of book was thus reduced sharply, and copies of the *Siddur* were placed in the hands of many and in time all worshippers. The prayers and piyutim which had accumulated during the centuries could now be read by the congregation...

The format of the *Siddur* also received due attention. Various sizes, from folio volumes to pocket-sized miniatures, were published. The former were meant for the reader's desk, while the miniatures were designed for those who traveled to fairs and other trading centers....

The Beloved Siddur

Before the printing press was invented it was customary to adorn the manuscript *Siddur* with beautiful illuminations. Some *Siddurim* contained elaborate initial letters, decorative margins, and colorful illustrations of the text. These pictorial illustrations have been studied and admired. And the writing, too, was often masterful. The specimens that have survived are few, especially when compared with the favorites of Jewish illuminators--the Haggadah, the *Megillah*, and the marriage contracts--but the few illuminated *Siddurim* that have endured are exquisite and are deservedly treasured with pride....

When the printing press was invented, the woodcut replaced the hand-painted embellishments of the manuscripts. Unfortunately, the woodcuts were often crude. It can be said generally that the introduction of printing led to the discontinuance of the artistic illumination of the prayer book.

But the Jew did not cease to express his love of the *Siddur* by artistic means. During the Middle Ages bookbinding was often an art rather than a craft. When the prayer book was handwritten, it was usually bound in parchment which was hand painted in vivid colors. The printed book was often adorned with silver covers, frequently of delicately wrought filigree. During the Renaissance it was quite fashionable for a young man to present his bride with a prayer book bound in an exquisite silver binding, and many a bride would proudly carry her gift to the synagogue.

Beginning with the sixteenth century an increasing number of Jews began to possess their own *Siddurim*. These prayer books were generally not bound in silver covers, but they were just as precious to their owners. The *Siddur*, adorned or unadorned, was the Jew's daily companion....

For your consideration:

1. What might have been the development of the liturgy had the printing press been invented earlier or later? What might have happened had the medieval rabbis forbidden the mechanical printing of the Siddur?

2. In recent years there has been an exciting resurgence of the ancient art of calligraphy. See the *Jewish Catalog* (Philadelphia: The Jewish Publication Society of America, 1973) Vol I, 184-209, for details.

3. You might want to try your hand at illuminating and embellishing part of a Siddur (which you may first write): The b'rachot which follow can be a starting point.

בָּרוּךְ אַתָּה
ה׳ אֱלֹהֵינוּ
מֶלֶךְ הָעוֹלָם,
שֶׁהַכֹּל נִהְיֶה
בִּדְבָרוֹ.

רוּךְ אַתָּה
ה׳ אֱלֹהֵינוּ
מֶלֶךְ הָעוֹלָם
הַנּוֹתֵן
רֵיחַ טוֹב
בַּפֵּירוֹת.

68

SECTION II
THE HISTORY AND STRUCTURE
OF JEWISH PRAYER

CHAPTER 3 THE HISTORY OF JEWISH PRAYER
Development of Jewish Prayer

In the following pages we shall trace the origins and development of Jewish prayer, the synagogue and the Siddur.

Excerpts in this section are from Evelyn Garfiel, *The Service of the Heart* (Cranbury, New Jersey: Thomas Yoseloff, Inc., 1958), 24-39.

> Prayer is probably as old as man. But early worship all over the world, certainly formal worship, consisted chiefly of sacrifices. This obtained in Judaism as late as the days of the Second Temple, and very much later among other peoples. Sacrifice-services were necessarily conducted by members of a priest-class especially trained in the intricate ceremonies established by tradition. But among the Jews, the people, too, had some share in these services. They brought their sacrifices to the Temple, the fine meal and the appropriate animals; they recited a simple formula of confession, and they responded to the songs and praises of the Levites.... The evidence seems clear tht even in the days of the First Temple, prayers as well as sacrifices were part of the regular Temple service. The Levites sang and probably composed many of the Psalms. The most famous prayer of all the *Shema Yisrael*, and the Ten Commandments were also recited daily...

In addition to prayers recited at the Temple, there are numerous prayers found in the Bible. These are generally personal prayers covering the entire range of human feelings, from sorrow to joy, and from frustration to hope and trust. What follows is a listing of our earliest recorded t'fillot, found in the Bible. Look up some of the passages and apply the analysis questions at the beginning of Section III to them.

This chart is from Pinchas Wollmam-Tsamir, *The Graphic History of the Jewish Heritage* (New York: Shengold Publishers, 1963), 211:

PRAYERS IN THE BIBLE

#	UTTERED BY	OBJECT OF PRAYER	OUTCOME OF PRAYER	SOURCE
1.	Abraham	That God forgive the sin of Sodom.	God agrees to forgive Sodom if ten righteous persons can be found in the city.	Genesis 18.23-33
2.	Abraham	That Abimelech's wives no longer be barren.	The house of Abimelech is healed.	Genesis 20.17-18
3.	Abraham's Servant	That he succeed in his mission.	He meets Rebekah.	Genesis 24.12-14
4.	Isaac	That Rebekah bear children.	Jacob and Esau are born.	Genesis 25.21
5.	Jacob	That he be protected from Esau.	The brothers make peace with each other.	Genesis 32.9-12
6.	Moses	That Israel be forgiven for the sin of the golden calf.	God forgives the people.	Exodus 32.31-35
7.	Moses	That God continue to show grace to His people.	God continues to be gracious to Israel.	Exodus 33.12-18
8.	Moses	That Miriam be cured of her leprosy.	Miriam is cured after seven days.	Numbers 12.18
9.	Moses	That the people be forgiven for having believed the spies sent into Canaan.	God forgives the people.	Numbers 14.13-19
10.	Moses	That he be permitted to enter the Promised Land.	God shows Moses the Promised Land before his death.	Deuteronomy 3.23-25
11.	Samson	That he be avenged upon his enemies.	With his death he avenges himself.	Judges 16.28
12.	Hannah	That she be given a son.	Samuel is born.	1 Samuel 1.11
13.	David	That God make good His promise concerning David.	The Davidic line continues as the reigning dynasty	2 Samuel 7.18-29
14.	Solomon	That God cause His Presence to dwell in the Temple.	God causes His Presence to dwell in the Temple.	1 Kings 8.23-62
15.	Elijah	That the Lord vanquish Baal.	Fire descends from heaven and consumes Elijah's offering.	1 Kings 18.36-37
16.	Hezekiah	That Israel be saved from Sennacherib.	An angel smites the Assyrian camp.	2 Kings 19.15-20
17.	Asa	That God help his army defeat the Ethiopians.	God smites the Ethiopians.	2 Chronicles 14.11
18.	Jehoshaphat	That God defend His people against the armies of Moab and Ammon.	God grants Jehoshaphat the victory.	2 Chronicles 20.6-12
19.	Hezekiah	That God forgive the people for not having sanctified themselves before eating the paschal lamb.	God forgives the people.	2 Chronicles 30.18-19
20.	Nehemiah	That God aid His captive people.	God promises that He will rebuild the walls of Jerusalem.	Nehemiah 1.5-11
21.	Daniel	That God rebuild Jerusalem.	Jerusalem will be rebuilt in 70 weeks.	Daniel 9.4-19
22.	Jonah	That he be taken out of the whale.	The whale casts Jonah out upon dry land.	Jonah 2.2-9

POST-BIBLICAL ANCIENT PRAYERS

Here are some additional samples of our earliest recorded prayers. These are post-biblical.

Rabbi Neḥunya ben HaKaneh used to offer a short prayer upon entering the Beit HaMidrash, and upon leaving. They said to him, "What type of prayer is it?" He said to them, "Upon entering I pray that no misfortune will occur because of me and when leaving I give thanks for my portion." What did he say when entering? "May it be Your desire, O Lord my God and God of my Fathers, that I not be too strict with my colleagues and they not be too strict with me, that I not declare impure something which is pure or vice versa, that I not forbid something permitted or permit something forbidden, for that would cause embarrassment for this world or the world to come." And what did he say upon leaving? "I thank you, O Lord my God and God of my Fathers, that You have made my lot among those who dwell in the House of Study and synagogue and not among those who dwell in theaters or circuses. For I labor and they labor; I am industrious and they are industrious. I labor to inherit 'the Garden of Eden' and they labor too for the nethermost pit."

ר' נחוניא בן הקנה היה מתפלל בכניסתו לבית המדרש וביציאתו תפילה קצרה. אמרו לו: מה טיבה של תפילה זו? אמר להן: בכניסתי אני מתפלל שלא תארע תקלה על ידי וביציאתי אני נותן הודייה על חלקי. בכניסתו מהו אומר? "יהי רצון מלפניך ה' אלהי ואלהי אבותי שלא אקפיד כנגד חברי ולא חברי יקפידו כנגדי, שלא נטמא את הטהור ולא נטהר את הטמא, שלא נאסר את המותר ולא נתיר את האסור ונמצאת מתבייש לעולם הזה ולעולם הבא." וביציאתו מהו אומר? "מודה אני לפניך ה' אלהי ואלהי אבותי שנתת חלקי מיושבי בית מדרש ובתי כנסיות, ולא נתת חלקי בבתי תרטיות ובבתי קרקסיות, שאני עמל והן עמלין אני שוקד והן שוקדין, אני עמל לירש גן עדן, והן עמלין לבאר שחת."

Yerushalmi B'rachot 4:7d

It happened that Rabbi Eliezer went down to lead the congregational prayers before the ark, recited twenty-four b'rachot, and was not answered. Rabbi Akiva went down after him and said, "Avinu Malkenu, we have no King but You. Avinu Malkenu, be merciful to us for Your sake." And (he was answered:) it began to rain.

מעשה בר' אליעזר שירד לפני התיבה ואמר עשרים וארבע ברכות ולא נענה. ירד ר' עקיבה אחריו ואמר: אבינו מלכנו אין לנו מלך אלא אתה! אבינו מלכינו, למענך רחם עלינו! וירדו גשמים.

Ta'anit 25b

Notice that while there were prayers already uttered in the Temple, the talmudic rabbis also composed prayers they thought might have been uttered in earlier times.

Abraham's prayer after the Binding of Isaac:

Master of the Universe, it is revealed and known to You that when You asked me to sacrifice Isaac, my son, I could have answered and said to You, "Yesterday you said to me, 'Your future will be called through Isaac,' and now You say 'Sacrifice him there.' " Heaven forbid if I had not done it, but I overcame my natural impulse and did Your will. So may it be Your will, O Lord my God, that when the descendants of Isaac, my son, enter into trouble and have no one to defend them, You will be their Defender. "The Lord will see...."; You will remember the binding of Isaac their father for them, and be merciful toward them.

רבון עולמים, גלוי וידוע לפניך שבשעה שאמרת לי להעלות את יצחק בני, היה לי מה להשיב ולומר לפניך: אתמול אמרת לי "כי ביצחק יקרא לך זרע," ועכשיו אתה אומר "והעלהו שם לעולה!" חס ושלום לא עשיתי כן, אלא כבשתי את יצרי ועשיתי רצונך. כן יהי רצון מלפנך ה' אלהי, שבשעה שיהיו בניו של יצחק בני נכנסין לידי צרה ואין להם מי ילמד עליהם סניגוריא, אתה תהא מלמד עליהם סניגוריא! "ה' יראה" – את נזכר להם עקידתו של יצחק אביהם ותתמלא עליהם רחמים!

Yerushalmi Ta'anit 2:65d

73

Moses' prayer after his death had been decreed by God:

Master of the Universe, my toil and sorrow are revealed and known to you, that I suffered for Israel until they believed in Your name; oh, how I suffered for them...I said, "As I have seen their suffering, so may I see their success." And now that Israel's success has arrived You say to me, "You will not cross over this Jordan River." You make Your Torah a fraud, as it is written, "In his time You give his reward." Is this payment of forty years that I toiled, until they were a holy and faithful nation?

רבונו של עולם, גלוי וידוע לפניך יגיעי וצערי שנצטטערתי על ישראל עד שיהיו מאמינים לשמך, כמה צער נצטרתי עליהן . . . אמרתי כשראיתי בצערן, כך אראה בטובתן, ועכשיו שהגיעה טובתן של ישראל אתה אומר לי: "לא תעבר את הירדן הזה." הרי אתה עושה את תורתך פלסתר! דכתיב "ביומו תתן שכרו" זו היא שילום עבודה של מ' שנה שעמלתי, עד שהיו עם קדוש ונאמן?

D'varim Rabbah 11

Perhaps you could continue this tradition by writing some prayers that might have been uttered at a time of need or joy by other figures of Jewish history. Use the checklist on writing creative t'fillot found in Chapter 1. Notice the simple style of these prayers.

Development of the Synagogue

Many people are under the mistaken impression that Jewish prayer developed mainly as a substitute for the sacrificial system of worship used in the Temple. This is not exactly the case, however. If it were not for the fact that before, during, and after the days of the First Temple oral prayers and declarations of faith taken from the Torah were part of the religious life of the people, Judaism would not have survived into the Second Temple, or beyond. When the First Temple was destroyed in 586 B.C.E. and the Jews were exiled to Babylonia, lacking the central place of worship they were used to, they began to assemble regularly to talk, pray, and study. Thus, according to one theory, the synagogue was born. By the time of the Second Temple there were already many synagogues and increasing numbers of prayers. Therefore, when the Second Temple was destroyed in 70 C.E. -- and, again, a centralized worship system was no longer available--the institutions of prayer and the synagogue were able to take over. By the first centuries of the Common Era, the synagogue and the "House of Study" were guiding forces of Judaism.

<table>
<tr>
<td>Rav Abahu said, "Seek the Lord where He is found" (Isaiah 55:6). Where is He found? In synagogues and houses of study. "Call Him where He is close." Where is He close? (In synagogues and houses of study.)</td>
<td dir="rtl">רבי אבהו בשם ר' אבהו: "דרשו ה' בהמצאו" (יש' נה,
ו). איכן הוא מצוי? בבתי כנסיות ובבתי מדרשות!
"קראהו בהיותו קרוב" (שם). איכן הוא קרוב? (בבתי
כנסיות ובבתי מדרשות!</td>
</tr>
</table>

Yerushalmi Berachot 5:4d

There is another theory about the origin of the synagogue as well.

> After the return to Palestine, in Ezra's time, when the Temple had already been rebuilt -- that is, in the fifth century B.C.E. -- representatives of each hamlet and village in a district would gather in a central town to choose from among their number one man to go up to Jerusalem to represent Israel at large at the offering of the *Tamid* sacrifice, offered up daily in the Temple in the name of the people of Israel. While they awaited the return of their representative and his report that he had satisfactorily completed his mission, they would meet to read Torah, recite Psalms, perhaps some other prayers, and from this nucleus the service developed.

Whatever their origin, the prayer service and the synagogue were revolutionary ideas in the ancient world. This was due to the nature of prayers as opposed to sacrifice. It was also due to the democratic nature of Jewish worship, encouraging participation of all the people, not just the specialists, the priests.

> Perhaps this emphasis on the people instead of on the building accounts in large measure for the absence of a specific pattern of synagogue architecture. Its form has always varied with the local and contemporary styles of architecture current in the country in which it was built....
>
> Freedom from dependence on the specialized knowledge of a priest was not the only condition which contributed to the democratic spirit of the synagogue. The wide diffusion of knowledge of their religious culture among the Jews made it possible for the synagogue to function as it did. Torah and *Talmud Torah* (Study of Torah) together were the keys to the process of democratization not only in the synagogue, but in the religious life as a whole.... They certainly knew the basic prayers which then made up the synagogue service. It was on the basis of this educated laity that the synagogue was able to become the first genuinely democratic religious institution in the world.

EXERCISE 1

You are a Jew living in the Soviet Union. The only synagogue remaining in your town, which you had attended only once a year, has now been closed by the Russian authorities. You are growing in your Jewish consciousness, and have submitted an application for a visa to leave the country and go to Israel, though you are lacking a great deal of Jewish knowledge. Everyone seems to know a little, but no one seems to know everything that is involved in creating a synagogue service. Try now to create your own synagogue and synagogue worship service based on the knowledge you have and the Russian culture of which you are part.

Development of the Siddur

...It is reasonably certain that by the early days of the Second Temple, about 400 B.C.E., some form of group prayer service existed among the Jews....

The prayer service grew in importance during the next two or three hundred years until it became, in addition to the Temple service, an established mode of worship -- the synagogue. Its prayers increased in number; two benedictions were added before the *Shema* and one after it. The benedictions of the *Shemoneh Esray* (the "Eighteen Benedictions") were composed by various Rabbis, probably in large part during these years, and they became an essential element of every service.... By the generation after the destruction of the Temple in 70 C.E., the synagogue service was fairly well established, though there was as yet no written *Prayer Book* recording in one place all the prayers then already in use, nor any single written record of the order of the various services.

As we approach the Middle Ages, about the year 800, we find that differences in the service from place to place have increased--quite naturally, in the circumstances. For Jewish communities were scattered over most of the then known world from Babylon to the far western reaches of the Roman Empire... The only connecting link was the tenuous one of whatever advice and legal opinion might come to them from the faraway Academies of Babylon and Palestine. In such circumstances, the possession and regular use of a written prayer book in common was imperative.... Jewish scholars in Spain appealed to Rav Amram, the Gaon of the Sura Academy in Babylon, to supply them with a guide to the correct order of the prayers. They turned to him because, as President of the Academy in Sura, the Gaon (literally, the great or illustrious one) was in effect the spiritual head of the Jews of the world. It was in response to the request for a definitive text of the prayer services that Rav Amram produced the first complete written *Prayer Book*.

He compiled it from oral tradition, from the service as he knew it in practice, and from numerous Talmudic sources. Since he was preparing his *Siddur* for the benefit of scholars and Rabbis, he accompanied the text with a brief running commentary from the Talmud. It has been said that Amram's *Siddur* appeared in 865 C.E., but that is no more than a "historical guess." ... Of course, his original manuscript no longer exists. Perhaps, as that great scholar, Louis Ginzberg, once suggested, it was "used until it was used up." ... But amended and much revised copies of this very ancient book do exist....

An even more famous Gaon of the Academy in Sura was Saadia, who was born in 882....

Amram's earlier *Siddur* had been prepared for scholars. Saadia's aim was quite different. In the preface to his *Siddur*, he tells how and why he came to write it. On his travels through many different Jewish communities in many different lands, he says, he found so many changes in their religious services that in a very short time a common liturgy might cease to exist among Jews and the traditional order of prayers be confused and forgotten. He decided therefore "to collect and arrange the established prayers, praises and benedictions so that the original form should be restored." He wrote not for scholars, but for the people everywhere, because he wanted "to see his (established) order of prayers used everywhere and by everyone." He included not only the traditional prayers but many new liturgical poems by leading poets of his time....

These two Prayer Books--of Amram and Saadia Gaon--have given to the traditional *Prayer Book* we know today its basic structure....

In addition, prayers and Siddur organization common among Western (Ashkenazic) Jews have their source in the eleventh century. Living in the city of Vitry, France, Rabbi Simhah ben Shmuel, a student of Rashi, the famous Bible commentator, completed a Siddur called *Mahzor Vitry* ("The

Cycle of Prayers from Vitry"), containing a commentary and collection of religious laws. This work was ten times the size of Amram's and Saadia's Siddurim.

> In 1868, Seligman Baer, a German Jewish scholar, published a definitive text of the *Siddur*. He had carefully compared all the manuscript versions available and had traced all the prayers back to their original sources in the Talmud and elsewhere. Baer's corrected texts of the *Siddur* is used in all recently published traditional Prayer Books.
>
> Until the nineteenth century, Jews had been concerned with having as full and as correct a version of their *Prayer Book* as could possibly be had. Besides, they kept adding to the prayers.... And so we find the *Prayer Book* growing longer and longer during the Middle Ages....
>
> But it was not only the desire to pray that stimulated the expansion of the *Siddur*. It was the fact that Jews could read....
>
> And yet, there must have been some Jews in the sixteenth century whose knowledge of the Hebrew language was not all that it should have been, for the very first translation of the *Siddur* .... was (in) Italian but the book was printed in Hebrew characters. Like so many people today, they seem to have mastered "mechanical reading" of Hebrew without understanding what they read.
>
> The first translation of the *Siddur* into English was made about two hundred years later....
>
> For generations after its basic form had been established, the *Prayer Book* continued to grow by accretion....
>
> No rabbinical synod met to vote on which new prayers to accept for inclusion in the *Prayer Book* and which to reject. But, by a process of sifting, the people themselves put their stamp of approval on more and more of these expressions of religious devotion....

Some movements within Judaism have published editions of the Siddur. A Reform prayer book was published, in Hebrew and German, in 1818 and by the late 19th century many English versions of the Siddur had appeared. After a tendency to cut out much of the ever-growing liturgy, the *Union Prayer Book for Jewish Worship* was published in 1895 by the Reform rabbinate. It restored some of the Hebrew omitted in earlier editions.[1]

The Conservative Movement, too, felt the need for its own Siddur translation. The principles stated in the "Foreward" to the 1946 *Sabbath and Festival Prayer Book* outline the need for "continuity with tradition...relevance to the needs and ideals of our generation...(and) intellectual integrity."[2] In consonance with these values, the text retains the traditional structure of services, supplemented by new translations, interpretations, and readings. The Movement has also produced a new edition of the High Holiday Maḥzor, Passover Haggadah, Weekday Prayer Book, and other works. It is continuing the process with a *Siddur Shalem* ("Complete Prayer Book") and liturgical publications to aid our devotion and understanding.

Future of Prayer and the Siddur

We have examined the development and origin of the liturgy and synagogue. In the last twenty-five years more versions of the Siddur and Maḥzor have been created than in our entire previous history. Problems of understanding Hebrew and identifying with the poetic language, idioms, values, and institutions of the past have motivated many to re-edit and reinterpret the Siddur and Maḥzor. New and beautiful translations and formats, the appearance of directions and explanations, the replacement of some piyyutim (liturgical poems) and the elimination of others, and the addition of modern religious poetry have shaped these new editions.

All this raises the question of our liturgical future and its direction. Will people know more or less Hebrew? Will they return to prayer and Judaism during a period of economic crisis, energy shortages, reduced standards of living? Will we see a return to traditional values of people, faith, and family in North America? These are interesting questions for you to contemplate. The next activity is presented to stimulate your thinking on the future of prayer and how it might affect you.

EXERCISE 1

Place yourself twenty years in the future. What prayers that you find will then be most meaningful in your life? What will the synagogue service look like? What kinds of music will accompany the prayer service? What kinds of audio or visual aids might be employed by people to highlight or intensify the prayer experience? What will the synagogue look like twenty years from now? Whom will you be standing with in the synagogue? What will you know Jewishly? What will your Jewish lifestyle be like? Consider these issues and what influence they may have on the Siddur and synagogue.

CHAPTER 4 STRUCTURE OF THE SIDDUR
Introduction

The Siddur is a complex but logical arrangement of prayers, hopes, dreams, and goals of our people. In fact, the word סִדּוּר means "arrangement" or "order," as in סֵדֶר הַתְּפִילוֹת , "order of prayer" (or the Passover סֵדֶר , the order of that night's ritual). It is organized according to the nature, use, content, and history of the t'fillot it contains.

Understanding the order of the Siddur as a whole, certain values and Jewish world views are conveyed. In placing t'fillot in order within a particular service, important intellectual, religious, ethical, and aesthetic statements are made. What at first seems like an overwhelming task -- to understand why the prayers are ordered as they are--becomes quite simple when underlying principles of organization are mastered.

Once you have this key, the very meaning of prayers often becomes clear by the order in which they occur in the Siddur as a whole or in specific services. The traditional (complete) Siddur is organized according to three main principles:

> A. *Frequency of use*--prayers said more often are placed before those said less frequently.

> B. *The Daily routine of the Jew*--prayers within a given section are placed in the order they are said during the day.

> C. *The Jewish calendar*--some prayers are placed in the order in which they are recited during the year, beginning with Rosh HaShanah.

The following examples will clarify these principles.

> 1. Daily morning prayers are said most frequently, and thus placed first in the Siddur.

> 2. *Birkat HaMazon* (the "Grace after eating") follows the morning service in the Siddur, since it is next in a Jew's routine; (recall that we do not eat until after we pray).

> 3. Shabbat prayers follow weekday prayers, because they are said less frequently. Similarly, Hallel and Rosh Hodesh Amidot follow Shabbat prayers, but precede the Amidot for the Festivals.

> 4. Blessings for Hanukah follow prayers for Simhat Torah and precede those for Purim.

EXERCISE 1

Look at a full traditional Siddur and number the following prayers, according to their order in the Siddur. See if the order agrees with the organizing principles outlined above.

_____ Kabbalat Shabbat

_____ Weekday Minhah (afternoon service)

_____ Kiddush for Festivals

_____ Bedtime Shema

_____ Amidah for Festivals

_____ Hoshanot for Sukkot

_____ Shabbat Musaf (additional service)

The B'rachah -- Building Block of Worship

The basic building block of all Jewish prayer is the b'rachah. This liturgical formula is the source for all of the poetry and expansion which took place over the centuries in the Siddur. Understanding the formula of the B'rachah, how it works, what it intends, and how it is structured will give you a deep and important understanding of all of Jewish prayer in general. Let us now analyze the nature of b'rachot and see how they function and what they contain. We shall begin with an analysis of each word of the standard, basic b'rachah formula, *Baruch attah adonai elohaynu melech ha'olam...*

BARUCH בָּרוּךְ

Most of us are familiar with this word and the most common English translation of it, namely "blessed" ("are You, O Lord, our God..."). But, when we look at the meaning of the English word "blessed," a problem arises. In English, to bless implies a hierarchical relationship between the one doing the blessing and the one who is blessed. Therefore, we raise the question, "Who are *we* to bless God?" The common translation "blessed" doesn't seem to be particularly appropriate for this Hebrew word.

It is usually suggested that the word baruch, comes from a root used in the Hebrew word בִרך knee, and that baruch has something to do with bowing or bending the knee. That, however, is a very uncertain theory; baruch may simply come from a word in another ancient language which also means "to praise" or "to bless." The word baruch is a complicated passive Hebrew word which, in this usage, implies a relationship with God. To define the relationships between a person, or people, and God is an extremely difficult thing to do. It implies that God is He who is deserving of our praise, awe, worship, serving, and looking towards. Have you ever tried to define the love that you feel for your parents or for a close friend? It is even more complicated to describe such relationships with God. So the word baruch stands for a great many things and is a very difficult word to define or translate.

ATTAH אַתָּה

Seeing the word attah, "you" in the formula of the b'rachah, should give us pause, for it is used to address God. It is interesting that in Hebrew the same word, attah, can be used to talk to your father, your brother, your close friend, as well as to God. In some foreign languages a difference is made between addressing someone who is familiar to you and speaking with someone who is in a position of authority or responsibility over you. So, for example, in French the formal second person word of address is *vous*, and the familiar form of address is *tu*. In German, the same division is made, with the word *Sie* used as the formal second person address, and *du* used for the familiar. (Old English, too, had a similar distinction between formal and familiar.) In Hebrew, however, we have one word which is used for both formal and personal address. That implies that we approach God on at least two levels: we can look to God as someone personal and intimate with whom we can relate and, at the same time, as our Master and Ruler.

You may be familiar with lines beginning, *Avinu Malkenu*, "Our Father, our King." To address God as both Father and King implies that we are at once intimate with God and at the same time subservient to Him. The word attah speaks to both of these relationships. God is near and, at the same time, distant and commanding. Again, attah implies a relationship, and is not easy to define. The Jewish philosopher Martin Buber spoke of two basic kinds of relationships between people and between things. On the one hand, said Buber, we relate in an *I-it* fashion to objects in the world. We use an object, like a chair, which is only in relationship to us as long as we need it. The other type of relationship is *I-Thou*, which involves human beings related to one another with the sum of their relationship being much greater than the sum of the parts. Our relationship to God is much like this *I-Thou* relationship, a back and forth growing and experiencing of two souls. This simple word attah, then, is most complicated to understand for it speaks about our fundamental relationships with the Divine.

ADONAI

This word has often been translated "Lord" and the question arises of how we differentiate *Adonai* from the following word *Elohaynu*. Adonai as it is used here is really the personal name of the God of Israel. Just as each one of us has a first name, so, too, the God of Israel has a personal, private name. In Jewish tradition the real name of God (which uses the Hebrew letters *Yod, Hay, Vov, Hay*) is never pronounced as it was originally, out of a deep respect and love for God, and through the ages became lost to us. The word is often abbreviated as ה' , which stands for "The" (Name of God). Adonai literally means "my master" or "my Lord" and has come to stand for the personal name of God. It also comes to represent God's qualities of mercy, and His unchanging nature.

ELOHAYNU אֱלֹהֵינוּ

Elohaynu means "our God." It is based on the words *elohim*, a more general term for God. (In fact, even the gods of other nations are referred to as elohim.) We may answer the question "Who is our God?" by stating "Adonai Elohaynu," "Adonai is our God." Notice, too, that we have used the second person word of address (attah) and now we are using the first person plural as the suffix. Another switch from second to third person occurs when we reach a later part of the b'rachah, as well. These shifts enable us to relate, again, on many different levels as individuals, as a community, personally, and publicly to God. Both words, Adonai and elohaynu, which stand for God, are almost impossible to define, for how do you define God? Elohaynu has also developed to be associated with God's attributes of justice.

MELECH מֶלֶךְ

At first glance the word *melech*, King, might seem like a simple expression derived from a time in history when the supreme ruler of any country was a king. Therefore, God was considered the Absolute Ruler, the King of kings. But when we examine the word in greater depth and consider the implications of sovereignty, we realize how complicated a word it is. As explained before, our relationship to this King is not the common variety. We are at once the King's subjects and His children. So this use of melech implies a relationship which is hard to define. Moreover, the concepts involved in sovereignty, such as rulership, benevolence, authority, responsibility, leadership, control, and power, all make this word extremely powerful and difficult to define. So again we see an extremely abstract word used in this basic liturgical formula.

HA'OLAM הָעוֹלָם

Ha'olam means "the universe." When we use a word to mean everything, in a way it means nothing. For how can one define the universe? A definition implies setting something apart so that it is distinct from other things. When a word stands for everything, it is almost meaningless, because it can't be defined. Therefore, this word, too, is extremely abstract and difficult for us to comprehend.

Now look back over the first six words of the b'rachah. As you reread the words, thinking about the analysis of each, you may feel a bit uncomfortable. What you thought you understood before has suddenly become much more complex and difficult to understand. Indeed, that is part of what those six words are meant to do. They are meant to complicate. They are meant to expand our horizons. For God to be God we cannot understand what God is. If we understood totally, that would diminish God's power; we could be God. But as human beings we have a need to relate to the Divine. We have a need to call out to something greater than ourselves. Our easiest and most common way of communicating and relating is through the use of words. So, in addition to their "meaning," the first six words of a bracha are almost, but not quite, nonsense syllables. They mean so much, that they almost mean nothing.

We have a deep desire to call out to God, but we're not quite sure what to say or how to express ourselves. We, therefore, use these six highly abstract words as a way of starting the process of relating to something so far beyond ourselves. Indeed, as we read earlier, they are very much the pebbles thrown into the pool of meaning which radiate out vast waves of connotations and implications.

Now let's look at one of the most well-known b'rachot:

Praised Be You, Adonai Our God, King of the universe, who brings bread out of the earth.	בָּרוּךְ אַתָּה ה' אֱלֹהֵינוּ מֶלֶךְ הָעוֹלָם הַמּוֹצִיא לֶחֶם מִן הָאָרֶץ.

Compare the first half of the b'rachah with the second half. Let's look at the words which make up the second half.

What part of speech is the word *Hamotzee*, "who brings out"? If you guessed a verb, you're correct; if you guessed a noun, you're also correct. (It is a verb which signifies the person doing the act.) It is a measurable, seeable, touchable, action word, which comes from the verb לְהוֹצִיא "to bring out," and is a measurable, physical action. *Lehem*, bread, a noun, is also obviously a very touchable, smellable, seeable, eatable, tastable object. *Min* is a linking word necessary for language to work properly, (a preposition). *Ha'aretz*, the earth, is also to be sure a very touchable word. Now look what has happened.

The second half of the b'rachah is made up of extremely concrete, definable, clearly understandable words. They are set in juxtaposition to the first six words of the b'rachah which are incredibly abstract. Each b'rachah makes the following type of theological statements: for God to be God, He has to be greater than anything we can understand, but we do have to relate to God and want God to know that we are aware of His presence in the world. So out of a desire to relate, we say "We don't really know what God is" *(baruch attah adonai elohaynu melech ha'olam)*, but we do know, *hamotzee lehem min ha'aretz*, "He brings bread out of the earth." Therefore, every time a Jew makes a b'rachah he or she is defining a belief in God and making a theological statement about the nature and attributes of Divinity. This is, perhaps, one reason why over the course of Jewish history there were not many books written as theologies. Jews had a kind of practical theology inherent in statements of b'rachot, prayers, and halachah. We don't know what God is, but we do see His actions in the world, which we attribute to Him. In those actions we get a glimpse of the Divine nature and power.

A second aspect of the liturgical formula of the b'racha stems from its basic purpose, to thank God for the many blessings we have received from His hand. Implied in thanking someone for a gift is a relationship to the giver. When a parent gives a child a bicycle, there are certain expectations of that child. In addition to saying "thank you" we expect the child to take care of the gift. Were the child to leave the bike in the rain or out on the playground, getting rusty or being stolen, the parents would have every right to be disappointed. Likewise, when we thank God for the gifts we have received, we assume a certain ethical responsibility for those gifts. For example, when one recites HaMotzee, one must take ethical responsibility for the food. Therefore, not wasting food (the mitzvah of *bal tash-heet*) is part of that responsibility. Likewise, concern for all of the human beings it took to bring that bread to our table must also become part of our responsibility in thanking God for the gift. Try tracing backwards, step by step, from the table, to the grocery, to the bakery, to the farmer, to the field, all of the people it took to bring that bread to your table. So, when hearing of labor problems, or farm problems, a sensitive Jew who takes his ethical responsibilities seriously, will be concerned. Not to look at these problems is, in essence, a direct slap at the gift Giver. It is one part of what we might consider making a b'rachah *l'vatalah* (in vain). To thank God for a gift and not take responsibility for it, to abuse food or to deny the rights of those it took to bring us that food, is to deny God and the gift He has given us.

Other examples of ethical responsibility stem from other b'rachot. When we eat fruit or vegetables from the ground, we recite the b'rachah praising God "who creates fruits of the earth." Obviously, one ethical implication of someone who is grateful for fresh food involves taking care of the earth.

This is a picture of a forest which has been strip-mined. Nothing will ever grow again on that land unless it is properly and extensively reclaimed.

Therefore, those of us who have the possibility of influencing decisions in regard to the use of land have a responsibility to care for the land from which our blessings come. The use of toxic fertilizers and insecticides are concerns for a sensitive Jew who makes this b'rachah.

Another example is found in the b'rachah for smelling fragrant fruit, "...who gives fruit pleasant fragrance." If we think about our sense of smell, we are immediately reminded of the problems of air pollution. Therefore, a Jew who thanks God for this sense of smell must also take responsibility for not abusing that sense, and not abusing the air which carries the fragrant scents. Similarly, when we praise God "who makes the Great Sea", upon seeing the (Mediterranean) Sea, our concern with water pollution must come to mind, especially in this day of oil crisis and exploitation of the oceans.

Perhaps, one more example will suffice to make this point of our ethical responsibility for the world around us. When a Jew sees beautiful sights in nature such as a sunset or a magnificent landscape, the b'rachah "Praised are You...who re-enacts the work of Creation," is recited. The world is continually being re-created by God, and we have a certain aesthetic responsibility in maintaining the natural beauty of the world; we are obligated not to clutter the earth with our debris. Thus, the second part of the formula of a b'rachah involves our ethical responsibility when we thank God for one of his gifts.

Sensitivity to Life

A third aspect of the b'rachah involves sensitivity to and appreciation of the world around us. Our tradition teaches that every Jew is responsible for saying מֵאָה בְּרָכוֹת , one hundred b'rachot each day. Counting up all of the b'rachot in the three services each day, and adding to them the b'rachot in Birkat HaMazon as well as some of the extra b'rachot recited in the course of the day, it is easy to reach the one hundred minimum. Why did the Rabbis set this number of b'rachot -- or any number at all? They wanted us to be sensitive to the beauty and joy of the world God has given us, by looking for opportunities to praise God and thank Him for the magnificence of the world. We don't let life pass us by; we look for every opportunity to savor it. How often do we attend to our daily business without ever giving a thought to the beauty of the sky, or the flowers, or the birds, or the little things that make life pleasant? "Don't take life for granted," say the Rabbis when they tell us to recite 100 b'rachot every day. And each b'rachah says, "Life is too short to be missed. Don't let the world pass you by."

A fourth concept underlying the b'rachah formula stems from its ability to change an experience significantly. All of us get hungry, but so do animals. What makes us different from animals? How can we strive to be more human, and therefore, more in the image of God? The purpose of saying a b'rachah before gulping down a meal is to stop and say, "I am a human being, not an animal. I am aware of the beauty and the gifts of the world; I want to relate to that world on a higher level than that of beasts."

Besides that, we are not all great religious poets. Very often when we have a particularly beautiful experience we feel the need to respond. A b'rachah gives us the opportunity to raise the level of our response and make it more spiritual, more human. Uttering a b'rachah when experiencing an event in life significantly changes that event, raising it, making it more important and enriching. Each time we undergo a situation in which we utter a b'rachah, we add to our own personal history of religious experiences.

So it was, for instance, when the author of this source book witnessed the birth of his son and, together with his wife in the delivery room, recited the b'rachah, *sheheh-hehyanu.* All of the previous times that b'rachah had been recited somehow came together in this magnificent moment of life. The need to address God at that moment, to go beyond oneself, was extremely profound. The fact that we were comfortable in saying the b'rachah at that time, because we had said it so many times before, made that moment all the more significant.

It is interesting to note that the Rabbis were not interested in people uttering b'rachot for any and all reasons at any time. The b'rachah has to be "caused" by an event, the stimulus for reciting the b'rachah. The reason for this is stated in the Talmud *(B'rachot: 33a):*

"Anyone who makes a b'rachah without it being necessary debases the name of God by taking His name 'in vain,' " (i.e., taking it lightly).

כָּל הַמְבָרֵךְ בְּרָכָה שֶׁאֵינָה צְרִיכָה עוֹבֵר מִשׁוּם ״לֹא תִשָּׂא.״

The Rabbis do not want us to minimize the significance of b'rachot. Since the b'rachah effects the experience, we are also prohibited from any interruption between the b'rachah and the appropriate action or happening. The recitation of the b'rachah raises the commonplace to a higher, spiritual level. Finally, by including both the second person singular pronoun of address (attah, You) and the first person plural suffix noun (*our* God), the b'rachah reminds us that each one of us is responsible for relating to God as individuals and as part of a people. The world was created by God for all people. We are caretakers of His world and together we are responsible to the ultimate creator for the use of that world. Each time we say a b'rachah we reaffirm the statement of the Psalms (115:16),

הַשָּׁמַיִם שָׁמַיִם לַה׳ וְהָאָרֶץ נָתַן לִבְנֵי־אָדָם.
"The heaven is God's, but He has given the earth to mankind."

We are also saying that God is the owner of the property from which we are deriving interest or benefit. To summarize, every time we utter a b'rachah, the basic building block of all Jewish prayer, we are

1. making a theological statement, defining our beliefs and attitudes toward God;

2. thanking God for a gift and acknowledging our ethical responsibility for taking care of it;

3. making ourselves sensitive to the world around us, trying not to take life for granted;

4. changing the common variety of experience, raising it and, in the process, making ourselves closer to the image of God we seek to emulate.

Below are listed the *Birchot HaNehehnin*, (Blessings for things we enjoy on various occasions). As you read each b'rachah, see if you can determine when it is recited and what personal or communal responsibility is evoked. At the end of the b'rachot is a list of the appropriate occasions for reciting each one, and also an exercise for you to try in order to increase your understanding and awareness of the importance of this part of our tradition.

BLESSINGS ON VARIOUS OCCASIONS

1. בָּרוּךְ אַתָּה ה' אֱלֹהֵינוּ מֶלֶךְ הָעוֹלָם בּוֹרֵא מִינֵי מְזוֹנוֹת.
Praised are You, O Lord, our God, King of the Universe who creates various types of foods.

2. בא״י אמ״ה בּוֹרֵא פְּרִי הָעֵץ.
...who creates the fruit of the tree.

3. בא״י אמ״ה בּוֹרֵא פְּרִי הָאֲדָמָה.
...who creates the fruit of the earth.

4. בא״י אמ״ה שֶׁהַכֹּל נִהְיֶה בִּדְבָרוֹ.
...by whose word all things exist.

5. בא״י אמ״ה בּוֹרֵא נְפָשׁוֹת רַבּוֹת וְחֶסְרוֹנָן עַל כָּל מַה שֶּׁבָּרֵאתָ לְהַחֲיוֹת בָּהֶם נֶפֶשׁ כָּל חָי. בָּרוּךְ חֵי הָעוֹלָמִים.
...who creates many living beings with their needs and provides food for them in addition to that which He has provided to sustain life. Praised be the eternal source of all life.

6. בא״י אמ״ה בּוֹרֵא עֲצֵי בְשָׂמִים.
...who creates fragrant woods.

7. בא״י אמ״ה בּוֹרֵא עִשְׂבוֹת בְּשָׂמִים.
...who creates fragrant plants.

8. בא״י אמ״ה הַנּוֹתֵן רֵיחַ טוֹב בַּפֵּרוֹת.
...who gives fruits a pleasant fragrance.

9. בא״י אמ״ה בּוֹרֵא שֶׁמֶן עָרֵב.
...who creates fragrant oil.

10. בא״י אמ״ה בּוֹרֵא מִינֵי בְשָׂמִים.
...who creates various kinds of spices.

11. בא״י אמ״ה זוֹכֵר הַבְּרִית וְנֶאֱמָן בִּבְרִיתוֹ וְקַיָּם בְּמַאֲמָרוֹ.
...who remembers the covenant and who is faithful to His covenant and keeps His word.

12. בא״י אמ״ה שֶׁלֹּא חִסַּר בְּעוֹלָמוֹ דָּבָר וּבָרָא בוֹ בְּרִיּוֹת טוֹבוֹת וְאִילָנוֹת טוֹבִים לְהַנּוֹת בָּהֶם בְּנֵי אָדָם.
...who has withheld nothing from His world and has created beautiful creatures and beautiful trees in it, to give mankind delight in them.

13. בא״י אמ״ה שֶׁעָשָׂה אֶת הַיָּם הַגָּדוֹל.
...who has made the great sea.

14. בא״י אמ״ה שֶׁכָּכָה לוֹ בְּעוֹלָמוֹ.
...who has such as this in His world.

15. בא״י אמ״ה מְשַׁנֶּה הַבְּרִיּוֹת.
...who makes people different.

16. בא״י אמ״ה עֹשֶׂה מַעֲשֵׂה בְרֵאשִׁית.
...who enacts the creation.

17. בא״י אמ״ה מַצִּיב גְּבוּל אַלְמָנָה.
...who restores the borders of the widow (Zion).

18. בא״י אמ״ה שֶׁחָלַק מֵחָכְמָתוֹ לִירֵאָיו.
...who has given of His wisdom to those who revere Him.

19. בא״י אמ״ה שֶׁנָּתַן מֵחָכְמָתוֹ לְבָשָׂר וָדָם.
...who has given of His wisdom to mortals.

20. בא״י אמ״ה שֶׁנָּתַן מִכְּבוֹדוֹ לְבָשָׂר וָדָם.
...who has given of His glory to mortals.

21. בא״י אמ״ה שֶׁכֹּחוֹ וּגְבוּרָתוֹ מָלֵא עוֹלָם.
...whose strength and power fill the world.

22. בא״י אמ״ה הַטּוֹב וְהַמֵּטִיב.
...the Good, and who causes good.

23. בא״י אמ״ה דַּיַּן הָאֱמֶת.
...the true Judge.

24. בא״י אמ״ה שֶׁהֶחֱיָנוּ וְקִיְּמָנוּ וְהִגִּיעָנוּ לַזְּמַן הַזֶּה.
...who caused us to live and preserved us and enabled us to reach this season.

25. בא״י אמ״ה מַלְבִּישׁ עֲרוּמִים.
...who clothes the naked.

26. בא״י אמ״ה מְחַיֵּה הַמֵּתִים.
...who brings the dead to life.

27. בא״י אמ״ה אֲשֶׁר קִדְּשָׁנוּ בְּמִצְוֹתָיו וְצִוָּנוּ לִקְבּוֹעַ מְזוּזָה.
...who has made us distinct through His commandments and commanded us to attach the mezuzah.

28. בא״י אמ״ה אֲשֶׁר יָצַר אֶת הָאָדָם בְּחָכְמָה וּבָרָא בוֹ נְקָבִים נְקָבִים חֲלוּלִים חֲלוּלִים. גָּלוּי וְיָדוּעַ לִפְנֵי כִסֵּא כְבוֹדֶךָ שֶׁאִם יִפָּתֵחַ אֶחָד מֵהֶם אוֹ יִסָּתֵם אֶחָד מֵהֶם אִי אֶפְשָׁר לְהִתְקַיֵּם וְלַעֲמוֹד לְפָנֶיךָ. בא״י רוֹפֵא כָל בָּשָׂר וּמַפְלִיא לַעֲשׂוֹת.
...who has formed man in wisdom and created in him many orifices and many hollow tubes. It is well known before Your glorious throne, that if one of them be perforated or obstructed, it would be impossible to stay alive before You. Praised are You, O Lord, Healer of all flesh, who does wondrously.

The b'rachot are said on the following occasions. The numbers refer to the b'rachah number on the previous pages. Some b'rachot could actually fit in more than one "category," and traditions vary about when to use some of them.

Blessings for "taste":

1. ...Before eating food (other than bread) made from any of the "five species of grain": wheat, barley, rye, oats, and spelt; (such as cake, etc.).
2. ...Eating fruit which grows on trees.
3. ...Eating fruit or vegetables which grow in or on the ground.
4. ...Eating meat, fish, eggs, cheese, etc., or drinking beverages except wine.
5. ...After eating things listed in the prior three b'rachot.

Blessings for "smell":

6. ...Smelling fragrant woods or barks.
7. ...Smelling fragrant plants.
8. ...Smelling fragrant fruits.
9. ...Smelling fragrant oils.
10. ...Smelling fragrant spices.

Blessings for "sight":

11. ...Seeing a rainbow.
12. ...Seeing trees blossoming for the first time in the year.
13. ...Seeing the (Mediterranean) Sea.
14. ...Seeing unusually beautiful trees or creatures.
15. ...Seeing someone of abnormal appearance.
16. ...Seeing lightning, shooting stars, great deserts, high mountains, or a sunrise.
17. ...Seeing synagogues which have been restored.
18. ...Seeing a sage distinguished for knowledge of Torah.
19. ...Seeing someone distinguished for secular knowledge.
20. ...Seeing a ruler and his court.

Blessings for "hearing":

21. ...Hearing thunder.
22. ...Hearing good news.
23. ...Hearing tragic news.

Other blessings of gratitude:

24. ...Obtaining a new item, tasting a fruit for the first time in a season, entering a new home, and many other special occasions.
25. ...Wearing a new garment.
26. ...Seeing a friend after a long separation (one year or more).
27. ...Affixing a mezuzah to a doorpost.
28. ...After leaving the bathroom.

EXERCISE 1

In our discussion of b'rachot we have talked much about God as a gift-giver and us as receivers of His gifts. We have discussed our responsibility for taking care of those gifts in our need to thank God for them. The notion of giving gifts and appreciating gifts is quite important to most people. Birthdays, Ḥanukah, or graduations are all celebrated with gift giving and the necessary thank you's and appreciation that come with it. The kinds of gifts we give, the kinds of gifts we wish to receive, and the kinds of gifts for which we are truly grateful are mirrors of our own values and ideals. To highlight the expressions of thanks in all of the b'rachot, try the following exercise. In the first column list people who are very close to you, including family and friends. In the second column across the top list a gift that you have given that person. In the third column list a gift that you could give which would dramatically change some aspect of that person's behavior or life. Next, list a gift that that person could give you that could change your life. Finally, if possible, list the monetary values of the various gifts you have listed.

Name	Gift Given	Gift to change person	Gift to change me	Monetary Value
1.				
2.				
3.				
4.				
5.				
6.				
7.				
8.				
9.				
10.				

EXERCISE 2

After discussing the ethical responsibilities implicit in b'rachot, consider the dimension of which we are reminded in the following story.

THANKS FOR BREAD

Once a boy who had just eaten lunch turned to his mother and said, "Thank you very much." But his mother said, "You should not thank me alone, for I only prepared the food."

The boy wondered, "Whom should I thank?" He went to the grocery store and saw the grocer. "Thank you, Mr. Grocer, for the very fine bread that I ate at lunchtime."

"Oh," said the grocer, "you should not thank me alone. I only sell the bread. I do not bake it."

So the boy went to the bakery where all the bread was made; and there he saw the baker. "Mr. Baker," the boy said, "I want to thank you for the wonderful bread that you bake."

The baker laughed and said, "I bake the bread, but it is good because the flour is good. And the flour comes from the miller who grinds it."

"Then I will thank the miller," said the boy and he turned to leave. "But the miller only grinds the wheat," the baker said. "It is the farmer who grows the grain which makes the bread so good."

So the boy went off in search of the farmer. He walked until he came to the edge of the village and there he saw the farmer at work in the fields. "I want to thank you for the bread that I eat every day."

But the farmer said, "Do not thank me alone. I only plant the seed, tend the field, and harvest the grain. It is sunshine and good rain and the rich earth that makes the wheat so good."

"But who is left to thank?" asked the boy, and he was very sad, very tired, and very hungry again, for he had walked a long way in one day. The farmer said, "Come inside and eat with my family and then you will feel better."

So the boy went into the farmhouse with the farmer and sat down to eat with the farmer's family. Each person took a piece of bread and then, all together, they said,

בָּרוּךְ אַתָּה ה' אֱלֹהֵינוּ מֶלֶךְ הָעוֹלָם הַמּוֹצִיא לֶחֶם מִן הָאָרֶץ.
Praised are You, Lord, our God, Who brings bread out of the earth.

And then the boy discovered that it was God whom he had forgotten to thank.

From Seymour Rossel, *When a Jew Prays* (New York: Behrman House Publishers, Inc., 1973).

CHAPTER 5
The Structure of Weekday, Shabbat and Holiday Services

Having studied the overall plan of Siddur organization and the basic building block upon which most t'fillot are based, we can now turn to an examination of the structure and content of individual services. Amazingly, though your own experience may seem to prove otherwise, all of the morning services for every day of the year have the same basic structure. The same is true of all afternoon services and all evening services. Sometimes there are additions, or modifications, but each service of the day has a plan of organization similar to its counterparts every day of the year. The following charts present an overall view of the structure of the major services in the liturgy. Refer to them as your continue your studies.

GENERAL STRUCTURE OF THE FIXED PRAYER SERVICES[3]

Evening Service (Ma'ariv or Arvit)

SHEMA and its blessings + (Half Kaddish) + AMIDAH + (Full Kaddish) + (Alaynu)

Morning Service (Shaḥarit)

(Morning Blessings) + (Passages of Praise) + Half Kaddish) + (SHEMA and its blessings + AMIDAH* + (Full Kaddish) + (Alaynu)

*Additions as appropriate: (Petition Prayers) + (Half Kaddish) + (Hallel) + (Torah Reading) + (Half Kaddish) + (K'dushah D'sidra)

Afternoon Service (Minḥah)

(Half Kaddish) + AMIDAH + (Full Kaddish) + (Alaynu)

(This format also applies to the Musaf--Additional--Service and to Ne'ilah--the Yom Kippur concluding service.)

DIAGRAM OF MA'ARIV (EVENING) SERVICE

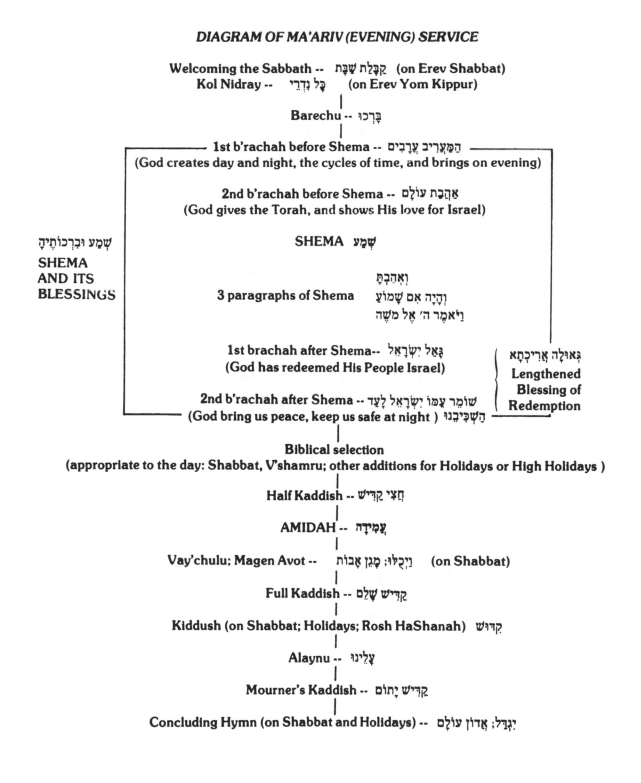

Welcoming the Sabbath -- קַבָּלַת שַׁבָּת (on Erev Shabbat)
Kol Nidray -- כָּל נִדְרֵי (on Erev Yom Kippur)

Barechu -- בָּרְכוּ

— 1st b'rachah before Shema -- הַמַּעֲרִיב עֲרָבִים —
(God creates day and night, the cycles of time, and brings on evening)

2nd b'rachah before Shema -- אַהֲבַת עוֹלָם
(God gives the Torah, and shows His love for Israel)

SHEMA   שְׁמַע

שְׁמַע וּבִרְכוֹתֶיהָ
SHEMA
AND ITS
BLESSINGS

3 paragraphs of Shema
וְאָהַבְתָּ
וְהָיָה אִם שָׁמֹעַ
וַיֹּאמֶר ה׳ אֶל מֹשֶׁה

1st brachah after Shema-- גָּאַל יִשְׂרָאֵל
(God has redeemed His People Israel)

גְּאוּלָה אֲרִיכְתָּא
Lengthened
Blessing of
Redemption

2nd b'rachah after Shema -- שׁוֹמֵר עַמּוֹ יִשְׂרָאֵל לָעַד
(God bring us peace, keep us safe at night) הַשְׁכִּיבֵנוּ

Biblical selection
(appropriate to the day: Shabbat, V'shamru; other additions for Holidays or High Holidays)

Half Kaddish -- חֲצִי קַדִּישׁ

AMIDAH -- עֲמִידָה

Vay'chulu; Magen Avot -- וַיְכֻלּוּ; מָגֵן אָבוֹת (on Shabbat)

Full Kaddish -- קַדִּישׁ שָׁלֵם

Kiddush (on Shabbat; Holidays; Rosh HaShanah) קִדּוּשׁ

Alaynu -- עָלֵינוּ

Mourner's Kaddish -- קַדִּישׁ יָתוֹם

Concluding Hymn (on Shabbat and Holidays) -- יִגְדַּל; אֲדוֹן עוֹלָם

95

DIAGRAM OF SHAHARIT (MORNING) SERVICE [4]

Early morning b'rachot -- בִּרְכוֹת הַשַּׁחַר

פְּסוּקֵי דְזִמְרָה
**HYMNS AND PSALMS
TO PREPARE US
FOR PRAYER**

Baruch She'amar -- בָּרוּךְ שֶׁאָמַר

PSALMS, SONGS, MEDITATIONS

Yishtabah Shimchah -- יִשְׁתַּבַּח שִׁמְךָ

Barechu   בָּרְכוּ

1st b'rachah before Shema -- יוֹצֵר הָאוֹר
(God creates the world anew every day; light)

2nd b'rachah before Shema -- אַהֲבָה רַבָּה
(God gives the Torah, and shows His special love for Israel)

שְׁמַע וּבִרְכוֹתֶיהָ
**SHEMA AND
ITS BLESSINGS**

SHEMA שְׁמַע

3 paragraphs of the Shema
וְאָהַבְתָּ
וְהָיָה אִם שָׁמֹעַ
וַיֹּאמֶר ה׳ אֶל מֹשֶׁה

B'rachah after Shema -- גָּאַל יִשְׂרָאֵל
(God has redeemed His people Israel)

AMIDAH -- עֲמִידָה
also known as
"18" Benedictions -- (שְׁמוֹנֶה עֶשְׂרֵה)

Hallel --   הַלֵּל   (on Rosh Hodesh and Holidays)

Half Kaddish   חֲצִי קַדִּישׁ

Torah Reading   קְרִיאַת הַתּוֹרָה   (on Monday and Thursday, Shabbat, Rosh Hodesh and Holidays)

(ADDITIONAL SERVICE) -- תְּפִלַּת מוּסָף   (Shabbat, Rosh Hodesh and Holidays)

Full Kadish -- קַדִּישׁ שָׁלֵם

Alaynu -- עָלֵינוּ

Mourner's Kaddish -- קַדִּישׁ יָתוֹם

Concluding Prayers

96

DIAGRAM OF MINḤAH (AFTERNOON) SERVICE

ASHRAY-- אַשְׁרֵי
(Supplemented Psalm 145)

|

"There comes a redeemer --   וּבָא לְצִיוֹן גּוֹאֵל   (on Shabbat and Holidays)

|

Half Kaddish-- חֲצִי קַדִּישׁ

|

Torah Reading --   קְרִיאַת הַתּוֹרָה   (On Shabbat and Fast Days)

|

Half Kaddish -- חֲצִי קַדִּישׁ

|

AMIDAH -- עֲמִידָה

|

Full Kaddish-- קַדִּישׁ שָׁלֵם

|

Alaynu-- עָלֵינוּ

|

Mourner's Kaddish-- קַדִּישׁ יָתוֹם

Thematic Organization of Morning and Evening Services:
The Creation, Revelation, Redemption Formula

The content and structure of services which include the Shema--Shaharit and Ma'ariv--are in accordance with a rabbinic statement:

In the morning recite two b'rachot before it (the Shema) and one following; and in the evening, two before it and two after it, one long and one short. Where they (the sages) established a long b'rachah, one may not recite a short one, and where they established a short one, one may not recite a long one. Where they said to recite the concluding formula ("Praised are You...") one may not omit it; where they said to omit it, one may not recite the concluding formula.

בשחר מברך שתיים לפניה ואחת לאחריה, ובערב שתיים לפניה ושתיים לאחריה, אחת ארוכה ואחת קצרה. מקום שאמרו להאריך אינו רשאי לקצר, לקצר אינו רשאי להאריך; לחתום אינו רשאי שלא לחתום ושלא לחתום אינו רשאי לחתום.

B'rachot 1:4

As mentioned in previous chapters, the process of evolution of the liturgy took place over a long period of time. Yet very early this basic, required structure shaped the content and form of our morning and evening services.

In the morning service, the first passage, beginning with the b'rachah *Birkat HaYotzayr*, deals with the Creator, God. The second b'rachah, ending with the words "who has chosen His people Israel in love" deals with God's gift of the Torah. The b'rachah following the Shema deals with the redemption of Israel by God. Thus the great trilogy of relationships in Judaism -- God, Torah, Israel -- is the basic subject matter for the liturgical structure.

On yet another level, a remarkable intellectual structure linking the prayers and their order stems from a basic notion of Jewish history and its overall purpose. Attention was first called to this schema by the modern philosopher, Franz Rosenzweig, in his work, *Star of Redemption*. Jewish history can be seen as a three-fold process: creation (of the world and humanity); revelation (the giving of the Torah to the Jewish people and our "rebirth" as followers of God's laws); redemption (historically at the exodus from Egypt, and conceptually since the ultimate goal of observing God's law is that we will be "redeemed" and made one with God--a rebirth of the spirit, if you will). Interestingly, our major festivals may be interpreted as following this order: Pesah, the holiday of our *creation* as a nation, took place in Nisan, the first month of the year in the Bible. Then follows Shavuot, the holiday of *revelation*, the giving of the Torah. Finally Sukkot can be seen as a holiday of *redemption*, since traditionally it was a time when wars ceased and peace treaties were concluded; when seventy oxen were sacrificed in the Temple on behalf of all the nations of the world; when all people were called to observe the harvest holiday which reflects all humanity's ultimate reliance on nature.

Rosenzweig applied the formulation of creation, revelation, redemption to the Siddur.

I. He suggested that in the first b'rachah before the Shema we see God as the Creator:
   a. in the morning we talk about the creation of light by God in mercy;
   b. in the evening we speak of God's continuing creation of the world each day and night.

II. In the second b'rachah before the Shema we see God as giving us the gift of the Torah (revelation) in love:

   a. in the morning introduced by "a great love";
   b. in the evening introduced by the variation "an everlasting love."
The Shema -- a citation from the Torah -- is a part of that revelation.

III. Finally, in the b'rachah after the Shema we see God as redeemer of Israel through history:

    a. in the morning by "The help of our ancestors...who redeemed Israel";
    b. in the evening by "True and certain...who redeemed Israel."

The same thematic structure appears in the organization of the three Amidot on Shabbat, as considered in detail later in the chapter.

EXERCISE 1

Find other examples of the "creation, revelation, redemption" pattern (in that order) in the Siddur. As one instance, read Psalm 19, which appears in P'sukay D'zimrah for Shabbat and Holidays.

The pattern applies nationally, as seen in the Bible:

    creation (Genesis)
    revelation (Exodus)
    redemption (the rest of the Bible).

Can you see how it would apply on an individual level? What stages in a person's life would correspond to each phase?

    creation _____

    revelation _____

    redemption _____

Format of the Service:

A. Shema and its Blessings

We shall now proceed to an analysis of the prayers which make up the fixed format of the daily service. Many of the other t'fillot which make up the Siddur are analyzed separately in Section III. First there are some technical concepts we must master to understand the arrangement of the Shema and its escort of blessings.

We refer to the passages preceding and following the Shema which lies at the core of the service, by the term בְּרָכָה אֲרוּכָּה (a "long b'rachah") for the long form, and בְּרָכָה קְצָרָה (a "short b'rachah") for the short form.

...The long b'rachah begins with the word baruch and concludes with baruch...The short b'rachah concludes with baruch, but does not begin with baruch.

... ארוכה שפותחת בברוך וחתומת בברוך ... קצרה שחותמת בברוך ואינה פותחת בברוך.

Bartenurah commenting on *B'rachot 1:4*

A paragraph beginning a b'rachah which follows another section ending in a b'rachah is called בְּרָכָה סְמוּכָה לַחֲבֶרְתָּהּ , a "b'rachah attached to another."

Now glance at the diagrams at the beginning of this chapter. The structure of the service is basically a system of blessings preceding and following passages of Scripture. The first part of the morning service, P'sukay D'zimrah (consisting of biblical passages) is preceded by a long b'rachah (Baruch She'amar) and followed by a short b'rachah (Yishtabah Shimchah). The Shema (also comprised of biblical selections) is preceded by two b'rachot in the morning, one long and one short, and followed by one (short) in the morning and two (short) in the evening. Notice that this pattern is similar to having an aliyah, where the reading of the Torah is preceded by a long b'rachah and followed by one. The same is true when we read a Haftarah, or the *Megillot* (such as *Megillat Esther*). We shall now look at the "core" prayers, beginning with the Shema and the b'rachot preceding and following it. Only after we understand the framework for the Shema will we examine the Shema itself.

First b'rachah before the Shema (morning service): בִּרְכַּת הַיוֹצֵר

BACKGROUND:

Birkat HaYotzayr, "...who forms light and creates darkness, who makes peace and creates all things," declares God to be the Creator. The first sentence of the b'rachah is based on Isaiah 45:7, which ends with "evil." However, the Rabbis changed this to "all things," stressing the compassionate side of God and the measure of love they felt appropriate in the Siddur. It may also have been used against the Persian belief of dualism: Ahuramazda was the god of light and goodness; Ahriman was the god of darkness and evil. Thus, to combat the idea that the god who created darkness could not also create light, the Talmud ordained the b'rachah in its present form.

The following sections of the b'rachah all expand the meaning of its first line, "who forms light":

HaMay-eer La'aretz, "who brings light to the earth," concludes Psalms 104:24;

Ayl Baruch, an acrostic following the Hebrew alphabet;

Titbarach...

Et Shaym...   which makes up the section known as the "K'dushah of Yotzayr."

Kadosh, Kadosh, Kadosh

L'ayl Baruch N'eemote, "to the blessed God," which concludes the section.

Note that on weekdays the poem "who brings light to the earth" is read, which takes its cue from the word "light" in the initial b'rachah. On Shabbat, however, another poem, "All acknowledge You" is read, taking its theme from the word "all." There are numerous other *Yotzrot* (poems inserted on special occasions in this section of the service) written through the ages. On Shabbat we continue with the hymn of praise *Ayl Adon* and the poem "To God, who rested from all His activity..." reflecting the themes of God as Master of the universe and the special sanctity of Shabbat.

CONCEPTS:

1. This b'rachah is a prelude to the Shema, negating the idea that there are different powers in the universe controlling different aspects of creation. God is the only Master of creation.
2. The creation of peace is parallel in importance to the creation of the universe itself.
3. The *K'dushah D'yotzayr* results from the tradition that even the angels praise God. This segment is seen as a parallel to the recitation of K'dushah in the Amidah, and enables us to sanctify God even if praying without a minyan (which is required for the K'dushah in the Amidah).
4. God creates a comfortable world of light and warmth because He is compassionate and merciful.
5. Dependability of the Cycles of time and the gradual change from night to day are essential for human well-being.
6. Admiration is expressed for the incredible assortment of God's creations.
7. All creatures and heavenly bodies praise God and sanctify Him--all are subject to His rule.

"Prayer Analysis"

1. The words "light" and "darkness" are central to this entire section. Write below as many synonyms and connotations for each of these words as occur to you, in order to sense their poetic beauty and force.
2. In Judaism light is a crucial part of our rituals. List all the rituals that involve the use of light and the kind of light which is used.
3. These prayers may be a refutation of the notion of dualism (two gods) or of polytheism (many gods). Accordingly, how do you explain the list of phrases at the end of the first b'rachah before the Shema such as "who makes new things"; "triumphs in battles"; "sowing righteousness"; "who creates healing."
4. Compare the alphabetic words of Ayl Baruch (recited weekdays) and Ayl Adon (recited Shabbat). These poems use the letters of the alphabet themselves to praise God and His works. In this context, read the following story.

> A simple man came to the synagogue once. During most of the service, he just sat and listened, for he did not know very much. He could not even read the Hebrew of the prayerbook.
> All around him the members of the congregation were standing in prayer, each man speaking with God in a whisper. And the simple man wished to speak with God, too. He wished to tell God what a magnificent world He had made. He wished to thank the Lord for the blessings of health and life. But he could not find the right words to say.
> When he thought his heart would break from shame and sadness, he said, "O God, I cannot speak a beautiful prayer for You because I am a simple man and I have forgotten what I studied. I am not good with words. But You, O Lord, You know how to do everything. So I will give You the Alef Bet and You can make a beautiful prayer for Yourself." Then he recited, "Alef...Bet...Gimel...Dalet..."[5]

5. Can you think of "gods" worshipped even by people who profess to believe in the one true God? Why is it so important to be reminded continually that God alone is Supreme?

EXERCISE 1

Since the act of creation is central to many of our prayers, an understanding of what creation and creativity are about is vital to an appreciation of Jewish prayer. Many of you are creative in many areas of your life. You play musical instruments, paint or sculpt, act, or even develop new athletic plays and procedures. Creativity is a fundamental part of living, but creativity brings with it certain responsibilities and problems. To understand a bit more how difficult it must have been to create the world and how easy it is for us to forget how many conflicting problems and pressures there are in the creative process, try the following exercise:

Close your eyes and think about what it would be like if you could be the "creator of the world" for a while. What kind of world would you build? Would it have many people? Would there be wars? How would people make a living? Would there be schools? Would there be different races and religions? Would there be oceans and mountains? Would people own the land? Would there be nations and flags?

Based on Howe, *Personalizing Education*, 132.

First b'rachah before the Shema (evening service): הַמַּעֲרִיב עֲרָבִים

BACKGROUND

The evening service equivalent of Birkat HaYotzayr is the prayer which immediately follows Barechu, our call to worship. The K'dushah of Yotzayr is absent at night, possibly because of a midrashic idea that the angels proclaim God's holiness (K'dushah) only in the daytime when the perception of creation can be more intense, or because in the biblical story, God created light, but not darkness. The section *V'hu Raḥum* (Psalms 78:38), which precedes Barechu, appeals to God for mercy as we complete our day, with its success and failures behind us.

CONCEPTS:

1. Concepts are similar to the morning Birkat HaYotzayr.
2. Regular changes in time and season are a source of comfort and security.
3. We note the aesthetic of time changes happening gradually, not abruptly.

"Prayer Analysis"

1. Imagine life on earth without regular seasons or normal nights and say. Suppose earth were thrown out of its orbit around the sun, doomed to wander the universe, never knowing when it would pass a sun. If we could survive, how would life be different?
2. Write a description of the onset of night, expressing your own feelings and perceptions.

Second b'rachah before Shema (morning and evening services): אַהֲבָה רַבָּה; אַהֲבַת עוֹלָם

BACKGROUND:

Both Ahavah Rabbah (said during Shaḥarit) and Ahavat Olam (said during Ma'ariv) have their origin in talmudic times. The Rabbis debated which should be said when *(B'rachot 11b)* though it wasn't till the time of the Ge'onim (650-1050) that the present positioning was decided. Interestingly, the Sephardic and Italian rituals use only Ahavat Olam, both morning and evening.

Both of these are b'rachot attached to another, as described previously. They serve as a kind of Torah blessing for the Shema which follows immediately, with no pause permitted. (No interruption is allowed for the whole section from Barechu through the Shema. In this context, "Amen" is not considered an interruption and may be said). Elsewhere, even responding "Amen" is not permitted.

CONCEPTS:

1. God shows His love for Israel by giving us the Torah.
2. God is both our Father and our King.
3. We implore God to teach us as He taught our ancestors--to understand, learn, teach and observe His law.
4. The study of Torah is central to our lives.
5. At the end of Ahavah Rabbah we find the notion of gathering the entire Jewish people to one place in strength and unity. Symbolically, we gather the four fringes of the tallit as though we were gathering the Jews from the four "corners" of the globe.
6. God's love for Israel precedes the first paragraph of the Shema--V'ahavta--which speaks of Israel's return love for God.

> It is impossible to conceive a more categorical repudiation of the assertion that Judaism is a dry legalistic burden to its adherents....No matter how horribly Israel suffered at the hands of her oppressors, she always reassured herself and affirmed once more: Ahavah Rabbah "With great love hast Thou loved us." The blissful conviction that she was beloved of the Highest One, instilled new strength in Israel each day to fight with the courage of a lion for the Shema Yisrael, to suffer for it, to live, and if need be, to die for it.[6]

7. As night approaches we are reminded in Ahavat Olam that Torah study never ceases.

"Prayer Analysis"

To understand God's love for the Jewish people it's important to understand the connotations of the word "love." Obviously, this is one of the richest poetic words in any language. To help you focus on this prayer which expounds God showing His love for the people of Israel, try the following exercise. List the people in your life whom you have loved, or have loved you. After each name, state in a sentence or two how you know they loved you or you loved them. After you have finished your list and descriptions, see if you can detect any patterns of what love means to you. Compare your list of things which show love to Ahavah Rabbah and its list of the way God shows His love to the Jewish people. You can also compare this to Ahavat Olam in the evening service. Now answer these questions:

What is love?

What do you love most?

Is there a difference between loving a person and loving a thing?

What Jewish thing (book, time, event) do you love most?

What do you think God might love most about you?

2. Fill in the following Jewish knowledge self evaluation chart based on the abilities we ask of God in Ahavah Rabbah.

List a mitzvah, custom, fact, or skill you possess or do, or would like to try.	וְתֵן בְּלִבֵּנוּ לְהָבִין וּלְהַשְׂכִּיל Do you understand why, what, how to do it?	לִשְׁמֹעַ לִלְמֹד Have you learned it with mastery?	וּלְלַמֵּד Can you teach it to others?	וּלְעֲשׂוֹת וּלְקַיֵּם Do you observe, practice, or use it?
Example: Putting on t'fillin.	How, not why.	Yes, I can put them on in 1 min.	The how, not the why.	Once in a while; could be more often.

Look over your lists and make some priorities for self-improvement.

First b'rachah following the Shema (morning and evening): עֶזְרַת אֲבוֹתֵינוּ; אֱמֶת וֶאֱמוּנָה

BACKGROUND:

Products of talmudic times, the two paragraphs *(Ezrat Avotaynu* said mornings, and *Emet V'emunah* said evenings) are parallel in meaning. In the evening, the paragraph is the first of two b'rachot following the Shema. In the morning it is the only b'rachah following the Shema as an accompanying blessing, and is introduced by the word emet, taken from the last word in the Shema. The fringes (tzitziyot) held by the worshipper throughout the Shema (during Shaharit) are released after the words וְנֶחֱמָדִים לָעַד since it is believed they are the last words officially relating to the Shema.[7]

CONCEPTS:

1. The main theme is the redemption *(ge'ulah)* of Israel from Egypt in the past; redemption hoped for in the future is implicit, as well.
2. God is faithful, kind and loving every day; we can depend on God.
3. God's actions in history in the past give us hope for His continued activity in the present and future.
4. We remember our humble slave origins in preparation for the petitions we are about to make in the Amidah blessings to come. In fact, we find this concept in a talmudic principle, סוֹמְכִין גְּאוּלָה לִתְפִלָּה "we join redemption to the Amidah" *(B'rachot 4b).* This means that no interruption is permitted between the "redemption" blessing and the Amidah. This is a way of stating that "our petition and prayers...should flow out of historical experience...The Kabbalist commentators however, explain (this concept) in a different way. To them redemption comprises the sum total of all our individual and national aspirations. Only he who ...links his hope for redemption to fervent prayer...has a share in the future."[8]
5. God is again referred to as perfect, with no peer or equal.
6. God is also intimate, close, approachable.
7. We praise God for His actions which shaped our people's history.
8. Whereas love for God was offered before the Shema, now Truth, affirmation of God, becomes central.

"Prayer Analysis"

1. Mystical Math: How many times is the word אֱמֶת repeated after the morning Shema? Can you find a parallel to the number, representing something else in our tradition?
2. Compare the verb tenses in the morning and evening introductory paragraphs. Why is there a difference; what does it signify?
3. Upon reading Ezrat Avotaynu we realize how many times the exodus from Egypt is recalled in our liturgy every day. This major event in our history is referred to time and again because it lies at the base of every subsequent Jewish happening and development. Turning points can be crucial not only in the life of a people, but in the life of an individual. One event, one instance can change an entire life or an entire world view. The story is told of Franz Rosenzweig who was a most assimilated, non-observant Jew. Before going to be baptized for conversion, he wanted to participate in one last Kol Nidre service on Yom Kippur Eve. The inspiration resulting from that service completely changed his life, turning him to Jewish study, thought, prayer, and ritual. At that moment he took the first step in becoming one of the great modern Jewish philosophers. Try the following exercise as a way of locating some pivotal events in your own life you might want to think about when you read Emet V'emunah or Ezrat Avotaynu. Describe an event such as the first day of school, first haircut, the birth of a younger brother or sister, a time when you got lost, a trip, an important school event, etc. Then answer the following questions:

Why was the event important?

What actually happened?

What did you learn from the event?

How did it change your life?

Did it change your attitude towards people? If so, how?

Did the event affect others? How?

Did it change their behavior? How?

Now try the same exercise for an important Jewish event in your life, e.g., Bar or Bat Mitzvah, trip to Israel, etc.

_____

Based on Howe, *Personalizing Education*, 164.

Second b'rachah following the Shema (evening)   הַשְׁכִּיבֵנוּ

BACKGROUND:
Hashkeyvanu, cited in the Talmud, appears in different forms in different communities. It is considered a lengthening of the Ge'ulah (redemption) benediction. The weekday version ends in the phrase "who guards Your people Israel forever" while the Shabbat and Festival version uses the ending created in Palestine, "who spreads the Sukkah of peace over us, over Israel, and over Jerusalem" (*Yerushalmi B'rachot 4:5*).

CONCEPTS:

1. Whereas the preceding b'rachah declared God our Redeemer in the past, the ending of this prayer declares Him our Redeemer now and in the future.
2. The Midrash on Psalm 6 tells us that this b'rachah comes to replace the obligation of *tzitzit*, which is not observed at night. As we are reminded in the day by the fringes to follow God's laws, at night we challenge God to protect us beneath His wings so we can continue to follow those laws and have hope for the future.
3. The normal tensions and insecurity that come with night are mirrored in this prayer, as is the concern for reawakening in the morning.
4. Night is a time for taking counsel, for evaluating our day, our life, and planning for tomorrow.

"Prayer Analysis"

1. Compare the concerns expressed in Hashkeyvaynu with any of the English bedtime prayers you may have said as a child before going to sleep.
2. What is meant by the phrase "Guard our going out and our coming in unto life and peace"?
3. Are you different at night from in the day? Which time of day do you prefer? Why?
4. The following incident contains a letter written by the author of this source book a long time ago:

> On November 23, 1968 a terrorist bomb exploded in the Mahane Yehuda open-air market in Jerusalem. It was erev Shabbat, and as usual, the narrow streets of the market swarmed with shoppers. Eleven people were killed; fifty injured. One young man who was unharmed in the explosion...asked to lead the davening of Kaballat Shabbat. "When I got to the prayer Hashkeyvaynu, it hit me as it never did before. 'Help us to lie down in peace; and awaken us to life again. Shield us from enemies...remove the evil forces that surround us. Spread over us the shelter of Your peace...Baruch Atah Adonai...who spreads a shelter of peace over us, over all His people Israel and over Jerusalem!"[9]

106

Special addition to Ma'ariv: בָּרוּךְ ה' לְעוֹלָם

BACKGROUND:

This passage, probably written in Babylonia, was added in post-talmudic times. Some say it was included as a substitute for the Amidah, since it repeats God's name eighteen times. Either because people were afraid to remain till the end of the evening service (since the synagogues were outside the town) or because the Ma'ariv service used to be optional, this passage came to replace the Amidah. By the way, the Rabbis originally felt that the evening service was not obligatory since there was no evening sacrifice in the Temple.

Today, some traditions do not include the passage and some recite only part of it. 10 On Shabbat and holidays, the passage is omitted, being replaced with a special quotation appropriate to the day: *V'shamru* (on Shabbat); *Vahy'dabayr Mosheh* (on festivals); or *Tik'u Vahodesh* (on the High Holidays).

CONCEPTS:

1. The welfare of the community was seriously considered by the Rabbis in the demands they placed on people.
2. This particular prayer is a general summary of many of the major themes of the whole prayer service.
3. *Note:* The Ma'ariv service continues after this prayer as shown in the diagram at the beginning of the chapter. During the Rosh HaShanah season, from Rosh Ḥodesh Elul through Hoshana Rabbah, Psalm 27 is added at the end of the service, morning and evening. The psalm reflects the theme of God's compassion, and our reliance on Him.

SHEMA שְׁמַע

BACKGROUND:

The Shema was recited publicly after the Ten Commandments in the Temple service. Later, by the first century C.E., the three paragraphs constituting the Shema became the core of the synagogue service along with the Amidah.

When the Shema is recited publicly, the shaliaḥ tzibbur repeats the three concluding words, ה' אֱלֹהֵיכֶם אֱמֶת , "the Lord your God is faithful," bringing the total number of words in the Shema to 248. (When reciting the Shema alone we begin by adding the three words אֵל מֶלֶךְ נֶאֱמָן , "God, faithful King," which form an acrostic, אָמֵן , and which keeps the number of words at 248.) According to rabbinic tradition, this is the number of parts of the body, thus symbolizing our love and devotion to God with all our body.

It is also believed that Rabbi Yehudah HaNasi, the 3rd century Palestinian editor of the Mishnah, began the custom of covering his eyes when reciting the first line of the Shema, to devote complete concentration to the words. Another custom is to stress the word *Eḥad*, "one," by prolonging the final *d*, to emphasize our encompassing belief in the unity of God. In the Torah itself, the last letter of the word שְׁמַע , and of אֶחָד are written larger to form the word עֵד , witness, thus attesting to our serving as witnesses to God's unity and sovereignty every time we recite the Shema.

The second line of the Shema, *Baruch Shaym K'vod Malchuto* ... was added as a declaration of our accepting the yoke of the Kingdom of God annunciated in the Shema. In Palestine it was always pronounced aloud to counter the claims of "Jewish Christians," accusing those who said it quietly of heretical (under-their-breath) interpretations. In Babylonia, as in most synagogues today, it was said quietly, since it is a non-biblical passage inserted among passages all taken from the Torah. We are to pronounce the Shema with great care and precision, because of its importance and the power of its words.

Rabbi Yehoshu'a ben Korḥah explained the order of three sections of the Shema (which are not recited in the order they are found in the Bible) as follows:

Why do we read *Shema* before *Vehayah im shamoa?* Because one must first accept the yoke of the Kingship of God and then accept the yoke of the *Mitzvot.* Why does *Vehayah im shamoa* precede *Vayyomer?* Because the latter makes reference to the *tzitzit,* a *mitzvah* which is to be observed only during the day, while in *Vehayah,* we are told "And you shall teach them to your children," and the *mitzvah* of studying and teaching the Torah devolves on us both day and night (Mishnah Ber. 2:3).[11]

CONCEPTS:

From Max Arzt, *Justice and Mercy* (New York: The Burning Bush Press, 1963), 69-70.

1. The first section (Deut. 6:4-9) affirms that God alone is to be our God. When we say that God is One, we declare that all our loyalties are conditioned by the primary loyalty owed to Him alone. We are to love God with all that we have and with all that we are. If love, any love, is to be more than a casual experience, it must be founded on the consciousness of the proximity of the beloved. The love of God is articulated in the nearness of God, in the fact that it will inspire diligent efforts to teach "these words" to our children, to make these teachings the guide-posts of our daily life, evening and morning, when at home and when abroad. As reminders of this supreme loyalty, "these words" are to be placed on the forehead (*tefillin*) and inscribed on the doorposts (*mezuzah*).

2. The second section of the *Shema* is also taken from the Book of Deuteronomy (11:13-21). In the context in which it is found, Moses tells the people that unlike the soil of Egypt which was cultivated largely by irrigation, the land of Canaan which they were about to occupy depended on rain -- which is a gift of God. There follows the warning that these rains would come down regularly and plentifully if the Israelites would obey God's commandments, but they would be withheld if Israel allowed itself to be lured into the worship of strange gods. As further punishment for the violation of their covenant with God, they would be driven into exile from the very land which God had given them. As frequent reminders of the promise and the warning, "these words" are to be inserted in the capsules of the *tefillin* and inscribed on the parchment of the *mezuzah.* However unsophisticated the second paragraph of the *Shema* may be, it offers a concrete warning that the moral law cannot be violated with impunity.

Modern history has confirmed all too accurately that in the wake of idolatries based on racial and class imperialisms, severe economic hardship and tragic dislocations of peoples result. The interdependence of moral integrity and physical security can be seen to have a global significance, for the effects of the maltreatment of the weak by the strong offer horrifying validation of the warning here expressed with such simple profundity.

3. In this, the third section of the *Shema*, mention is made of the fringes (*tzitzit*) "with a blue thread on the fringe of each corner" which the Israelites are to put on their garments. When looking at them, the Israelites will remember "all the commandments of the Lord and do them" (Num. 15:39).

Perhaps because he was apprehensive that the literal meaning of this verse might lead to the telescoping of all the commandments into the one *mitzvah* of the *tzitzit,* Rabbi Meir allegorized it in this comment:

The verse does not say: "And you shall look at them" (namely, the *tzitzit),* but rather "and you shall look at Him *(oto)."* We are here told that one who observes this *mitzvah* is as if he were greeting the Divine Presence, for the blue thread in the *tzitzit* is comparable to the sea, the sea to the verdure, the verdure to the firmament, and the firmament is comparable to the Throne of Glory (TP Ber. 3a).

4. The Shema--even in its first paragraph--embodies various elements of Jewish life. Perhaps one reason the passage is so important is that it presents all these elements together.

"...The Lord is One"--the unity of God (monotheism);

"And you shall love..."---emotion;

"And you shall teach them..."--intellect;

"And you shall bind them..."--ritual.

All these aspects are necessary for a full Jewish existence.

"Prayer Analysis"

1. V'HAYAH EEM SHAMO'A
An Essay to Complete...

The second paragraph of the Shema deals with some profoundly difficult theological and moral questions. It involves the Jewish people's obeying God's laws and demands. When God's laws are obeyed, the people will prosper. Their crops will thrive, rains will come at the appropriate times and, in general, all will be well with the world. When the Jewish people forgets God's ways and turns from His laws, nature will respond by punishing the Jewish people and causing them great hardship. Biblical man believed in a theocentric world: all things are attributable to God and God's will. If nature were violent, it was due to the sinning of people. Though biblical man might not have understood why he was being punished, generally he knew it must have been for some good reason, even if unknown to him, but certainly known to God. Many modern Jews have great difficulty with the notion that people who suffer from natural catastrophes, from diseases, or from the evil doings of others are being punished for some ethical or religious transgression. The phrase "the righteous person has trouble and the evil person prospers" seems to be a fact of life. We look around at the world and see that many people whom we count as criminals are quite well off, while righteous, God-fearing people often suffer terribly. The problem of why there is evil in the world--if God is good and cares about us--has been a problem central to all religious thought.

Some people interpret this paragraph of the Shema as referring to natural processes, i.e., if mankind treats the earth and nature well, then nature will respond by caring for us. If we exploit nature, polluting and destroying the beauty of the world, we will be made to suffer the consequences, which are really due to our own hand. Others interpret this passage as dealing not with individual righteousness, but rather with entire peoples. History seems to teach that entire nations receive the reward or punishment due them. There is apparently some practical truth to this, for if evil peoples were not punished and not eliminated from the face of the earth, most of us would not be here today. Nazi Germany did not gain the upper hand and conquer the world; it was defeated.

For others, this problem of evil is dealt with by saying that God gave man free choice. In other words, for man to be man, God enables us to choose between good and evil. Were we to do only good things, we would be like angels. Were we not to know the difference between good and evil, we would be like animals. So we are at once blessed and cursed. We can see what could be and what should be in the world, but often are foiled by our baser instincts and animalistic needs for power and control. So, evil comes from human beings misusing the potential which God has given them. Were we to direct our talents toward helping people rather than for destruction, the world could be a better place. So the Holocaust, this theory goes, is not God's doing, but man's. Man let the Holocaust happen by not using his potential for good, but letting his potential for evil win out.

These are some of the ideas that have been suggested to understand the very difficult concept of reward and punishment in this world. A strongly traditional belief is that God will reward or punish us when we die. For many of us this type of philosophy is a bit difficult to accept. Nevertheless, the question must be confronted, though no one has yet found a satisfactory answer for all situations and places. Being religiously alive means constantly seeking answers to this question.

Continue this essay by writing your own position on the problem of evil in the world. Try to relate it to the second paragraph of the Shema.

2. Why has the Shema come to symbolize the core of Judaism? Why is it the last thing we say before sleeping and before dying?

3. How does the attitude toward God's unity in the Shema compare with the Christian notions of the Trinity?

4. How do Jews demonstrate their love for God?

5. If you wear a tallit and t'fillin, do you feel different when praying with them from when you pray without them?

6. What "reminder," other than tzitzit, might you suggest for us today to remind us of obligations and values?

Format of the Service:

B. *THE Prayer, Amidah (Sh'moneh Esray)* -- הַתְּפִלָּה, עֲמִידָה, (שְׁמוֹנֶה עֶשְׂרֵה)

Central to every Jewish service is the Amidah (literally, "standing") or Standing Devotion. It is also known as HaT'fillah (literally, *"The* Prayer") or Sh'moneh Esray ("Eighteen" Benedictions). Along with the Shema and accompanying blessings, the Amidah makes up the core of every morning and evening service; it also constitutes the basis of every afternoon service. Since the structure of this complex prayer is essentially the same in all cases, we will treat here all the Amidot in the liturgy. This section will include:

1. A general background to the origin and growth of the Amidah;

2. Overall structures and comparisons;

3. Analysis of all basic concepts in all sections;

4. Laws and customs related to recitation of the Amidah;

5. Prayer analysis of selected sections.

BACKGROUND:

From Abraham Millgram, *Jewish Worship* (Philadelphia: The Jewish Publication Society of America, 1971), 104, 106.

> The development of the *Tefillah* is shrouded in mystery. Its formative period goes back to the days of the Persian rule in Palestine, a period which is particularly lacking in Jewish historic documents. According to a ... rabbinic tradition, "a hundred and twenty elders, among whom were many prophets, drew up eighteen blessings" (Meg. 17b). Elsewhere in the Talmud we read: "It was the Men of the Great Synagogue who instituted for Israel blessings and prayers, sanctifications (Kedushot) and *habdalahs*" (Ber. 33a).... One thing is certain: it was only after the destruction of the Temple that the order of the benedictions and the exact wording of their concluding blessings were established. Also, the general content (though not the exact wording) of each benediction was decided upon. The *Tefillah* was thus left largely in a fluid state...

Somewhat later, probably late in the 1st century C.E., a b'rachah against apostates was composed.

> With the addition of this benediction against the Judeo-Christians (which will be described later) the weekday *Tefillah* achieved its official number of eighteen benedictions and thus derived its alternate name, *Shemoneh Esreh,* or the Eighteen Benedictions. The number was obviously fortuitous. It just happened that the number of benedictions of the *Tefillah,* as edited and arranged by Rabbi Gamaliel and his associates, was eighteen. But in later times some tried to find special significance in that number....

Even after the Amidah was expanded to include nineteen b'rachot, the name Sh'moneh Esray ("Eighteen") remained!

STRUCTURE AND CONTENT:

The logic underlying the structure of the Amidah is expressed in the Talmud as follows:

Rav Yehudah said, "One should never request his needs in the first three (b'rachot) or in the last three (b'rachot), but only in the middle ones," since Rabbi Hanina said, "The first section -- like a servant who organizes his praise of his master; the middle -- like a servant requesting payment from his master; the end -- like a servant who received payment from his master and takes his leave.

אמר ר׳ יהודה: לעולם אל ישאל אדם צרכיו לא בשלוש ראשונות ולא בשלוש אחרונות אלא באמצעיות, דאמר ר׳ חנינא: ראשונות – דומה לעבד שמסדר שבחו לפני רבו; אמצעיות – דומה לעבד שמבקש פרס מרבו; אחרונות – דומה לעבד שקיבל פרס מרבו ונפטר והולך לו.

B'rachot 34a

OVERALL STRUCTURE OF AMIDOT[12]

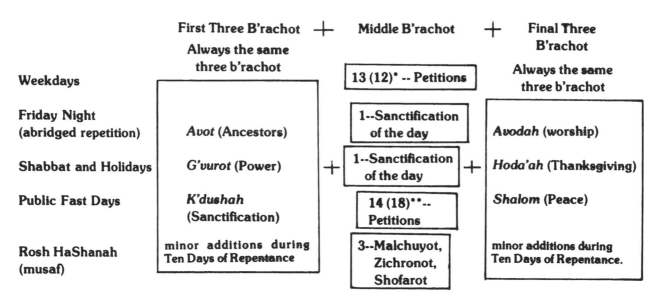

* 13 now; originally 12.
** 14 today; 18 in Mishnaic times.

1. The Amidah begins with three major blessings, passages of praise. It is introduced, however, by a verse from Psalms (51:17):

ה' שְׂפָתַי תִּפְתָּח וּפִי יַגִּיד תְּהִלָּתֶךָ.

O Lord, open my lips and my mouth will declare Your praise.

This introduction -- and a somewhat longer one at certain services -- asks God's help for the ability to pray easily, with concentration and conviction. It uses the most personal name of God, to set an intimate and warm tone.

1. *AVOT* אָבוֹת : (Ancestors). God is the God of our fathers and was their protector as He is ours. He appeared differently to each of them and is different to each of us; He is the God of history, awesome and all-powerful. We appeal to the "merit" or "virtue" of our ancestors as a way of urging God to care for us. (During the Ten Days of Penitence we add the refrain זָכְרֵנוּ לַחַיִּים "Remember us for life," which furthers the appeal to God, who desires life, to protect us with life.)

2. *G'VUROT* גְּבוּרוֹת : (Power). God's power to perform wondrous works and His concern for providing for all our needs are declared. So great is His power that He can even revive the dead. By acknowledging God's powers we hope to benefit from them. (During the High Holiday season the line beginning מִי כָמוֹךָ "Who is like You?" is added to laud God for His mercy in addition to His power.)

3. *K'DUSHAH* קְדוּשָׁה : (Sanctification). God is separate, unique and beyond earthly pressures in executing His rule and judgment. There are individual and public forms of the Sanctification. The public proclamation of God's uniqueness -- K'dushat HaShaym -- is based on biblical passages (Isaiah 6:3; Ezekiel 3:12; and Psalms 146:10). There are different introductions for weekday and Shabbat musaf versions. (During the Ten Days of Repentance we replace the concluding phrase, "the holy God," with "God the King.") The sanctity of God gives us pause for reflection before we begin to ask for our own petitions.

"Prayer Analysis" for opening b'rachot:

1. Why is "God of..." repeated before each patriarch's name? Based on your knowledge of the patriarchs, can you describe how each related to God?

2. Why do we say "our God and God of our fathers," repeating the word "God"?

3. When you want to ask your parents for something important, how do you go about it? Is your approach in any way similar to the talmudic statement regarding the structure of the Amidah?

4. Why do we appeal to the "merit of our fathers"? How do parents and ancestors influence us? How much a part of that influence do you feel? How independent of it are you? How bound are you to family ties? Try the following exercise to examine where your own values and beliefs seem to come from.

EXERCISE 1

Sources of Personal Influence

Value Areas	List one thing you've learned about the topic	Who taught you the value	How do you feel now compared to the way you felt when first taught about the topic?
Money			
Politics			
Habits			
Race			
Love			
Sex			
Marriage			
Charity			
Religion			
Education			
Drugs			
Friends			
(other values:)			

*Use the following code: SA--strongly agree; PA--partially agree; N--neutral; PD--partially disagree; SD--strongly disagree.

Adapted from Howe, *Personalizing Education,* 310.

5. The concept of "resurrection of the dead" has been interpreted differently over the years. No one interpretation is dogma. Here are some alternative ways of looking at this idea; see which ideas seem reasonable to you, and consider other interpretations.

     a. Physical resurrection of the dead when the Messiah comes.
     b. People live on in the memories of others.
     c. People's good works in life live on after them (e.g., Tzedakah, public service, artistic creations, etc.).
     d. The soul is resurrected and comes back in another body (reincarnation).
     e. People are revived spiritually, so life takes on new meaning.
     f. People recuperate after a severe illness.
     g. Someone pronounced dead can be revived by C.P.R. (Cardiopulmonary resuscitation).

When we recite the phrase "May the memory of the Righteous be for a blessing" it is with the thought that by having someone's memory influence our actions, that person remains very much alive. On a personal level, I was privileged to have many great and wonderful teachers in my life. One of the greatest of those teachers and friends was Rabbi David Mogilner, a former director of Camp Ramah, who taught me a great deal about Judaism and education. I went to him for advice; he influenced my educational thinking, and my Judaic thinking. Every day since his death at a very untimely young age, I think about something he taught me, or ask myself what he'd have done in any given situation. Even though he is no longer around physically, he is very much alive, influencing my deeds and beliefs. This example may stimulate us to ask what type of influence we will leave on other people. What kind of ancestors do we hope to be for our future descendants?

6. The public K'dushah can only be recited in a minyan because, in the words of the Talmud (B'rachot 21b), "And I shall be sanctified among the children of Israel." This suggests that only in the presence of the congregation is it appropriate to recite K'dushah, the "Sanctification." Why do you think this is the case? Why are the Kaddish, Barechu, and Torah reading included only in the presence of a minyan?

II. The Amidah concludes with three major b'rachot:

17. *AVODAH:* עֲבוֹדָה : (Worship). Originally recited by the priest at the end of the Temple service, this section came to be a reminder of our special form of worship in the Temple and the hope that Zion would always remain the center of the Jewish spiritual world. We also ask God to accept our worship and the prayers of the entire people. (On Rosh Hodesh and Festivals the beautiful prayer *Ya'aleh V'yavo* is added here, since it, too, recalls the Temple service and centrality of Jerusalem. Similarly, the commemorative nature of the Avodah benediction is highlighted in Ya'aleh V'yavo with its threefold division of history: past, "the remembrance of our ancestors"; present, "the remembrance of Jerusalem"; and future, "remembrance of the Messiah, son of David...").

18. *HODA'AH* הוֹדָאָה : (Thanksgiving; Acknowledgement). Originially recited after the sacrifice in the Temple, when people bowed down on the floor. Today we bow at the beginning and end of this benediction, which is introduced by a phrase from I Chronicles 29:13, *Modim anaḥnu lach*, stating our acknowledgment of God and our gratitude. (לְהוֹדוֹת means both to thank and to acknowledge.) We thank God for the daily miracles of life -- those miracles visible and invisible, of which we are aware, and those which occur daily without our knowing.[13] On Ḥanukah and Purim *Al HaNeeseem* paragraphs, which thank God for our miraculous deliverance from persecution, are appropriately added here. Again we see that the greatest praise of God is found in our acknowledging His acts in history.

When the reader repeats the Amidah the congregation adds the *Modim D'rabbanan* (Modim of the Rabbis), bowing slightly from their seats. This is done since no one else can acknowledge or thank God for us. (Since Ge'onic times, the passage "inscribe all the children of Your Covenant for a good life" is inserted here during the High Holiday season.)

19. *SHALOM* שָׁלוֹם : (Peace). The passage from Numbers 6:24-26, the Priestly Blessing, is added here as a prelude to the closing benediction when the Amidah is repeated. The shaliaḥ tzibbur -- or the Kohanim -- seek blessing for the entire congregation; this procedure is described in detail in Chapter 2 of the source book. The blessing was probably inserted here because it is reminiscent of the Temple service, seen in the Avodah benediction. It is a stimulus to continued well-being reflected in the previous blessing, and anticipates the greatest of all blessings -- peace. Though the priestly blessing was once the end of the Amidah, *Sim Shalom*, "Grant Peace," was a later addition, codified by the time of Rav Amram's Siddur. In the Ashkenazic ritual, an alternate version, *Shalom Rav,* is recited in the afternoon and evening. Interestingly, on fast days, when the Kohanim would naturally not eat or drink wine, the version of Sim Shalom -- including the priestly benediction -- was retained for services even after lunch, i.e., even for Minḥah. (During the Ten Days of Penitence we add a paragraph in this b'rachah asking God to inscribe us in the book of life, referring to Him as the one who makes peace.)

"Prayer Analysis" for concluding b'rachot:

1. One of the highlights of *Modim* (Birkat Hoda'ah) is its reference to "the miracles which are with us daily." Often we think of miracles only in terms of the supernatural, out of the ordinary, events sometimes described in the Bible. However, there are many miracles which happen every day. For example, the orderliness of the rising sun which we can count on every day has to be considered a miracle. The fact that our bodies usually function well, given the stress and load that we place on them, has to be considered a miracle. The opening of a flower and its closing, the majestic splendor of a sunrise or sunset, all fit into these categories. List below all of the daily miracles you can think of in your world. In the left-hand column list events and processes which are miracles; in the right-hand column list those people you consider to be miracle workers, who do their miracles every day, e.g., doctors, or teachers of young children.

MIRACLE EVENTS AND PROCESSES	PEOPLE MIRACLE WORKERS

2. The start of world peace will come, perhaps, when each of us learns to live in peace with those immediately around us. Below, write a peace agreement with a friend, relative, or teacher with whom you've had tension or trouble. Include obligations and responsibilities for both parties. Set a timetable for implementation of each step, to the final signing of this interpersonal peace agreement. You may even want to write a prayer for peace to be included at the beginning or end of the document.

III. The middle section of the Amidah varies, depending on the day, as shown on the diagram earlier in the chapter. On weekdays, the central section consists of thirteen b'rachot of request. This section can be divided into three categories, each following a logical plan of organization:

Spiritual Needs

4. *DA'AT* דַּעַת : Our first request is for knowledge and understanding -- to know how to use God's blessings and gifts.

5. *T'SHUVAH* תְּשׁוּבָה : When we know how to reason, we can then be responsible for our actions. Jewish tradition is our guide to righteous living, and we pray that we may be brought closer to it. If we stray from the path, our hope is to have our repentance accepted.

6. *SELIḤAH* סְלִיחָה : After engaging in true repentance, we ask that forgiveness by God will be granted.

7. *GE'ULAH* גְּאוּלָה : We seek redemption. Once we are forgiven, as individuals and as a people, we can begin anew. Relieved of anguish and guilt, we are redeemed.

Physical Needs -- Personal

(These can be requested only after we have made our spiritual requests. Then to be free to pursue matters of the spirit, we must be secure in health and physical necessities.)

8. *R'FU'AH* רְפוּאָה : Physical health is paramount to enjoying God's blessings and doing His will. (Personal prayers for a sick relative or friend are traditionally added as part of this b'rachah.)

9 *BIRKAT HASHANIM* בִּרְכַּת הַשָּׁנִים : The produce of our fields, our means for earning a living, should provide us with enough so we can be secure in body to pursue a complete Jewish life. Judaism is not ascetic in nature; this and the previous blessing testify to the need to enjoy life's many pleasures.

Physical Needs -- National

10 *KIBBUTZ GALUYOT* קִבּוּץ גָּלֻיּוֹת : First the people of Israel must be gathered together into its homeland, Israel. All Jews are responsible one for the other in this regard. The Jewish people is unified in diversity since Jews have been influenced by so many lands, but hold so much in common.

11. *TZEDAKAH U'MISHPAT* צְדָקָה וּמִשְׁפָּט : Self-rule, the ability to establish our own leadership, and the right to self-determination in our own land underlie this b'rachah. It was developed when Jews were not in control of their own destiny.

12. *MINIM* מִנִים : The justice resulting from self-rule will punish wrongdoers and forces opposing our people. (This b'rachah was added as a statement against Judeo-Christians of the early centuries C.E., heretics among our own people who professed to be Jews but denied the essence of Judaism.) According to one theory, this b'rachah made the Sh'moneh Esray into nineteen benedictions. The Rabbis first combined blessings 14 and 15 to keep the number at

eighteen, but later separated them, resulting in nineteen. The original name "Eighteen benedictions" has remained the same.

13. *TZADIKIM* צַדִּיקִים : The righteous of all nations will be duly rewarded in a society of just self-rule and self-determination. Righteous non-Jews also have a place in that society.

14. *YERUSHALAYIM* יְרוּשָׁלַיִם : God's presence will dwell in the Land of Israel, with Jerusalem its capital. In a rebuilt and rejuvenated Jerusalem, God's will can surely be carried out. For centuries since this prayer was written, the Jews' attachment to Israel and Jerusalem was uttered clearly and proudly three times daily.

15. *DAVID* דָּוִד : When all the previous national requests are granted, salvation will come and the messianic age will be upon us. The Messiah has traditionally been associated with the dynasty of David.

16. *SHOME'A T'FILLAH* שׁוֹמֵעַ תְּפִלָּה : This is the final petition: that God hear and accept our prayers. Our Rabbis taught that our own private requests may be added throughout the Amidah in the appropriate b'rachah, but may especially be added here.

Rabbi Hiyya bar Ashi said in the name of Rav: Even though one requests his needs in the blessing Shome'a T'fillah, if someone in his home is ill, he says (a personal prayer) in the blessing for those who are ill. If he needs sustenance, he says (a personal prayer) in the blessing of sustenance.

אמר ר׳ חייא בר אשי אמר רב: אף על פי שאמרו שואל אדם צרכיו בשומע תפילה, אם יש לו חולה בתוך ביתו אומר בברכת חולים, ואם צריך לפרנסה אומר בברכת השנים.

Avodah Zarah 8a

"Prayer Analysis" for middle b'rachot (weekdays):

1. Try to state the underlying ethical responsibility each b'rachah challenges us to uphold.

2. The fourth b'rachah (knowledge). Try to think of an argument you had recently. On what basis did you disagree: emotion? logic? prejudice? whim? Try to analyze your confrontation in terms of how you used your powers of reason and logic.

3. The fifth b'rachah (repentance). According to Rambam, there are four stages of true repentence:

a. being aware of the wrong committed;
b. admitting the wrong to oneself and the affected party;
c. Asking forgiveness from the offended party; (that individual gets three chances to forgive us or else the injured party is considered guilty!);
d. Resisting if presented with an opportunity to commit the same transgression again.

Taking examples from your own life, go through these four stages to see how you measure up. Consider why we are taught (Pirkay Avot 2:15):

וְשׁוּב יוֹם אֶחָד לִפְנֵי מִיתָתְךָ.
Repent one day before your death.

4. **The sixth b'rachah (forgiveness).** Each day as part of the Amidah (and especially on Yom Kippur when we go through a list of transgressions) we remind ourselves towards what we should be striving. Sometimes, this can be a very negative experience. If we look only at our faults we tend to get upset, angry, or depressed. No one likes to look only at his bad side, so this might make people avoid such experiences. Sometimes, it might be possible to do the same task of self-evaluation but from a more positive standpoint. Our prayers of forgiveness are written in the plural, because all of us share many shortcomings. It makes it easier for us to admit them in common. Likewise, it would be nice to know that we share certain strengths and that other people recognize those strengths.

EXERCISE 1

List all the things you do well, including the way you relate to others. Make another list of all your faults and compare lists. See if the things in the positive list can help you overcome problems in the other one.

5. The seventh b'rachah (redemption). What role or responsibility do you personally have for helping "redeem" or "ransom" Russian Jews or Jews in Arab lands? What prevents you from being more active in these causes? Be honest with yourself.

6. The eighth b'rachah (healing). In our tradition we are partners with God, and take an active role in the healing process; thus the doctor's role is essential. Have you ever been in a hospital? How many different people were involved in your care? What personal responsibility do you have for those people and that institution?

7. Ninth b'rachah (sustenance). We ask for a successful harvest and livelihood in this b'rachah. But, what is success? List the ten biggest successes in your life. Why did you choose these? What do they say about your values? Fantasize great future success you would like to achieve for yourself, or see in a friend, in your family, or in the Jewish people.

8. Tenth b'rachah (gathering the dispersed people). What should be the attitude of Jews in the diaspora and in Israel towards Russian Jews who emigrate from Russia ostensibly to go to Israel, but end up coming to the United States or Canada? Should the Jewish Agency continue to be responsible for them? What is the responsibility of the North American Jewish community for these Jews? What is their responsibility toward us?

9. Eleventh b'rachah (righteousness and justice). What are the implications of this b'rachah for the relationship between the modern Jewish state and Palestinian Arabs?

10. Twelfth b'rachah (slanderers; sectarians). This was directed against Jews who adopted certain Christian beliefs and were feared as a menace to the Jewish community. Does the b'rachah still have an important place in the liturgy today? Apply the ideas in this blessing to groups such as the Jews for Jesus or Beit Sar Shalom.

11. Thirteenth b'rachah (the righeous ones). This b'rachah places before us role models of ideal human behavior. To understand the nature of this type of living, answer the following questions:

For what are we willing to sacrifice?
For what are we willing to give up everything?

As a way of rewriting this paragraph of the Amidah, answer these questions:

What if anything, seems worth dying for?
How did you come to believe this?
What seems worth living for?
How did you come to believe this?

From Howe, *Personalizing Education*, 158.

12. Fourteenth b'rachah (Jerusalem). There is a traditional notion of a Jerusalem on earth and a parallel "heavenly" Jerusalem, of perfection and peace. The hope of the Jewish people that Jerusalem will be rebuilt and brought back to its former glory has been a central hope in various periods of our history. Even now that Jerusalem is again being rebuilt, there still remains the task of achieving the values and goals that a rebuilt State of Israel should aspire to. Try to design a model of the ideal Jerusalem. What would it look like? What would people in it do? What values would it hold? What social, economic, and political philosophies would guide its inhabitants? How would you build the ideal Jerusalem, center and capital of the Jewish people?

13. Fifteenth b'rachah (Davidic dynasty). What are the Jewish notions of the messiah? How do they differ from the Christian understanding? What is your own image of the messianic era? What would your own life be like in that time? Interestingly, whereas some other faiths picture heavenly bliss and singing angels, one Jewish view is that in the end of days we will sit and study Torah with God! What lesson does this idea[14] teach us about the Jewish world view?

14. Sixteenth b'rachah ("who listens to prayer"). As we've already seen, tradition bids us pause at this prayer to recite our own personal devotion. When you are in the appropriate mood, write a prayer you have offered mentally. Examine what you've said by studying your thoughts in writing.

IV. Closing Prayers.

A number of closing prayers for the Amidah were written by different Rabbis in the Talmud, on the assumption that after the formal prayer one should add his own private mediation. *Elohai N'tzor,* O Lord guard my tongue from evil," is the most popular closing prayer. Originally said as a private meditation, it contains the following ideas:

    a. Life and death are in the power of the tongue.
    b. Now that we've completed the Amidah, let us not be overcome by those who would try to stop us from improving ourselves.
    c. God should answer our prayer because He is gracious and loving.
    d. Our intellect and emotions should be open to God's teachings.

Here are some other examples of closing prayers written by the Rabbis:

Rava's Prayer (also included as the conclusion of the Amidah on Yom Kippur in some Maḥzorim).

My God, before I was formed I was worthless, and now that I am formed it is as if I had not been formed. I am dust in my life, and all the more so in my death. Before You, I am like a vessel filled with shame and disgrace. May it be Your will, O Lord my God, that I sin no longer. Cleanse my past sins in Your great mercy, but not by means of suffering.

רבא בתר צלותיה אמר הכי: ''אלהי, עד שלא נוצרתי
איני כדאי, ועכשיו שנוצרתי כאילו לא נוצרתי, עפר
אני בחיי, קל וחומר במיתתי, הרי אני לפניך ככלי מלא
בושה וכלימה. יהי רצון מלפניך ה' אלהי שלא אחטא
עוד, ומה שחטאתי לפניך מרק רחמיך הרבים, אבל לא
על ידי יסורין וחלאים רעים.''

B'rachot 17a

Rabbi Eliezer's Prayer.

May it be Your will, O Lord my God and God of my fathers, that hatred not arise in someone else, and that we not hate another person. And that jealousy not arise in someone else and that we not be jealous of another person. May Your Torah be our occupation all the days of our lives and may our words be supplication to You.

יהי רצון מלפניך ה' אלהי אבותי שלא תעלה שנאתנו
על לב אדם, ולא שנאת אדם תעלה על לבנו. ולא תעלה
קנאתנו על לב אדם, ולא קנאת אדם תעלה על לבנו.
ותהא תורתך מלאכתנו כל ימי חיינו ויהיו דברינו
תחנונים לפניך.

Yerushalmi B'rachot 4:7d

Rav's Prayer (This later became the basis for Birkat HaHodesh, blessing the new month).

May it be Your will, O Lord our God, to give us long life, a life of peace, a life of goodness, of blessing, of sustenance, a life of bodily strength, of fearing sin, a life with no shame or disgrace, a life of riches and honor, a life in which the love of Torah and fear of heaven are in us, a life which fulfills all our desires for good.

יהי רצון מלפניך ה' אלהינו שתתן לנו חיים ארוכים, חיים של שלום, חיים של טובה, חיים של ברכה, חיים של פרנסה, חיים של חילוץ עצמות, חיים שיש בהם יראת חטא, חיים שאין בהם בושה וכלימה, חיים של עושר וכבוד, חיים שתהא בנו אהבת תורה ויראת שמים, חיים שתמלא לנו את כל משאלות לבנו לטובה."

B'rachot 16b

"Prayer Analysis" for Closing Prayer

1. Upon concluding the Amidah between the lines "May the words of my mouth..." and "who makes peace in heaven..." our tradition has given us a way of "signing our own name." For most names in Hebrew there is a biblical verse which begins with the first letter of one's Hebrew name and ends with the last letter of the name.

For example, the name Sh'muel, which begins with the letter שׁ and ends with the letter ל . The verse chosen to represent that name is שָׁלוֹם רָב לְאֹהֲבֵי תוֹרָתֶךָ וְאֵין־לָמוֹ מִכְשׁוֹל "Grant peace to those who love Your Torah, and they will have no stumbling block" (Psalms 119:165). Look for a biblical verse that can represent your Hebrew name in this manner. A few good places to start your search are chapters which follow the Hebrew alphabet, such as Psalms 34, 119, 145; Proverbs 31; Lamentations 1-4. Some Siddurim also include such name-verse lists.

The verse may be recited at the end of the Amidah as a way of saying to God that it is *you* who is talking. It is also a way of personalizing the prayer experience. Your verse can also become a meaningful slogan for your own life. And you may even want to use it on a personalized tallit *atarah* (neckband), on a wedding invitation, or elsewhere. Try to find out the meaning of your Hebrew and English names by using a name dictionary. Compare the meaning of your name in Hebrew or English with the verse selected. See if you can come up with a relationship or if you can find a way of learning something as a goal or hope for yourself from the verse and from the meaning of your name.

2. The ability of our tongues to do evil is obvious to us all. To highlight this power and the difficulty in controlling our tongue perform and "Insult Survey." During a school day, or at a gathering of friends, jot down all the insults you hear uttered during the day; e.g., you stink; she's crazy; etc. See how many you are personally responsible for and devise a plan to modify your behavior. How about trying the same for profanity, on the theory that the same mouth which opens in praise to God shouldn't emit foul language.

V. Additions to the Weekday Amidah.

1. On most public fast days, the prayer *Anaynu*, "Answer us," is added between Ge'ulah and R'fuah, during the Minḥah service. This prayer asks that especially on fast days our fervent prayer be heard and answered. In addition, at Minhah on Tishah B'av we add the prayer *Nahaym*, "Comfort," which asks for the rebuilding of Jerusalem. The revised version of the prayer, which appears in *The Weekday Prayer Book* of the Rabbinical Assembly, now includes phrases such as "rebuilt from its destruction" and "reestablished from its desolation." The blessing is recited before the closing line of Birkat Yerushalayim.

2. During the winter months, when rain is crucial to the agriculture of Israel, we add the words "who causes the wind to blow and the rain to fall" between the first and second parts of the blessing G'vurot. (It is added beginning with Musaf on Sh'mini Atzeret until the first day of Pesaḥ.) As a parallel ritual, Sefardim and most communities in Israel add, "who causes the dew to fall" during the summer months, when great quantities of dew are necessary for agriculture in Israel.

Shortened Version of the Weekday Amidah

BACKGROUND:

A shortened version of the Amidah, *Haveenaynu*, is used in times of emergency or when recitation of the entire Amidah might take too long and be dangerous, (e.g., someone working on a high place and stopping to say Minhah). It is recited in place of the middle thirteen b'rachot of the weekday Amidah. There are two versions of this short form (one in the Jerusalem Talmud and one in the Babylonian). We use the Babylonian version *(B'rachot 29a)*, printed below, since it generally does not appear in Siddurim:

O Lord our God, cause us to understand, to know Your ways; prepare our hearts to be in awe of You; forgive us so we may be redeemed; keep us from pain; satisfy us with produce of Your land; gather our dispersed people from the four corners of the world. Judge those who stray from Your knowledge; punish the wicked; may the righteous rejoice in building Your city and repairing Your Temple, the flourishing of the dynasty of David, Your servant, and the continuance of the son of Jesse, Your anointed one. Before we call, You answer. Blessed are You, O Lord, who hears prayer.

הֲבִינֵנוּ, ה' אֱלֹהֵינוּ, לָדַעַת דְּרָכֶיךָ; וּמוֹל אֶת לְבָבֵנוּ לְיִרְאָתֶךָ; וְתִסְלַח לָנוּ לִהְיוֹת גְּאוּלִים; וְרַחֲקֵנוּ מִמַּכְאוֹב; וְתַשְׂבִּיעֵנוּ בִּנְאוֹת אַרְצֶךָ; וּנְפוּצוֹתֵינוּ מֵאַרְבַּע כַּנְפוֹת הָאָרֶץ תְּקַבֵּץ. וְהַתּוֹעִים עַל דַּעְתְּךָ יִשָּׁפֵטוּ; וְעַל הָרְשָׁעִים תָּנִיף יָדֶךָ; וְיִשְׂמְחוּ צַדִּיקִים בְּבִנְיַן עִירֶךָ, וּבְתִקּוּן הֵיכָלֶךָ, וּבִצְמִיחַת קֶרֶן לְדָוִד עַבְדֶּךָ, וּבַעֲרִיכַת גֵּר לְבֶן יִשַׁי מְשִׁיחֶךָ; טֶרֶם נִקְרָא אַתָּה תַעֲנֶה. בָּרוּךְ אַתָּה, ה', שׁוֹמֵעַ תְּפִלָּה.

"Prayer Analysis"

1. Make a chart showing which phrase of Haveenaynu corresponds to which b'rachah in the Amidah.

2. If you find reciting t'fillot in the morning takes too long, would you be more willing to begin the process if you could recite Haveenaynu instead of the entire Amidah? (See below for methods of abridging the service.)

EXERCISE 1
General Summary for Amidah

Below is a list of values and ideas to be explored. Look at each item and see if you can find a b'rachah in the Amidah which deals with the same theme, or which might serve as a jumping off point for your own thoughts about any one of these ideas. In the column to the left of each item indicate which b'rachah from the Amidah contains the kernel of the idea in the item listed. List the first word or two of the b'rachah, or its number in the Amidah.

Brachah	Values / Ideas
	Something you are proud of about your family.
	How you spend your free time.
	Something you are proud of that you own.
	Something you can do now that you couldn't do a year ago.
	A gift you have given or received of which you are proud.
	How you helped someone.
	Something you have written, drawn, or made with your hands of which you are proud.
	Something good that has happened as a result of a choice you made.
	Something important you are planning to do.
	Something you are proud of that you have worked hard for.
	Something you are good at that not many people know about.
	Something you did that took courage.
	A belief or value that you hold strongly and act upon.
	Something difficult you learned of which you are proud.
	An important pattern of behavior or a habit in your life.
	A mistake you made recently of which you are ashamed.
	A change you would like to make in yourself.
	Something you want for yourself or for others.
	Something you have said for which you are sorry.
	Something you didn't say and are glad you didn't.
	A sacrifice you have made.

An important memory in your own life.

Something for which you are deeply grateful.

Adapted from Howe, *Personalizing Education*, 208-213.

EXERCISE 2

As a review exercise for the entire Amidah try the following exercise. Go through each paragraph and *ḥatimah* (closing line of the blessing) of the Amidah. Write a slogan or one line advertisement which sums up that particular paragraph for you. For example, you might look at Sim Shalom and write the slogan "End the War Now." Share your slogans with others and see what values they may attach or what understandings they derive from each of the paragraphs in the Amidah.

Based on Simon, *Values Clarification*, 255-6.

Recitation and Repetition of the Amidah

As we already have learned, there is no break between the blessing of the "redemption" and the Amidah. Accordingly, when the Amidah is recited together, the shaliaḥ tzibbur lowers his voice at the b'rachah (Ga'al Yisrael) just prior to the Amidah, so we do not even answer "Amen," which is considered to be an interruption.

During the evening service, the Amidah is always recited silently by the entire congregation. During the morning and afternoon, however, there are two methods of reciting the Amidah, outlined in the following guidelines. In the first instance, the congregation recites the Amidah silently, and then the shaliaḥ tzibbur repeats the Amidah, being joined by the congregation for K'dushah:

When the congregation has completed the Amidah, the shaliah tzibbur repeats the Amidah, so if someone who doesn't know the prayer is attentive to the repetition, he can fulfill his obligation. One who fulfills his obligation in this manner must be attentive to everything the shaliah tzibbur says from beginning to end.

לאחר שסיימו הצבור תפלתן, יחזור שליח צבור
התפלה, שאם יש מי שאינו יודע להתפלל, יכוין למה
שהוא אומר ויוצא בו; וצריך אותו שיצוא בתפילת
שליח צבור, לכוין לכל מה שאומר שליח צבור, מראש
ועד סוף . . .

Shulhan Aruch, Orah Hayyim 124:1

In the second case -- the "Hoeche K'dushah" -- the shaliaḥ tzibbur begins the Amidah aloud, through the K'dushah. For Shaharit, the congregation joins with the shaliah tzibbur through the K'dushah, continuing silently after that. For other services at which this procedure is followed, the congregation joins aloud only for K'dushah, and then recites the entire Amidah silently, from the beginning.

In "emergency," for instance if the time for reciting the Amidah were passing, the shaliah tzibbur may recite the Amidah aloud at once and the congregation recites with him, word for word, in an undertone, through the words *Ha'Ayl HaKadosh* (at the end of K'dushah).

אם הוא שעת הדחק, כגון שירא שיעבור זמן התפלה, יוכל [שליח הצבור] להתפלל מיד בקול רם, והצבור מתפללין עמו מלה במלה בלחש עד לאחר "האל הקדוש."

Shulḥan Aruch Oraḥ Ḥayyim 124:2

Practices today vary among synagogues, though many use the "Hoeche K'dushah" in order to shorten the length of the service.

K'DUSHAH קְדוּשָׁה

Many of our t'fillot are concerned with the notion of k'dushah, "sanctification." We have the Kaddish, Kiddush, K'dushah of the Amidah as well as other references to the word *Kadosh*. Often translated as "holy," the word really means much more. In Hebrew, Kadosh implies specialness or being set apart for a particular purpose. Kadosh means unique, different, something which leads us to higher spiritual ends. In everyone's life there are things which we make separate or special in order to make life more meaningful. We all set apart things to be used only on special occasions or as a reminder of important events. Someone graduating high school might keep the tassel from the mortarboard as a remembrance of that special event. Someone else might have a trophy won in a competition, and kept in a special place at home.

As Jews, we attach great importance to special things and special times. The uniqueness of the Jewish people is that we have attached more specialness to time then to space. A Jew can pray almost anywhere, as long as the place is clean and neat and is conducive to prayer. We don't need large synagogues or edifices to enable us to communicate with God. Similarly, for the Jewish people holiness is often expressed through the way we observe time. We set aside times and make them special or different. Shabbat, holidays, and moments of t'fillah make time special, unique. To help you better understand this concept of differentness and separateness, answer the following questions:

1. Do you have a favorite place to be by yourself?
2. Do you go there at any special time?
3. Do you have a special spot in your house or room which is particularly important to you?
4. Is there a particular time of day or week which is special for you that you set aside?
5. Do you have a special piece of clothing or jewelry?
6. Name someone who seems special to you.
7. Now name someone who seems kadosh to you.
8. Name an object which is kadosh for you.
9. Name three activities which are k'doshim for you.

Based on Chug T'fillah Program, New England USY Region, January, 1979.

126

AMIDOT FOR SHABBAT AND HOLIDAYS

A. STRUCTURE:

The structure of these Amidot is the same as for the weekday, with the major exception that the central blessings -- petitions or requests made on weekdays -- are replaced with a b'rachah called *K'dushat HaYom,* "Sanctification of the Day." This b'rachah proclaims the uniqueness of the Shabbat or holiday. The reasoning for this (in this case dealing with Shabbat) is mentioned in the Midrash:

There are eighteen (blessings) we pray every day, but they are not entirely of praise of the Holy One, blessed be He. Only the first three and last three are; twelve blessings consist of requests. Therefore, they are not recited in the Shabbat Sh'money Esray, for if someone has an ill (relative) at home, he is remembered in the blessing "heal the sick people of Israel," and is troubled. But Shabbat is given to Israel for holiness, pleasure and rest, and not for distress. Therefore, we recite the first three b'rachot and last three, and speak of rest in the middle.

אתה מוצא י"ח שמתפללין בכל יום ואינן כולן לשבחו של הקב"ה אלא שלוש ראשונות ושלוש אחרונות, ושתים עשרה ברכות כולן לצורכו של אדם. ולפיכך אין מתפללין בשבת שמונה עשרה, שאם יהיה לו חולה בתוך ביתו נזכר ברופא חולי עמו ישראל והוא מיצר. והשבת נתנה לישראל לקדושה ולעונג ולמנוחה ולא לצער, לכך מתפלל שלוש ברכות ראשונות ושלוש אחרונות והמנוחה באמצע.

Tanhuma Va'yayra 1

The intellectual pattern structure we saw in the morning and evening service (creation, revelation, and redemption) appears in the themes of the K'dushat Hayom for Shabbat Amidot as well:

Erev Shabbat: We speak of the first Shabbat celebrating the finish of *creation.*

Shaharit L'Shabbat: We recount Moses' happiness upon receiving God's law at Sinai -- *revelation.*

Minhah L'Shabbat: We pray for the future joy and happiness of a redeemed people of Israel -- *redemption.*

A special "repetition" of the Amidah occurs Friday evening when praying with a congregation. In earlier times, people came to the synagogue only on Shabbat. Out of a desire that latecomers should not miss the Amidah on Friday night, *Magen Avot,* a short summary of the Amidah, was recited. It contains, in outline form, all the sections of the seven b'rachot of the Shabbat and Amidah. Accordingly, this poem is called בְּרָכָה מֵעֵין שֶׁבַע "the prayer similar to seven."

127

Read Magen Avot,[15] and compare it to the Shabbat Amidah. Examine the similarities and differences. The basic themes are listed below:

1.

   Our fathers' shield, God's word has ever been;

2.

   He gives life eternal to the dead.

3.

   Holy is He; no other can compare

4.

   With Him who gives rest each Sabbath day
   Unto His people whom He loves.

5.

   With veneration and with awe we serve Him;

6.

   We praise Him every day and bless His name.
   To God all thanks are due,

7.

   The Lord of peace, He hallows the Sabbath and blesses the seventh day; He gives rest unto a people knowing its delight, in remembrance of creation.

¹מָגֵן אָבוֹת בִּדְבָרוֹ ²מְחַיֵּה מֵתִים בְּמַאֲמָרוֹ ³הָאֵל הַקָּדוֹשׁ שֶׁאֵין כָּמוֹהוּ ⁴הַמֵּנִיחַ לְעַמּוֹ בְּיוֹם שַׁבַּת קָדְשׁוֹ. כִּי בָם רָצָה לְהָנִיחַ לָהֶם. ⁵לְפָנָיו נַעֲבוֹד בְּיִרְאָה וָפַחַד ⁶וְנוֹדֶה לִשְׁמ בְּכָל־יוֹם תָּמִיד מֵעֵין הַבְּרָכוֹת. אֵל הַהוֹדָאוֹת ⁷אֲדוֹן הַשָּׁלוֹם מְקַדֵּשׁ הַשַּׁבָּת וּמְבָרֵךְ שְׁבִיעִי. וּמֵנִיחַ בִּקְדֻשָּׁה לְעַם מְדֻשְּׁנֵי עֹנֶג. זֵכֶר לְמַעֲשֵׂה בְרֵאשִׁית:

Section of Magen Avot		Blessing in Amidah
1	=	Avot (Ancestors)
2	=	G'vurot (Power)
3	=	K'dushah (Sanctification)
4	=	K'dushat HaYom (Uniqueness of day)
5	=	Avodah (Worship)
6	=	Hoda'ah (Acknowledgement)
7	=	Shalom (Peace).

B. CONTENT:

The Musaf Amidot for Shabbat and Holidays recall the various sacrifices made in the Temple on those occasions. The Amidah for holidays also claims that we were exiled from our land and can no longer sacrifice in the Temple, because Israel had strayed from God's ways. The Conservative Movement, uncomfortable with the notion that the sacrificial system should be restored, has revised those texts (wording them in the past tense) and included interpretive meditations. The following excerpt from the *Sabbath and Festival Prayer Book 16* explains this view:

> In all our striving for intellectual integrity and historical truth, it must not be forgotten that the Prayer Book is couched in poetry and not in prose. It must be approached with warm emotion and not in a mood of cold intellectuality....
>
> There will naturally be instances, however, where reinterpretation is impossible and the traditional formulation cannot be made to serve our modern outlook. Such preeminently are the passages dealing concretely with animal sacrifices. Passages like *ezehu mekoman* and *pittum haketoret* or the phrase *v'ishei Yisrael* "the fire offerings of Israel in *"Retzeh,"* can be dropped without injuring the rubric of the service. The deletion of the Musaf service as a whole, however, would mean destroying the entire structure of the traditional liturgy, besides eliminating several valuable ideas and aspirations from the Prayer Book. Primarily, the Musaf service voices our hope for the restoration of Palestine as the homeland of the Jewish people. But that is not all. Also implied in the prayer is the recognition that sacrifice is essential for the fulfillment of all human ideals. Then too, we cherish the hope that Palestine will again become significant not only for Israel but for the spiritual life of mankind as a whole. Finally, it is characteristic of Judaism to recall the sacrificial system which represents a legitimage stage in the evolution of Judaism and religion generally. As Israel Abrahams wrote, "This is the virtue of a historical religion, that the traces of history are never obliterated.... The lower did not perish in the birth of the higher, but persisted." For all these reasons neither the deletion of the Musaf nor its retention unchanged would satisfy the basic principles of a Jewish Prayer Book for the modern age.

Just as on Festivals, K'dushat HaYom refers specifically to each festival, so, too, on Rosh Hodesh (in the Musaf Amidah) the sacrifices offered in the Temple are recalled, as we hope for a renewed month of life, health, and blessing.

The High Holiday Amidot are considered separately, in Chapter 8.

Format of the Service:

C. Torah Reading

One of the core elements in the morning service on Shabbat and holidays, as well as Monday and Thursday, is the reading of the Torah. The relationship between study and prayer is discussed in Chapter 1. Procedures for removing the Torah from the ark, calling congregants for aliyot, reading the Torah, and returning it to the ark, can be found in Isaac Klein, *A Guide to Jewish Religious Practice* (New York: The Jewish Theological Seminary of America, 1979), 27-33.

The heading of this page, however, is included to help clarify the structure of the service, outlining its major components: Shema, Amidah, and (on certain days), *K'riyat HaTorah,* the Torah reading.

Format of the Service:

D. Kaddish

The Kaddish is used to separate segments of the service. Below we consider many aspects of the Kaddish, not just its role in the structure of t'fillot.

BACKGROUND:

The Kaddish originated as an ending formula following a lecture or Torah study session. The Talmud *(B'rachot 3a; 21b)* relates that after hearing an explanation or interpretation of Torah, one was to respond אָמֵן. יְהֵא שְׁמֵהּ רַבָּא מְבָרַךְ. , "Amen. May His great name be praised." The Kaddish probably originated in Palestine in the last century B.C.E. and was written in the vernacular of the times, Aramaic. Its later use as a prayer said by mourners is said to derive from the fact that a Torah study session was often held in memory of the person who had died. As time passed, the Torah session was dropped, but the Kaddish remained associated with death rituals. In time, the Kaddish grew from a formula of dismissal from a study experience to a passage of praise affirming God's sovereignty and our faith in Him at all times.

There are five basic forms of the Kaddish:

a. Half Kaddish, חֲצִי קַדִּישׁ --contains two paragraphs separated by the main "response." This form is generally used to mark the conclusion of a section of the service.

b. Full Kaddish, קַדִּישׁ שָׁלֵם, קַדִּישׁ תִּתְקַבֵּל-- contains three additional lines asking that our prayers be accepted. It is generally recited at the conclusion of major parts of the service.

c. Orphan's (Mourner's) Kaddish. קַדִּישׁ יָתוֹם --recited by mourners during the first eleven months after the death of a close relative, and yearly on the anniversary of the death. It omits one line from the Full Kaddish which asks for acceptance of our prayers.

d. Rabbinic Kaddish, קַדִּישׁ דְּרַבָּנָן -- is similar to the Full Kaddish with a special paragraph for the well-being of all who study. It is recited after studying portions of rabbinic literature.

e. Kaddish of Renewal (Burial Kaddish), קַדִּישׁ לְאִתְחַדְתָּא --recited only by mourners at a funeral after the burial.

CONCEPTS:

1. Acts as a summary of praise and faith, concluding sections of the service.

2. It is a statement of hope and faith that God's blessings will pervade the world.

3. The participatory nature of Kaddish, being said only with a minyan, underscores the Jewish attitude of the importance of individuals within the community.

4. Public recitation of Kaddish by mourners helps link them to others, and grant immortality to the deceased by perpetuating a person's memory.

5. The mourner's recitation affirms life, even when faced with the inevitable fact of death.

6. For God to be God, He is beyond all words of praise.

7. It contains hope for the ultimate blessing -- peace.

8. Kaddish D'rabbanan underscores the holiness and importance of study in Jewish life.

9. The Kaddish as a whole reminds us that through our *actions* we sanctify God's name and demonstrate our faith.

"Prayer Analysis"

1. Why does the prayer said by mourners not contain any references to death?

2. What does the fact that the Kaddish was composed in Aramaic (the language spoken in Jewish Palestine) mean to you?

3. Do you agree with the practice some people follow of paying to have the Kaddish said for a relative rather than going to the synagogue to say it personally?

4. Could you write an appropriate prayer which would be used to conclude sections of the service? What concepts or ideas would it contain?

5. Listen to Leonard Bernstein's *Kaddish* symphony and compare his understanding of the Kaddish with your own.

TIME, PLACE, AND PREPARATION FOR PRAYER

The desire to regulate the prayer experience and the desire to maintain a parallel to the Temple worship services gave rise to guidelines on the times of prayer. The sources of the three daily services are many and varied. One tradition suggests that the Patriarchs instituted the daily services: Abraham originated Shaharit; Isaac, Minhah; and Jacob, Ma'ariv. Yet another tradition tells us that people should pray at each change of the day. Rabbenu Ya'akov Ba'al Haturim (15th century) said this was because we pray in the morning before we start our daily tasks, in the evening when we are finished with them and in the middle of the day, to put aside our tasks and acknowledge the source of our strength and life. In the Bible, reference is made to praying three times a day: "And he kneeled upon his knees three times a day, and prayed, and gave thanks before his God" (Daniel 6:11). Since in the Temple a sacrifice was only offered twice a day, morning and afternoon, the institution of the evening service was hotly debated and thought by many not to be mandatory. However, the force of universal Jewish practice over the years has given it a mandatory status.

The Rabbis divided the "24-hour day" into two parts, the daylight (from sunrise to sunset), and the evening (from sunset to the next sunrise). They subdivided each of these parts into twelve segments, each being a "relative hour." (The length of an "hour," however, varied depending on the length of daylight. Thus, for instance on a day when sunrise is 7:00 A.M., and sunset is 5:00 P.M., the day is ten hours; each of the twelve "hours," therefore, is fifty minutes.) Knowing this structure, you can understand the following guidelines for the times of each service.

Shaharit (morning service):

May be recited beginning at dawn through the fourth "hour" of the day (the Shema through the third "hour").

Minhah (afternoon service):

May be recited between 12:30 P.M. and sunset. The optimum time prescribed was from 3:30 P.M. until an hour and a quarter before nightfall, or 4:45 P.M., assuming the days and nights were of equal length. (Times are one hour later when daylight saving is in effect.) The period between 12:30 and sunset is called "the great Minhah," while the period between 3:30 and sunset is called "the small Minhah."[17] It is often the custom to recite Minhah close to sunset, followed immediately by Ma'ariv, so worshippers will not have to go back to the synagogue two separate times.

Ma'ariv (evening service):

May be recited when three stars appear in the sky, though we often use the sunset as a guide. Many communities recite Ma'ariv earlier on Erev Shabbat, thereby adding to the length of Shabbat.

We've seen much about the nature and structure or prayer. The Rabbis realized that it is not easy to move from the everyday worries and concerns of living to the spiritual world of prayer. Preparation and the setting for prayer were crucial components to the overall experience:

One should not pray in a place which has something to destroy his concentration or at a time which destroys his concentration.

לא יתפלל במקום שיש דבר שמבטל כוונתו ולא בשעה
המבטלת כוונתו.

Shulhan Aruch, Orah Hayyim 98:2

Similarly, one must not pray in a dirty place or even in a synagogue which is not clean. (Many times when stopping for a Minḥah or Ma'ariv service we may not give enough attention to the aesthetics of the place, and may be distracted as a result.)

Synagogues and study houses (schools) are to be treated with honor. They are to be swept and mopped....

Synagogues and schools should not be treated with irreverence, such as joking, kidding, or having worthless conversation. We do not eat, drink, have pleasures, or stroll around in them. We do not come inside them on hot days because of the heat, or come into them because of the rain. Scholars and students are permitted to eat and drink in them, if absolutely necessary.

We don't conduct business in the synagogue unless it is for religious purposes, such as the proceeds of tzedakah or redeeming captives, or similar activities. Eulogies are not recited in them unless in the public interest, such as the eulogy of an important community scholar, when the entire community gathers in attendance.

בָּתֵּי כְנֵסִיּוֹת וּבָתֵּי מִדְרָשׁוֹת נוֹהֲגִין בָּהֶן כָּבוֹד, וּמְרַבִּיצִין אוֹתָן ...

בָּתֵּי כְנֵסִיּוֹת וּבָתֵּי מִדְרָשׁוֹת אֵין נוֹהֲגִין בָּהֶן קַלּוּת רֹאשׁ, כְּגוֹן שְׂחוֹק וְהִתּוּל וְשִׂיחָה בְטֵלָה. וְאֵין אוֹכְלִין בָּהֶן וְאֵין שׁוֹתִין בָּהֶן וְאֵין נֵאוֹתִין בָּהֶן וְאֵין מְטַיְּלִין בָּהֶן; וְאֵין נִכְנָסִין בָּהֶן בְּחַמָּה – מִפְּנֵי הַחַמָּה, וּבִגְשָׁמִים – מִפְּנֵי הַגְּשָׁמִים. וַחֲכָמִים וְתַלְמִידֵיהֶם מֻתָּרִין לֶאֱכֹל וְלִשְׁתּוֹת בָּהֶן מִדֹּחַק.

וְאֵין מְחַשְּׁבִין בָּהֶן חֶשְׁבּוֹנוֹת אֶלָּא אִם כֵּן הָיוּ חֶשְׁבּוֹנוֹת שֶׁל מִצְוָה, כְּגוֹן קֻפָּה שֶׁל צְדָקָה וּפִדְיוֹן שְׁבוּיִם וְכַיּוֹצֵא בָהֶן. וְאֵין מַסְפִּידִין בָּהֶן אֶלָּא הֶסְפֵּד שֶׁל רַבִּים, כְּגוֹן שֶׁיִּהְיֶה שָׁם הֶסְפֵּד גְּדוֹלֵי חַכְמֵי אוֹתָהּ הָעִיר שֶׁכָּל הָעָם מִתְקַבְּצִין וּבָאִין בִּגְלָלָן.

Rambam, Hilchot T'fillah 11:5-7

133

OBLIGATORY AND OPTIONAL PRAYERS
OR:
HOW TO ABRIDGE THE SERVICE LEGITIMATELY AND INTELLIGENTLY

Not all of the prayers in the Siddur have the same status as being required each time one prays in order to fulfill the obligation of prayer. There are generally two categories of prayers:

1. obligatory, legally-mandated prayers-- תְּפִלּוֹת חוֹבָה
2. optional, non-obligatory prayers-- תְּפִלּוֹת רְשׁוּת

The diagrams at the beginning of the chapter contain the more-important parts of the service, but even some of those can be omitted if time or circumstances require.

The most essential prayers are those involved with the Shema and the Amidah. Prayers such as meditations before performing a given mitzvah (recited by individuals), penitential prayers like Taḥanun, and even the Psalms for the Day are considered voluntary. The prayers preceding Barechu might also be considered non-obligatory. Especially given the busy schedules and rushed existence of most people, and the fact that prayer doesn't come easily to begin with, we offer some carefully suggested methods of abridgement, while still being consistent with the fundamental structures of our prayer traditions.

What follows are some alternatives to reciting every prayer in the service. These suggestions might make it easier for you, given your own schedule and priorities, to make daily prayer more a part of yourself. If even these outlines seem too ambitious as a starting point, or if you have questions about any method of abridging the service, discuss other options with your rabbi. Other variations are possible, as well.

METHODS OF ABRIDGING THE SERVICE
WEEKDAY EVENING -- מַעֲרִיב לְחוֹל

Case I. For an individual:

1. Two b'rachot before the Shema.
2. Shema (the three paragraphs).
3. Two b'rachot following the Shema.
4. Amidah, (If necessary, recite one paragraph--Haveenaynu--in place of thirteen middle b'rachot.)
5. Alaynu (optional).

Case II. For a Congregation:

1. Barechu.
2. Case I, above.

The Kaddish is recited to separate segments of the service. When it is recited will be determined by what parts of the service are included. Mourner's Kaddish is added as well.

METHODS OF ABRIDGING THE SERVICE
WEEKDAY MORNING -- שַׁחֲרִית לְחוֹל

Case I. For an Individual:

1. Two b'rachot before the Shema.
2. Shema (the three paragraphs).
3. B'rachah following the Shema.
4. Amidah. (If necessary, recite one paragraph--Haveenaynu--in place of thirteen middle b'rachot.)
5. Alaynu (optional).

Case II. For a Congregation:

1. Barechu.
2. Same as numbers 1, 2, and 3 above.
3. Amidah, including K'dushah. (May be short form, "Hoeche K'dushah"--Yiddish meaning "high K'dushah." Shaliah tzibbur and congregation begin aloud through K'dushah. Then all continue silently. Congregation does not go back to beginning, as in afternoon, Case I, because of principle of joining the "redemption" b'rachah to the Amidah, without interruption.)
4. Kaddish*
5. Alaynu (optional).
6. Adon Olam (optional).

---

*The Kaddish is recited to separate segments of the service. When it is recited will be determined by what parts of the service are included. Mourner's Kaddish is added as well.

Case III.

A. For an individual:

1. Birchot HaShaḥar.
2. Baruch She'amar.
3. Ashray (or other selected psalms).
4. Yishtabaḥ Shimchah.
5. Case I, above.

B. For a Congregation:

1. Case IIIA.
2. Case II.

This is generally the norm for USY services, and has its origin in *Shulhan Aruch, Orah Hayyim,* 52.

METHODS OF ABRIDGING THE SERVICE
WEEKDAY AFTERNOON -- מִנְחָה לְחוֹל

Case I. For an individual:

1. Ashray (optional).
2. Amidah. (If necessary, recite one paragraph -- Haveenaynu -- in place of thirteen middle b'rachot.)
3. Alaynu (optional).

Case II. For a Congregation:

1. Ashray (optional).
2. Amidah. (May be short form: Shaliah tzibbur begins aloud. Congregation joins for K'dushah. The Shaliaḥ tzibbur continues silently, congregation goes back to beginning, reciting silently, without repeating K'dushah.)
3. Alaynu (optional).

The Kaddish is recited to separate segments of the service. When it is recited will be determined by what parts of the service are included. Mourner's Kaddish is added as well.

METHODS OF ABRIDGING THE SERVICE
SHABBAT SERVICES -- תְּפִלּוֹת לְשַׁבָּת

Case I. Erev Shabbat (if you can't go to the synagogue).

1. Select favorite psalms from Kabbalat Shabbat.
2. L'chah Dodi.
3. Psalm 92 (Psalm for Shabbat.)
4. Weekday evening Case I. Add V'shamru before Amidah.
5. Yigdal.

Case II. Shabbat morning:

1. Weekday morning, Case III A. Add favorite Shabbat psalms for P'sukay D'zimrah after number 2, Baruch She'amar.
2. When reciting Amidah, Haveenaynu cannot be included, since middle b'rachot--petitions--are not said.
3. Study the Torah portion for the week and read Haftorah portion.
4. Musaf Amidah.
5. Ayn Kayloheynu.
6. Alaynu.
7. Adon Olam.

Case III. Shabbat Afternoon:

1. Ashray.
2. U'va l'tziyon.
3. Amidah.
4. Study first aliyah of next week's Torah portion.
5. Alaynu.

Passages added to the weekday outlines are not obligatory, but are listed to enhance the spirit of Shabbat worship. Since Shabbat is for relaxing, you don't have to rush and abridge that much!

SECTION III
HOW DOES A PRAYER MEAN

QUESTIONS FOR ANALYZING PRAYERS

Below are questions which can be applied to analyzing any t'fillah, and should be applied to each prayer in the following chapters. These questions are designed to help you interpret prayers for yourself, since sophisticated prayer analysis can be exciting and deeply rewarding.

1. What does the prayer say?

2. Can it be divided into units of thought or style? This can be determined by tense, person, form of address, mood, style, literary device, poetic structure, or ideas.

3. Are there any striking grammatical forms?

4. When was the prayer written?

5. For whom was the prayer intended?

6. What kind of experience might have stimulated the writing of such a prayer? Can we have a similar experience today?

7. What related experiences (both positive and negative) do we have that the author did not have?

8. What questions is the prayer attempting to answer?

9. When is it recited?

10. Where is the prayer located in the Siddur?

11. What ideas are in the prayer? Most important? Next?

12. How does the writer feel about these ideas?

13. What has happened to these ideas in Judaism?

14. What role has this prayer played among Jews?

15. What role has this prayer played in your life?

16. How do you feel about this prayer?

17. If a person took this prayer seriously, how might it affect his behavior?

18. What senses, abilities, or processes are involved in making this prayer a real part of one's life (aside from saying it)?

From Saul P. Wachs, *An Application of Inquiry Teaching to the Seedur* (The Ohio State University, unpublished doctoral dissertation, 1970).

CHAPTER 6
Weekday Prayers
MODEH ANI מוֹדֶה אֲנִי

BACKGROUND:

Modeh Ani is probably based on an interpretation of the verse "They are new every morning; great is Your faithfulness" (Lamentations 3:23). In the Midrash (Gen. Rabbah 78:1), Rabbi Shimon ben Abba interpreted, "Because You renew us every morning, we know that Your faithfulness is great to redeem." This short prayer (printed below, since it does not appear in many Siddurim) is said immediately upon awakening.

I thank You, ever-living King, that You have compassionately returned my soul within me. Your faithfulness is abundant.

מוֹדֶה אֲנִי לְפָנֶיךָ מֶלֶךְ חַי וְקַיָּם שֶׁהֶחֱזַרְתָּ בִּי נִשְׁמָתִי
בְּחֶמְלָה; רַבָּה אֱמוּנָתֶךָ.

CONCEPTS:

1. We express our gratitude for daily renewal of physical and mental strength and ability.

2. The prayer attests the dependability of the cycle of nature, and God's faithfulness in maintaining that order.

3. It may be said even before washing, since we are so anxious to acknowledge the gift of renewed life. Since it is said before we are washed, it does not include God's name.

4. We re-establish a personal relationship to God every day.

"Prayer Analysis"

1. When you awaken during the next few mornings see if you can remember your first thoughts. What do you feel and how does this prayer relate to or contradict those feelings? What personal prayer might you add?

2. What is a "soul"? How would you define your own special essence; what makes you, you?

MAH TOVU מַה טֹבוּ

BACKGROUND:

This passage, said upon entering the synagogue, consists of the biblical verses (Numbers 24:5; Psalms 5:8; 26:8; 95:6; 69:14). The first verse was originally recited by Bilam. He was hired by a foreign king to curse Israel, but when he saw the Israelites' camp, was compelled to offer the words of Mah Tovu, a blessing. Reciting it on entering the synagogue is derived from the talmudic interpretation of "your tents" as houses of study and "your dwelling places" as synagogues.

CONCEPTS:

1. This reflects the beauty of communal worship and institutions.

2. A beautiful Jewish place is one where words of God are spoken and Torah is studied.

3. Part of the passage is written in first person singular to highlight the worshipper's personal relationship to God.

4. We worship God and relate to Him in awe and love and joy.

"Prayer Analysis"

1. What impressions or feelings do you get when you walk into your own synagogue? Which synagogues have you entered which particularly pleased you and why? Which have not pleased you and why not?

2. Where have you felt the presence of God most--in a synagogue, at home, or out of doors?

3. What different opening ceremony might you construct for Jews upon entering the synagogue for prayer?

4. Historically, most synagogues have been simple and functional. More recently in affluent communities in North America, large synagogue edifices have become the norm. How do you feel about this? What kind of building would you erect as a house of worship and study?

5. Below are verses which appear as "decoration" in many Conservative synagogues. What do the verses imply about the synagogues in which they appear? What verses, words, symbols, or pictures appear in your synagogue? How were they chosen? What might you have chosen were you the architect or designer?

Most synagogues include the Hebrew quotation, but we are printing only the translations here. We are grateful to all those congregations which sent information for use in the source book.

"Light shines from the righteous and for those who are upright in heart there is joy"
    Congregation Sons of Israel
    Briarcliff Manor, New York

"This is none other than the house of God and this is the gate of heaven"
    North Shore Jewish Center
    Port Jefferson Station, New York

"Truth, Justice and Peace"
    Beth El Synagogue
    Minneapolis, Minnesota

"Happy are they who dwell in your house"
    Congregation Beth Shalom
    Pittsburgh, Pennsylvania

"Blessed be the man who dwells in the house of the Lord"
    Beth Shalom
    Pittsburgh, Pennsylvania

"Blessed are you in your entering"
    Adath Jeshurun
    Louisville, Kentucky

"Blessed art Thou O Lord our God King of the Universe"
    Beth Shalom
    Oak Park, Michigan

"With our young and with our old we go forth"
    Temple Beth Torah
    Ocean, New Jersey

"In the beginning, God created the heaven and the earth"
"And in all that mighty hand and in all the great terror which Moses performed in the sight of Israel"
(First and last verses of Torah)
    Temple Beth Sholom
    Hamden, Connecticut

"Every generation will extol His deeds"
    Beth Emeth Synagogue
    Larchmont, New York

"Know before Whom you stand"
    Ahavas Israel
    Grand Rapids, Michigan

    Beth Israel Center
    Madison, Wisconsin

    Beth Israel Temple Center
    Warren, Ohio

    Congregation Shomrei Emunah
    Montclair, New Jersey

    Temple Reyim
    Newton, Massachusetts

    Temple Sinai
    Middletown, New York

"Know before Whom you stand for You are with Me"
    Temple Beth Israel
    Maywood, New Jersey

"Seek the Lord while He may be found"
Adath Israel
Cincinatti, Ohio

"Seek the Lord while He may be found; call upon Him while He is near"
Congregation Beth Am
Cleveland, Ohio

Jericho Jewish Center
Jericho, New York

"Lord, I love the habitation of Your House and the place where Your glory dwells"
Temple Israel
Natick, Massachusetts

"The Lord shall reign forever and ever"
Emanuel Synagogue
Oklahoma City, Oklahoma

"The Lord will give strength to His people"
Temple Reyim
Newton, Massachusetts

"Ho, everyone that thirsteth, come ye for water"
Temple of Aaron
St. Paul, Minnesota

"Have we not all one Father? Has not one God created us all?"
Agudat Achim
Schenectady, New York

"Love thy neighbor as thyself"
The Brotherhood Synagogue
New York, New York

"Thou, O Lord art abundant in mercy and truth"
Congregation Mercy and Truth
Pottstown, Pennsylvania

"Therefore choose life, in order that you and your descendants may live"
Beth El Synagogue
Omaha, Nebraska

"When I go forth to seek Thee, I find Thee coming toward me"
B'nai Abraham Synagogue
Easton, Pennsylvania

"But the Lord is in His Holy Temple; Let all the earth keep silence before Him"
B'nai Israel
Alexandria, Louisiana

"Be Thou a Source of Blessing"
B'nai Abraham Synagogue
Easton, Pennsylania

"And you shall be holy to Me: for I, the Lord, am holy"
Emmanuel Synagogue
West Hartford, Connecticut

"Let justice well up as waters and righeousness as a mighty stream"
Temple of Aaron
St. Paul, Minnesota

"And the Bush was not consumed"
Beth El Synagogue
Minneapolis, Minnesota

Temple Beth Am
Warwick, Rhode Island

"And all your children will learn of the Lord"
Temple Sholom
Bridgewater, New Jersey

"And they will make Me a Sanctuary, that I may dwell among them"
Temple Ner Tamid
Peabody, Massachusetts

"Spread over us Your shelter of peace"
Congregation Beth Tefilah
San Diego, California

"They shall keep the way of the Lord -- By doing what is just and right"
B'nai Abraham Synagogue
Easton, Pennsylvania

"May the words of my mouth and the meditations of my heart be acceptable before You"
Agudath Israel
Caldwell, New Jersey

"For My house shall be called a house of prayer for all people"
Congregation Beth Israel
Vancouver, British Columbia

Temple Israel
Silver Springs, Maryland

"For the Lord has sent us unto Beth-El"
Temple Beth El
Cranford, New Jersey

"For I have given you good teaching; do not forsake my Torah"
Temple Beth-El
Lowell, Massachusetts

"For out of Zion will go forth Torah and the word of the Lord from Jerusalem"
Mosaic Law
Sacramento, California

"For the Commandment is the candle and the Torah its light"
Beth Hillel
Wilmette, Illinois

"From Generation to Generation, In Every Generation"
Temple Israel
Natick, Massachusetts

"The earth is the Lord's in all its fullness"
Beth El Synagogue
Minneapolis, Minnesota

"How beautiful upon the mountains are the feet of him that brings good tidings, that announces peace"
Shaare Tefila Congregation
Silver Spring, Maryland

"The spirit of man is the candle of the Lord"
Temple Israel
Silver Spring, Maryland

"Thy Word is a Lamp unto my Feet"
Adath Jeshurun
Louisville, Kentucky

"Serve the Lord with gladness"
Temple Beth Sholom
Sarasota, Florida

"Serve the Lord with gladness; come before Him with singing"
Highland Park Conservative
Temple and Center
Highland Park, New Jersey

"The Crown of the Elders are Children's Children"
Congregation Beth Israel
Worcester, Massachusetts

"The world stands on three things: truth, justice and peace"
Beth Israel Synagogue Center
Derby, Connecticut

"The people of Israel live"
Orange Synagogue Center
Orange, Connecticut

"It is a tree of life to those who hold fast to it"
Beth El Synagogue
Omaha, Nebraska

"Open the gates of righteousness to me"
Beth El Temple
Harrisburg, Pennsylvania

"Open the gates of righteousness for me; I will enter them and praise the Lord"
Beth El Suburban
Broomall, Pennsylvania

"Holy, Holy, Holy is the Lord of Hosts"
Brith Shalom
Bellaire, Texas

"I will set the Lord before me always"
B'nai Israel
Staten Island, New York

"I will greatly rejoice in the Lord; my soul shall be joyful in my God"
Shaare Tefila Congregation
Silver Spring, Maryland

"I rejoiced when they said unto me 'Let us go into the house of the Lord' "
Jewish Community Center
Summit, New Jersey

"Hear O Israel, ye come nigh this day unto battle against your enemies"
Congregation Sons of Israel
Briarcliff Manor, New York

"The Law of the Lord is perfect, restoring the soul"
Temple Beth El
Lowell, Massachusetts

"The Torah is Light"
Ohavi Zedek
Burlington, Vermont

"Man is Man because He was Created by God, but, He achieves the status of true humanity only to the extent that he creates his life according to the commandment of God"
Congregation Sherah Israel
Macon, Georgia

BACKGROUND:

Originally this entire section of the service was said by the individual while performing the regular routines of rising, washing, dressing, and preparing to pray. Later, because of people's lack of knowledge (don't forget, prayers were not written down until the ninth century these blessings were included in the communal worship:

Upon awakening, one says "My God, the soul..." When hearing the crow of a rooster, one recites the blessings "...who gives the mind (or the 'rooster') understanding..." While dressing, once recites "...who clothes the naked." When resting hands on one's eyes, one recites '...who opens the eyes of the blind." When sitting, recite "who releases the bound." When standing up, "...who raises those who are bowed down." When putting one's feet on the ground, recite "...who spreads the earth over the water." When putting on shoes, one recites "...who has provided all my needs." When walking, one recites "...who prepares the steps of man." When putting on a belt, one recites "...who girds Israel with might."

When putting on a hat, one recites "who crowns Israel with glory." Upon washing the hands, one recites "...on washing the hands." When washing the face, one recites "...who removes sleep from my eyes..."

Now, since our hands are not clean, and also since the average person does not know these blessings, it is customary to arrange them as part of the synagogue service, answering "Amen" after each, thus fulfilling their obligation.

כשיעור משנתו, יאמר "אלהי נשמה." כשישמע קול התרנגול, יברך "הנותן לשכוי בינה." כשלובש, יברך "מלביש ערומים." כשיניח ידיו על עיניו, יברך "פוקח עורים." כשישב, יברך "מתיר אסורים." כשזוקף יברך "זוקף כפופים." כשיניח רגליו בארץ, יברך "רוקע הארץ על המים." כשנועל מנעליו, יברך "שעשה לי כל צרכי." כשהולך, יברך "המכין מצעדי גבר." כשחוגר חגורו, יברך "אוזר ישראל בגבורה." כשמשים כובע על ראשו, יברך "עוטר ישראל בתפארה." כשיטול ידיו, יברך "על נטילת ידים." כשירחץ פניו, יברך "המעביר שינה מעיני"...

עכשיו, מפני שאין הידים נקיות, וגם מפני עמי הארץ שאינם יודעים אותם, נהגו לסדרם בבית הכנסת, ועונים אמן אחריהם, ויוצאים ידי חובתם.

Shulhan Aruch Orah Hayyim 46

Some debate arose concerning the appropriateness of reciting a benediction when not performing the specific actions. However, we follow the practice explained by Rabbi Moses Isserles (a sixteenth century law codifier, known by his initials, as *Rama*) whose commentary on the Shulhan Aruch (a law code accepted by Sephardic Jewry) was embraced by Ashkenazic Jewry:

Some say that even though we are not obligated, we recite them (the b'rachot), since the blessing does not apply only to the individual, but rather expresses praise of the Holy One, blessed be He, who created the needs of the world. This is the custom and should not be changed.

יש אומרים דאפילו לא נתחייב בהן, מברך אותן. דאין הברכה דווקא על עצמו, אלא מברכין שהקדוש ברוך הוא ברא צרכי העולם. וכן המנהג, ואין לשנות.

This early portion of the service also includes the first line (or, in some communities, the first paragraph) of the Shema. A tradition has it that its inclusion stems from a decree in 452, in Babylonia, when the king prohibited any monotheistic worship and stationed officials at synagogues to make sure such prayers as the Shema and K'dushah were not said. So the Rabbis secretly inserted the Shema at the beginning of the service before the officials arrived, and again in the Musaf K'dushah, after they had left.

CONCEPTS:

1. Judaism sensitizes us to the daily miracles of life without which our existence would be difficult and unbearable.

2. *Elohai N'shamah* ("My God, the soul...") was originally said upon waking but was transferred to the public worship because it was not deemed proper to pronounce God's name before washing. The b'rachah emphasizes that we are born with a pure soul; each human being has the choice of how to lead his or her life. We are born free of guilt, beginning anew our decision-making processes each morning. This idea is very different from the notion of original sin (held in varying degrees among different Christian denominations), in which men are viewed as being born corrupt, needing to spend their entire lives atoning for the sin of Adam in the Garden of Eden. Each day for the Jew is seen as a new beginning, a re-creation, giving us renewed hope and enthusiasm as we begin the day.

3. The concept of Talmud Torah, study, is emphasized.

4. One version of the fifteen benedictions, which speak of all the daily human needs, contains three negative blessings. They imply that non-Jews, slaves, and women are not commanded to observe all the mitzvot as are adult, Jewish males. The males, on the other hand, give thanks for their privilege. Our tradition views performing a mitzvah out of obligation as being of greater merit than fulfilling it without being obligated. (Though this might seem like reverse logic, it is considered a greater act of loyalty to perform a deed out of duty than to satisfy personal desire. When you do something only because you *want* to, not because you *have* to, there is a danger that when it is not convenient, or the reasoning behind the mitzvah is not clear, you'll refrain from acting.) However, since the negative wording of three b'rachot could be construed as deprecating non-Jews, slaves, and women, other versions were developed. For example, *The Sabbath and Festival Prayer Book,* based on earlier texts and the trend of tradition,[1] has worded the b'rachot in positive forms:...who has "made me in Thine image";...who has "made me free"; ... who has "made me an Israelite."

5. Realizing that though we are born pure, life does have its temptations. We possess both good inclinations and bad inclinations, and pray that God keep us far from evil influences and people. This idea is found in the paragraph (attributed to Rabbi Yehudah HaNasi, editor of the Mishnah) at the conclusion of the fifteen morning b'rachot.

6. In the meditation, "Master of all worlds ..." we appeal to God to show us mercy even though we make mistakes. In general, the Siddur appeals to God's qualities of mercy. We also realize how insignificant many of our problems are in the great scheme of things.

7. In the final paragraph of this section, "You are the Lord our God...," closure is brought by asking God to sanctify His name in the world, thus making it a special place where we can, in turn, sanctify God by righteous acts.

EXERCISE 1

Write a list of your early morning activities. Create a blessing of praise to God for each action. Then compare your list with the blessings of Birchot HaShaḥar.

EXERCISE 2

"...WHO CREATED ME IN HIS IMAGE." שֶׁעָשַׂנִי בְּצַלְמוֹ

When we think of ourselves as created in the image of God we may ask ourselves -- after considering what we understand as "God's image" -- what, indeed, is our image? How do others perceive us? How might God perceive us? How do we want others to perceive us? What image do we have of ourself? What would we like to change about that image?

EXERCISE 3

"...WHO CLOTHES THE NAKED." מַלְבִּישׁ עֲרוּמִים

In this b'rachah, we not only thank God for enabling us to be clothed properly, and given a certain amount of dignity, but also reflect a certain ethical responsibility as a way of showing that we are grateful. The expression "clothes makes the man" is common, but in our day and age, especially pointed. Status in clothes has been a measuring device for the worth of people. This standard by which we measure people should give us pause as Jews, and make us question whether the value is correct, whether we should be party to this value system. Try the following exercises and when you're finished, try to develop a b'rachah of your own on the same theme.

Have you ever worn clothes that your group considered daring or different?

If so, what happened to you?

What did your friends and family say?

If you haven't, how would you feel if you found yourself in a situation where your clothes were different from everyone else's?

146

What do clothes mean to you?

What defines the appropriateness of clothing?

Can clothing be too ostentatious?

What does what you're wearing right now say about who you are?

What image would you like people to receive from the way you dress?

Complete the following chart:

Item of Clothing	What I *want* my clothing to say about me	What my clothing *does* say about me to others
1. Shirt or blouse		
2. Slacks, skirt, etc.		
3. Shoes		
4. Sweater, sport jacket, etc.		
5. Watch or other jewelry on wrist or hands.		
6.		
7.		
8.		

From Howe, *Personalizing Education*, 165; and Simon, *Values clarification*, 32.

EXERCISE 4

"MAY IT BE YOUR WILL ... TO CAUSE US TO WALK ACCORDING TO YOUR TORAH..."

Many issues raised in this t'fillah lend themselves to extensive thought.

A. What is temptation? Have you ever been tempted to do something wrong? If so, describe the temptation. How did you handle the situation, and what was the final outcome?

Based on Howe, *Personalizing Education,* 152.

B. Consider some of the following scenarios which deal with problems of temptation, bad companions, and people who might influence you to do evil.

Value Dilemmas: What would you do?

Shoplifting

Sharon, a 16 year old, has just been hired as a salesgirl in a record store in her neighborhood. She had been trying to get a job for several months in order to add to the income at home. Her mother had been struggling financially since Sharon's father died.

The store's owner stresses over and over again how important it is for Sharon to keep her eyes open for shoplifters. He keeps a meticulous count on the inventory and cash register receipts. In fact, Sharon had a chance at the job because the owner had fired her predecessor for insufficient vigilance.

During the second week on the job, Sharon's best friend, Lucy, came into the store. Sharon watches as Lucy slips two records under her coat. Lucy then approaches Sharon at the cash register to pay for yet another record. Sharon whispers to Lucy that she ought to return the records. Lucy's response is a wink and a snicker.

Should Sharon tell the owner and risk a friendship as well as possible arrest of Lucy? Why?

Should Sharon charge Lucy for the one visible record and risk the same thing happening again, as well as risking an eventual loss of her job? Why?

Camp Dilemma

At summer camp, many of the campers smoke pot, even though it is illegal. One day, three girls are sitting behind their cabin while the rest of the girls are inside resting. Susan, a very shy girl, sits with the other two because she really likes the girls, and wants very much to be liked by them. The other girls start smoking, and offer Susan a drag. Susan has never smoked before. She doesn't want to break the law and also feels that it is harmful to her health. However, she knows these girls will reject her and laugh at her if she refuses to smoke. What should she do?

Cheating

Ronnie is taking a final exam in her English class. She has prepared diligently for the test. When she turns to the second page of the exam she realizes that she has studied the wrong material. Knowing that she needs a "B" in the final to get a "B" in the course, she becomes very flustered. Her grade is very important because it can qualify her for a summer music scholarship that a local bank is sponsoring.

Ronnie has always been against cheating and has never cheated, although it is common knowledge that cheating occurs as a daily practice in her class.

Going through her mind now is the knowledge that she can get the required information from her boy friend, who is sitting next to her. Her teacher has left the room because he feels that students should be trusted during tests.

Ronnie likes the idea of being trusted, but also likes the idea of the music shcolarship. Should she cheat just this once or not? Why?

Are there times when cheating (anywhere, not just in school) is justified? Why or why not?

_____

Dilemmas based on Howe, *Personalizing Education*, 254, 261, 263.

C. Make a list of the best friends you have had throughout your life. Write a little about how you met, what you did together, why you liked each other, why you may have drifted apart. Who is or are your best friends now? Is your present pattern with your friends similar to or different from your pattern in the past? Have you ever encountered a person who had been your friend and later turned into your enemy? Have you ever felt that you are friends with someone who really is not a good influence on you? On whom you are not a good influence?

BARUCH SHE'AMAR בָּרוּךְ שֶׁאָמַר

BACKGROUND:

This prayer serves as the introductory blessing of the section called P'sukay D'Zimrah, "Verses of Song." Post-talmudic in origin, it was first mentioned in the ninth century.

CONCEPTS:

1. God is praised for creating the world with merely a word; being faithful and trustworthy; being the first cause of everything; for having concern for His creations; for rewarding those who follow His ways; for being eternal.

2. The prayer conveys the notion that we are overflowing with a need to praise God and thank Him for the wonders and beauties of life.

3. By reciting, "Praised be His name" as a summary of God's attributes, we acknowledge that He is infinitely greater than we can conceive. Yet, since we must relate to God, we react in words, which help convey some, but not all, of our feelings.

"Prayer Analysis"

1. Were you to write an introductory prayer to this section of the service, what ideas might it contain?

2. How does the repetition of the word "Baruch" affect the tone and feeling of this poem?

PASSAGES OF PRAISE פְּסוּקֵי דְזִמְרָה

BACKGROUND:

The psalms which make up the latter part of P'sukay D'zimrah (Psalms 145-150) prepare us for the main part of the morning service, which begins at Barechu. They were added by Rabbi Yose, because they conclude the Book of Psalms, and he prayed "May my portion be with those who finish the praise," i.e., The Book of Praise--The Psalms.[2]

CONCEPTS:

The psalms are chosen to fulfill the obligations of remembering acts of creation and the Exodus from Egypt, as well as the ongoing re-creation of the world, as introduced by Baruch She'amar.

A. *Psalm 145 (ASHRAY)* אַשְׁרֵי

BACKGROUND:

The Talmud (*B'rachot 4b*) asserts that "whoever recites this psalm three times daily is assured of a part in the world to come, because it contains the verse 'You open Your hand, and satisfy every living thing with favor.' " For this reason, two verses (Psalms 84:5 and 144:15) in which the word "Ashray" occurs three times precede the psalm.[3] The psalm is an alphabetical acrostic from which the letter נ is missing, traditionally since that letter begins the word for "fall" or "downfall." The missing letter was "rediscovered" in the Dead Sea Scrolls version of the psalm, which reads "Faithful (נֶאֱמָן) is God in His works and loyal in all His doings." Ashray serves as a mini-Psukay D'zimrah for the Minḥah service.

CONCEPTS:

1. Ashray is an expression of joy at being able to dwell with and relate to God.

2. God's caring attitude to all the poor, oppressed, hungry, and fallen on earth is stressed. Written in the present tense, the psalm communicates the sense of a process being undertaken by man and God, toward reaching a world where problems are solved.

3. The concept of reward for the righteous and punishment for evildoers is stated.

4. Ultimately, human beings must accept God's judgment as beyond our understanding.

"Prayer Analysis"

1. Can you accept the statements that God does provide for the fallen and feed the poor?

2. Why do righteous people suffer and evildoers prosper?

3. Is the language of Ashray directed only towards Jews? Does the psalm concern itself only with Jews?

4. Which lines of Ashray mean the most to you personally, and why?

B. Psalm 146

1. The source of man's security is in "contemplation of God's omnipotence and His ever-readiness to help."[4]

2. God is in the process of helping man to help himself by improving the human condition.

"Prayer Analysis"

1. Why is this psalm introduced in the first person singular?

2. Consider the imagery of the verse, "When his spirit is gone he returns to the ground; that day marks the end of his thoughts."

C. Psalm 147

1. Personal needs discussed in the previous psalm are enlarged to include communal reliance upon, and trust, in God.

2. God extends His support and protection to all people.

3. God is ruler over people and nature.

4. The source of our security is not in power or things but in commitment to God.

5. The refuge of the Jewish people is in Israel.

"Prayer Analysis"

1. This psalm is filled with magnificent images. Make a collage or picture with drawings that visualizes the psalm.

2. Consider the "weather" metaphors and evaluate them.

D. Psalm 148

1. This psalm expands similar concepts of the previous psalms to include the entire universe, which joins in praise of God.

2. We hope that in the future, all rulers of earth, and all nations will praise the true God.

"Prayer Analysis"

1. Strength bombardment: this psalm is reaching to the highest level of praise of which language is capable. Pretend God's presence is in the center of a circle surrounded by you and your friends. Go around and around, and with a word or gesture demonstrate your praise of God and His works. Keep up the process even if it gets repetitious; this might lead you to a better understanding of the fervor and enthusiasm underlying the psalmist's poetic creation.

E. Psalm 149

The psalm is hopeful or future-oriented, i.e., "A new song." The earth will be freed from those who don't accept God's rule.

"Prayer Analysis"

1. Examine the verse, "Let Israel rejoice in its Creator, the Children of Zion exult in their King." Note the parallelism between the two halves of the verse.

   Biblical poetry is built on a structure of parallelism. Why did the poet choose the name "Israel" for the first half and the name "Children of Zion" for the second?

2. This particular psalm alludes to a religious war waged on behalf of God. Many religious wars have been fought through history, from the conquest of Canaan by Joshua through the Crusaders, to Islamic "holy wars." Discuss the issues and problems involved. Was Joshua's campaign different from the others mentioned?

F. Psalm 150

1. This is a final song of praise climaxing all the previous praises.

2. All mankind unites in praise of God.

3. "Halleluyah" appears (in various forms) a total of thirteen times, equivalent to the famous thirteen attributes of God (Exodus 34:6-7).

4. The psalm rises above words and calls on instruments and dance to express their praise. This reflects the inadequacy of language in conveying our most sublime and deeply-felt emotions.

"Prayer Analysis"

1. Can you think of ways in which this psalm reflects its message in its very form? (Look at the short, staccato phrasing compared to previous psalms.)

2. The issue of using musical instruments in the service is a complicated one. Instruments were used to supplement the singing of the Levites in the Temple even on Shabbat and Holidays. When the Temple was destroyed, the use of the instruments was either lost or no longer permitted during prayer as a sign of eternal mourning for the destruction. In modern times, some Conservative synagogues have permitted the use of organs or other instruments during the Shabbat or holiday services. How do you feel about this? Why have many synagogues not adapted musical instruments to modern worship? What do they add? How can they detract?

3. Since Psalm 150 is short, try writing a new melody for it to be sung, or played on your favorite instrument. How does your melody reflect the message of the psalm?

THE SONG OF THE SEA (SONG OF MOSES) שִׁירַת הַיָּם

BACKGROUND:

Chanted by the Levites in the Temple during the Shabbat Minḥah sacrifice, the Song of Moses or the Song of the Sea consists of biblical verses (Exodus 15:1-18; Psalm 22:29; Obadiah 1:21; Zechariah 14:9). Along with its introductory passages (1 Chronicles 29:10-23; Neḥemiah 9:6-11; Exodus 14:30-31), it was introduced into the daily Temple service to fulfill the obligation of remembering the Exodus.

CONCEPTS:

1. The introductory quotations continue the climactic praise from P'sukay D'zimrah and give a brief history of the Jewish people, leading to the Exodus.

2. We recall the covenental relationship between God and Israel.

3. In P'suaky D'zimrah up to this point, there has been no mention of miracles which seem to break with natural events; previous passages described praise for the regular cycle of nature. Accordingly, controversy arose as to the appropriateness of the Song of the Sea being placed here, since it deals with extraordinary Divine miracles and may be more appropriate following Birkat HaYotzayr (which praises God as the Creator). Its inclusion here, before Yishtabaḥ, the official end of P'sukay D'zimrah, is a subtle lesson for us. "The most perfect praise of God is not in the inspired (psalms of David...) but grow out of the actual events of history which our ancestors beheld with their own eyes."[5]

1. In Chapter 4 we saw that there is a b'rachah for almost everything. In the Song of the Sea we attribute all our blessings to God. Interestingly, there is a custom to give tzedakah at this point in the service, but there is no b'rachah to be said upon giving tzedakah. One reason for this may be that the tzedakah recipient should not be kept waiting, even during the time it takes to recite a b'rachah, especially when that person is in need. Could you suggest a phrase or formula to be said while giving tzedakah?

3. The Midrash tells us that when the Children of Israel crossed the sea, leaving the Egyptians to drown, the angels wanted to sing the praises of God for the great miracle He had just performed. God rebuked them, saying, "My children, the Egyptians, are drowning and you can sing and dance?" A more modern incident recounts that when Yigal Alon (then Deputy Prime Minister of Israel) heard of the death of Egyptian President Nasser, he responded with the biblical injunction "In the fall of your enemy do not rejoice." Still another story is told of Golda Meir who stated that she could forgive the Arabs for killing Israeli boys, but she could never forgive them for having made Israeli boys into killers.

What do these tales teach us about the approach of Judaism to our enemies?

YISHTABAH SHIMCHAH יִשְׁתַּבַּח שְׁמְךָ

BACKGROUND:

This final poem of praise concludes P'sukay D'zimrah, thus setting off the preceding biblical selections with a closing b'rachah. One tradition suggests that the name of the author of this paragraph is Sh'lomo (found in an acrostic of the first letters of the words beginning with "shimchah").

CONCEPTS:

1. Though ending the section of praise, the prayer calls on the Jew to continue the process with even greater enthusiasm.

2. Ultimately God is beyond any words of homage; we can only keep trying our best to express our feelings.

3. This passage is a summary of the happiness we feel at being alive and able to enjoy God's world.

"Prayer Analysis"

1. List the fifteen words of praise from the first paragraph and write an interpretation of each, linking it to your own conceptions of different aspects of God.

BARECHU בָּרְכוּ

BACKGROUND:

The custom of officially calling the congregation together to worship God has its origin in our tradition as early as the Bible (Neḥemiah 9:5). It calls us together as a community (so Yemenite Jews do not have someone "leading" the t'fillot prior to Barechu). Barechu has come to signal the start of the central part of the morning and evening services, consisting of the Shema with its surrounding blessings and the Amidah. Recitation of Barechu is a call to participate in the benedictions which follow. The shaliah tzibbur includes himself in the invitation to worship by repeating the congregation's response verbatim.

CONCEPTS:

1. All sacred acts require summoning.6

2. A leader must never separate himself from the Jewish people, feeling their obligations are not his.

3. A leader must lead by example.

"Prayer Analysis"

1. Compare Barechu with the Islamic tradition of the muezzin who calls the faithful to prayer from atop the minaret.

2. Can you think of a different way of getting everyone's attention and making an official start to the prayer service?

3. How is Barechu an appropriate introduction to the "creation, revelation, redemption" themes which follow?

4. Compare this Barechu with the Barechu recited as part of the opening blessing of a Torah aliyah. Do they serve the same function?

AVINU MALKENU ("OUR FATHER, OUR KING") אָבִינוּ מַלְכֵּנוּ

BACKGROUND:

We are told in the Talmud *(Ta'anit 25b)* that Rabbi Akiba (second century C.E.) first created part of this prayer, now said on fast days and--with a minor variation--during the Ten Days of Penitence. On Rosh HaShanah, Avinu Malkenu is added after the Shaharit Amidah in place of Hallel said on other festivals. Rabbi Abahu, explained *(Rosh HaShanah 32b)* that, "The angels said to the Lord, 'O Master of the universe, why does Israel not sing the Song of Praise (Hallel) on Rosh HaShanah and Yom Kippur?' And the Lord replied, 'Should Israel sing songs while the King sits in judgment upon His throne with the books of the living and the dead open before Him?' " God judges everyone on Rosh HaShanah and so it makes more sense to offer a plea for mercy than to sing hymns of praise. Avinu Malkenu is not recited on Shabbat since it was originally associated with fast days and thought unsuitable for the joyous nature of Shabbat. Patterned on the Amidah, it is said standing. Many verses were developed over the centuries in different communities.

CONCEPTS:

1. We can relate to God intimately as a child to a father with all the warmth, openness and security implied in that kind of relationship, and we can relate to God as the King, ruler, awesome and distant, mysterious and unknowable.

2. After petitioning for the fulfillment of many requests, we call on God to remember those who died in sanctification of His Name as a way of pleading for God's compassion and mercy.

3. The woeful chant of the prayer is a mirror of the deep emotion and soul-searching associated with it.

154

"Prayer Analysis"

1. Try to match each line of Avinu Malkenu to a b'rachah found in the Amidah.

2. Pick ten phrases of Avinu Malkenu which mean the most to you and add ten more of your own. Then go back to the original and see if any of your own have already covered by the poetry of others written long ago.

3. Describe the ideal relationship you'd like between yourself and your father. If possible, sit with him and ask him to describe his ideal of relating to you. (You may wish to do this with your mother, as well.) See if these activities can help you better understand the ideal implied in the Avinu Malkenu relationship between man and God.

PENITENTIAL PRAYERS פַּחֲנוּן

BACKGROUND:

Tahanun (the "Petition") is said on weekdays (a short form for Sunday, Tuesday, Wednesday, and Friday, and a longer one on Mondays and Thursdays) when no festive or commemorative historical occasion takes place. The custom of reciting a private petition dates back to Temple times when people would prostrate themselves after the sacrifice. This "falling on the face" was later carried over into the synagogue but actual prostration was abandoned because it looked too much like pagan worship. In Tahanun, it is the custom to lean on one's weaker arm (except when wearing t'fillin), with the face buried in the crook of the arm. (See Chapter 2, on Body Language.) Originally, the content of this petition was up to each individual, but by the sixteenth century it was standardized. Various forms exist today among different Jewish communities. The Ashkenazic ritual consists of biblical quotations and a poem, *Shomayr Yisrael,* "Guardian of Israel."

CONCEPTS:

1. When Israel breaks its side of the covenant agreement with God, it is punished for its misdeeds.

2. We appeal to God's mercy to forgive, since He loves His people and will not forsake them.

3. For medieval Jews, the opening verse dealing with Divine--rather than human--punishment related to the hope of escaping the wrath of the Crusaders, and that their rewards and punishments would come from God.

"Prayer Analysis"

1. Analyze the image of the "Guardian of Israel." What qualities or attributes make it an apt description of God's relationship with Israel. How is such a phrase different from "Shield of Abraham" or "Rock of Israel"?

2. Look up the story about David and Batsheva in II Samuel 24. Compare it with Psalm 6 and analyze David's feelings. Have you ever been so totally overwhelmed with guilt? What did you do; where did you turn?

AND A REDEEMER SHALL COME TO ZION גּוֹאֵל לְצִיּוֹן וּבָא

BACKGROUND:

A product of talmudic times, it is believed this prayer was said following a reading from the prophets with rabbinic interpretations, which used to be included at the end of the service. The biblical selections of this prayer--known as *K'dushah D'sidra*--were usually translated into Aramaic. Later, during a period of persecution when the secular authorities forbade Jews to recite K'dushah in the Amidah, the Rabbis "secretly" inserted a Hebrew-Aramic version here, near the end of the service, after the "informers" left. It also provides the latecomers or individuals unable to pray with a minyan, an opportunity of reciting a K'dushah. One reason this paragraph is not recited on Sabbaths and Festivals is that everybody is supposed to be present, and on time.[7] Latecomers on those occasions catch up as needed.

CONCEPTS:

1. This is a declaration of the specialness of God.

2. God is compassionate and forgiving.

3. God has shown us His love by giving us the Torah; we glorify Him and show our gratitude by doing His will.

4. Our ultimate trust should be placed in God.

5. The call for a sanctification of God in the normal actions of everyday life reminds each worshipper of the synthesis between spiritual and mundane aspects of serving God. This appears late in the service so we take the message with us when we leave the synagogue.

"Prayer Analysis"

1. Mystical math: See if you can determine how many times the Divine name appears in this prayer. (It equals the number of b'rachot in the weekday Amidah.)

2. Discuss the meaning and implications of the opening phrase, "A redeemer shall come to Zion." How does the Jewish understanding of these words differ from what Christians believe?

3. Keep a careful, hour-by-hour, diary of a weekday or week in your life. Then, mark "KH" (Kiddush HaShaym) for everything you did which sanctified God's name; "Ḥ H" (Ḥillul HaShaym) for everything you did which diminished or profaned God's name and your own self worth. Write "N" for neutral behaviors, and seek the advice of teachers and friends in classifying behaviors of which you are not certain.

ALAYNU עָלֵינוּ

BACKGROUND:

Alaynu, said daily, was originally part of the Musaf service for Rosh HaShanah (introducing the Malchuyot verses). It has been included at the end of all synagogue services since the fourteenth century, but probably has its origin in Temple days. The author is believed to be Rav (Babylonia, third century) one of the greatest talmudic scholars, although there are other traditions of authorship.

The prayer became very popular after its recitation by Jewish men and women in the town of Blois, France in 1171, who were burned at the stake because they refused to be baptized. They died reciting Alaynu, a statement of belief that Israel has been chosen by God to follow His law, containing the hope that idolatry would vanish and all men will worship God. During the Spanish Inquisition, Christian authorities censored the lines "For they worship and bow before idols and vanity and pray to that which does not avail..." which they felt demeaned Christians. Though the prayer was written centuries earlier, the Christian authorities were nevertheless convinced by far-fetched reasoning of a Jewish apostate who equated the word "vanity" with "Jesus," by Hebrew *gematria* (numerology). With the invention of the printing press, demands became even stronger that certain passages of the Siddur be removed. Jews developed their own censorship mechanisms to prevent local Christian authorities from removing words and prayers *they* felt objectionable. Interestingly, in Moslem lands, where censorship of Jewish books was not as prevalent, Alaynu kept its original form. Today, even though we need not fear censorship, the "revised" version still is used.

CONCEPTS:

1. We praise God for his creation of the universe and for chosing us to work for establishment of His Kingdom on earth.

2. Judaism's particular view of its responsibilities to God is linked to a universal hope that all humanity will acknowledge God as the Supreme Being and seek to do His will.

3. Hope is expressed for the messianic age.

4. On the High Holidays, some worshippers actually prostrate themselves on the ground as a sign of their acceptance of God's will.

"Prayer Analysis"

1. Compare the following version of the beginning of Alaynu found in the *Seder Avodah* prayer book, edited by Rabbi Max Klein for Congregation Adath Jeshurun, a Conservative congregation in Elkins Park, Pennsylvania. Why is the text changed? What is added? Omitted? Why?

> Let us now praise the Lord of the universe and acclaim the greatness of the Author of creation, who called the heavens into being and stretched them forth; who spread out the earth and all that emanates therefrom; who gives life to the nations that dwell upon it and breath to them that walk thereon.

2. Do you accept the notion of Israel's "chosenness"?

3. What does the phrase "To perfect the world under the Kingship of God" mean? (The name of the USY tzedakah program, *Tikkun Olam*, "Perfecting the world," is based on a similar phrase.) If you had three wishes that would improve the world, what would they be?

4. Write a short story about the martyrs who died in the Middle Ages, with Alaynu on their lips. Is there anything you would be willing to die for?

PSALM FOR THE DAY שִׁיר שֶׁל יוֹם

BACKGROUND:

During the Temple service, the Levites used to sing a special psalm for each day of the week. We continue that tradition by reciting a special psalm each day. Ashkenazim recite it after Alaynu (or early in the Shaḥarit service); Sephardic Jews recite it before Alaynu. Each psalm is introduced with the phrase, "Today is the first (second, third, etc.) day as we count towards Shabbat." We count down, so to speak, to Shabbat, highlight of the week. Psalms chosen for each day reflect the creation of the world in some way.

CONCEPTS:

1. First Day (Sunday)--Psalm 24: Heaven and earth were created by God, thus "The earth is the Lord's and the fullness thereof..."

2. Second Day--Psalm 48: God separated the waters (upper and lower) and though He dwelled on high "He left the knowledge of His glory on earth."

3. Third Day--Psalm 82: The dry land appeared and the psalmist recounts that unless man observes God's law "the very foundations of the earth tremble."

4. Fourth Day--Psalm 94: The heavenly bodies were created, and in this psalm where God is called a God of vengeance, we are reminded of those who would falsely idolize the creations of God, rather than worship God Himself.

5. Fifth Day--Psalm 81: The many, varied fish and fowl were created on that day and are remembered in the psalm, in its praise of the Creator who orders and guides the world.

6. Sixth Day--Psalm 93: The psalm recalls the completion of all the acts of creation which happened on this day by proclaiming, "The world is set on an unshakable foundation, never to yield."

7. Seventh Day (Shabbat)--Psalm 92: This psalm looks forward to the era of eternal Shabbat on earth, when God will be thanked by all and evildoers overcome, with harmony, and justice reigning.

"Prayer Analysis"

1. Mystical Math: Count the words in psalm 93. Take their numerical value in Hebrew and convert it to a person's Hebrew name. (This is called gematria, the practice of equating Hebrew words through their letter values. Hint: The psalm marks the day of his birth in the creation of the world.)

2. Many synagogues customarily conclude with a closing prayer or benediction rather than with one of these traditional psalms. Which practice do you prefer? Could you write a closing prayer based on the themes in each psalm to be used each day of the week, marking something special or unique about the day?

YIGDAL יִגְדַּל

BACKGROUND:

Probably written by Daniel ben Judah, Dayyan of Rome, at the end of the thirteenth century, this hymn is based on Maimonides' "Thirteen Principles of Faith." The poem is written in Hebrew influenced by Arabic meter. In some traditions it is a daily hymn; others recite it as a concluding hymn on Erev Shabbat. The Sephardic ritual adds a statement that "These are the Thirteen Principles of faith; they are the foundation of the Divine faith and of God's law."[9] It must be noted that these articles of faith were the personal opinion of their author and are not binding on Jews in a dogmatic fashion.

CONCEPTS:

1. Each of Maimonides' "Thirteen Articles of Faith" begins with the formula "I believe with perfect faith that..." The articles are

    1. the belief in the existence of a Creator;
    2. the belief in God's unity;
    3. His having no form;
    4. His eternity;
    5. all worship and adoration are due Him alone;
    6. belief in prophecy;
    7. Moses was the greatest of all prophets;
    8. the Torah was revealed to Moses at Sinai;
    9. the Torah is unchangeable;
    10. God knows the actions of people;
    11. He rewards and punishes in justice;
    12. the Messiah will come;
    13. the dead will be resurrected.

It will be noted that some of the articles were of a polemic nature, especially the ninth article. Obviously this was aimed at the Christians' claim that the New Testament superseded the Torah and the Moslems' claim that the Koran also superseded it (and the Christian Bible).[10]

"Prayer Analysis"

1. Compare Maimonides' "Principles" with Yigdal. Consider style (differences between prose and poetry) and theology (content). Discuss each idea and see which you can accept, which need interpretation, and which are troublesome for you.

2. The need for Rambam's polemic against Christian thought was vital in his day when Christianity and Islam were trying to convert Jews forcibly. Today, the challenge posed by various cults and missionary movements is a similar threat. Do you think it would help to have modern creed of beliefs to combat these cults? Could you list your own person thirteen principles of faith? If Judaism is a way of life concerned more with what Jews *do* than with what they *believe*, can Judaism really be reduced to a list of beliefs? Try to list below Jewish personal beliefs and activities toward which you strive.

I believe sincerely that...	*Jewish activities I must perform:*
1.	1.
2.	2.
3.	3.
4.	4.
5.	5.
6.	6.
7.	7.
8.	8.
9.	9.
10.	10.
11.	11.
12.	12.
13.	13.

ADON OLAM אֲדוֹן עוֹלָם

BACKGROUND:

Probably written by Solomon ibn Gabirol or Rav Hai Ga'on in the eleventh century, it is an alphabetic acrostic, in the meter and style of Spanish Hebrew poetry. It has been inserted in the beginning of the morning service since the fifteenth century,[11] and is now also used as a concluding hymn.

CONCEPTS:

1. Adon Olam is uttered at beginning of the day (in Shaharit) and the end of the day (as part of the bedtime Shema ritual), linking our lives to God and pointing to our ultimate source of security.

2. The ease of meter and verse reflect in poetic form the ease of our trusting relationship in God.

3. A dual conception of God is expressed: God's distance from us ("Lord of the world, who was King before existence was created, and who exists through all eternity") and God's closeness ("My God, my Redeemer, My Rock and my Protector").

4. This is a fundamental Jewish statement of monotheism.

"Prayer Analysis"

1. See if you can scan the rhythm of this prayer. How does it make you feel? Notice how many melodies fit its regular meter. Are all melodies appropriate to the words of the poem?

2. What are the qualities of paternal love which this prayer intimates as the way God loves His people?

3. Why do you think this poem came to be so popular?

4. In what do you trust and place your own sense of security: parents? friends? talents? material possessions? God?

CHAPTER 7 SHABBAT AND YOM TOV (FESTIVAL) PRAYERS
STRUCTURE OF SHABBAT AND HOLIDAY SERVICES

The structure of Shabbat and holiday prayers is very similar to the organization of weekday services. There are additions which reflect the special nature of those days, without changing the basic weekday structure. The additions include Kabbalat Shabbat, the service of "Welcoming the Shabbat," before Ma'ariv on Friday evening; extra passages of praise in P'sukay D'zimrah, in the morning; the Torah reading (also added on Rosh Ḥodesh) and Haftorah; Hallel, psalms of praise, on holidays (and part of it also on Rosh Hodesh); the Musaf, or "additional" service after Shaḥarit on Shabbat, Rosh Ḥodesh, and holiday mornings.

Since we can be more leisurely and relaxed on Shabbat and holidays, the service is somewhat lengthier and richer in the number and range of prayers. Some of the prayers added for Shabbat and Yom Tov are analyzed in this chapter.

SONG OF SONGS שִׁיר הַשִּׁירִים

BACKGROUND:

Shabbat traditionally was welcomed as a Bride or Queen, the beloved of Israel. It was thought fitting to read a love song to one's beloved, and so Jews began to read *Shir HaShirim,* the biblical book of love poetry, before the arrival of Shabbat. (Song of Songs is also read on the Shabbat of Pesah, since it is full of the imagery of spring, new life, and rebirth.)

CONCEPTS:

1. The imagery of Shabbat as a beloved partner is given added depth and beauty through the recitation of beautiful love poetry.

2. The poem has been variously interpreted as being a love poem between Israel and God, or between King Solomon (who is said to be its author, according to tradition) and God, or between a lover and his beloved. The overtones of these relationships add to the overall effect of the relationship of the worshipper to Shabbat, to God, and to other people.

3. The poem juxtaposes spiritual and physical love, both of which are essential to our health and well-being. Both delights are to be part of the Shabbat experience.

4. Reading or chanting Shir HaShirim helps prepare us for the proper mood of Shabbat.

"Prayer Analysis"

1. Even if the meaning of the Hebrew is difficult for you, read at least part of Shir HaShirim aloud to hear the music of its sounds. You will also discover how many popular Hebrew songs are taken from this text.

2. Often we tend to look at Shabbat as a long list of "don'ts." The concepts embodied in the recitation of the Song of Songs as a preparation for Shabbat gives us pause to think of the "do's" on Shabbat. Make a list of such items.

3. Write a love poem or song of your own addressed to Shabbat or to God. Use symbols and images which mean something special to you. Then ask someone else to interpret your creation.

WELCOMING THE SABBATH קַבָּלַת שַׁבָּת

BACKGROUND:

The idea of conceiving of Shabbat as a Queen or Bride and adding a special welcome to her go back to the sixteenth century. (The custom originally stems from talmudic statements, *Shabbat 119a,* which describe how the Rabbis would dress up on Friday night and say to each other "Come let us go out to meet the Sabbath Queen and receive her with festive ceremony.") A series of psalms (95-99, and 29) was introduced by the Kabbalists of Safed, particularly by Moses Cordovero, prior to the evening service. The six psalms stand for the six work days of the week; each praises God for the glory of His creations.

The well-known poem, L'chah Dodi--introduced by a short mystical prayer in some communities--was written by Solomon HaLevi Alkabetz, who lived in Safed in the 16th century. The author's name (Sh'lomo HaLevi) is forever memorialized in the first letters of each verse. The

Kabbalists of Safed used to go out to the fields surrounding the town on Friday evening, dressed in white, singing songs and psalms to welcome the Shabbat. Today, symbolic of that, we turn and face the synagogue entrance, bowing as we recite the words in the last verse, bidding the Shabbat Queen to enter. Following L'chah Dodi are two psalms: Psalm 92 was recited by the Levites on Shabbat in the Temple; Psalm 93 continues the image of God's splendor appropriate for Shabbat.

CONCEPTS:

1. In Psalms 95-99, and 29, we thank God for the world of creation in which we grow, work, and live.

2. We proclaim our hope for the universal goal of the establishment of God's kingdom on earth, a prelude to a world-wide, eternal Shabbat.

3. All the nations of the world are called to worship God and accept His rule (Psalm 96).

4. When all people know the Lord, He shall be enthroned in Zion (Psalm 99).

5. When all of the above will happen, the universe will hear the sound of God's voice and know the ultimate blessing of peace (Psalm 29).

6. The first stanza of L'chah Dodi recalls the midrashic interpretation of two commandments: "Remember the Sabbath" (Exodus 20:8); "Observe the Sabbath" (Deuteronomy 5:12). According to legend, God uttered both words simultaneously, but mortal men can only record them separately. This teaches that the observance of Shabbat and caring about Shabbat are equally important.

The second stanza (expressing the thought that, though made last, Shabbat was conceived of first) teaches that Shabbat is the symbolic ideal of all creation. The remaining stanzas (until the last) hope that Jerusalem will be rebuilt, the Messiah will come, and Israel will be redeemed. The final stanza is the official welcome to the Shabbat.

7. Psalms 92 and 93 speak of an ideal world where evildoers will be punished and when Shabbat and its beauty will pervade the universe.

"Prayer Analysis"

1. Read each of the first six psalms and paraphrase their ideas. See if you can find a way of linking each with the things created on the corresponding day in the creation story.

2. What do the following expressions in L'chah Dodi mean to you?

      a. "(Shabbat)...for it is a source of blessing."
      b. "The city shall be rebuilt on its mound."
      c. "Your God will rejoice over you (the city) as a groom rejoices over a bride."

3. What might we do during the recitation of L'chah Dodi to highlight this dramatic and important welcoming moment, as did the Kabbalists of Safed?

EVENING SERVICE FOR SHABBAT מַעֲרִיב לְעֶרֶב שַׁבָּת

BACKGROUND:

See the discussion of Ma'ariv and the Shabbat Amidot in Section II. Here we shall deal with several additions to Shabbat Ma'ariv.

1. Hashkeyvanu. The final blessing is changed from "...who guards His people Israel forever" to "...who spreads the Sukkah of peace over us, over all His people Israel, and over Jerusalem." It was felt the weekday blessing was more appropriate to the workaday world, asking God to watch over our daily activities. On Shabbat and holidays, when we rest, it is more appropriate to ask God for His blessing of peace to go with the peace of Shabbat, and to ask for the peace of Jerusalem, symbol of our greatest joy.

2. V'shamru (Exodus 31:16-17). Considered part of the lengthened blessing of redemption, it was placed here as the logical continuation of the blessing for peace which will be attained if, and when, the people of Israel keep the Shabbat. The Shabbat itself is a guardian of Israel. The great Hebrew essayist, Aḥad Ha'Am said, "More than Israel kept the Sabbath, the Sabbath kept Israel." On holidays, a brief reference to the observance of the festivals is added here. The weekday prayer "Blessed be the Lord forever" is omitted, since it was seen as a substitute for the weekday Amidah.

3. Vay'chulu (Genesis 2:1-3). This biblical selection deals with God's resting on the seventh day. Originally coming only after the Amidah, this paragraph was later inserted into the Amidah itself, so each person could recite it. Now it occurs three times on Friday evening: in the Amidah, following the Amidah, and preceding Kiddush (when recited at home).

"Prayer Analysis"

1. What is so special about Kabbalat Shabbat and the Friday evening service which makes them so enjoyable?

2. Consider these phrases from the Amidah of Erev Shabbat:
   a. "You have sanctified the seventh day for Your name, the end of creation of heaven and earth. You blessed it more than all days, and sanctified it more than all the seasons."

   b. "Grant our portion in your Torah."

   c. "Purify our hearts to worship You in truth."

KIDDUSH FOR SHABBAT AND FESTIVALS קִדּוּשׁ

BACKGROUND:

The custom of reciting Kiddush ("Sanctification" of God, made over wine) in the synagogue arose in talmudic times as a way of fulfilling the mitzvah of hospitality, or providing for wayfarers and the poor. Travelers would eat their Shabbat meals in the synagogue and were provided for by the community. Though conditions changed over the centuries, the inclusion of Kiddush in the Friday evening service was retained primarily in Ashkenazic synagogues. But the full Kiddush is said in the warmth of our homes before the Shabbat meal, which mirrors the true enjoyment and holiness of Shabbat. It is preceded by Vay'chulu which, in turn, is preceded by the last words of Genesis, Chapter 1. Those words, "It was evening, it was morning, the sixth day" are said silently, with only the last words, "Yom HaSheeshee," said aloud. Along with the first words of Vay'chulu, this creates an acrostic for God's name: יוֹם הַשִּׁשִּׁי וַיְכֻלּוּ הַשָּׁמַיִם

In many homes, making Kiddush is the central act in making Shabbat. Singing the Kiddush on Friday night or holidays makes the occasions different and special, and reciting Kiddush or hearing it recited adds to the sense of belonging to a people. Kiddush has a way of making us feel as if we belong to something much greater than ourselves.

CONCEPTS:

1. The use of wine for "sanctification" is derived from the place wine occupies in the Tanach (Bible). "Wine makes glad the heart of man" (Psalm 104:15); "It cheers God and man" (Judge 9:13). It was offered at the sacrifices in the Temple, and from there was introduced into the home as a symbol of joy to usher in the festivals.

2. Kiddush is recited as a remembrance of the creation of the world, remembrance of the Exodus from Egypt, and the creation of the Jewish people.

3. The specialness of Shabbat is underlined.

4. God shows love for His people by giving them the gift of the Shabbat.

5. Kiddush speaks of the chosenness of Israel, for the purpose of observing God's law and receiving His special gifts of the Torah and Shabbat.

Note: Kiddush for the day of Shabbat is shorter than the evening version. It includes V'shamru, (optional) recitation of the Fifth Commandment, an introductory line to the b'rachah over wine. On Festivals, the b'rachah is introduced by the verse announcing the Festivals to the people.

"Prayer Analysis"

1. Consider the statement by Abrahams, on the topic of drinking, "It has been very plausibly maintained that such a custom as this is sanctified by use and degraded by abuse."[12] The issues involved in alcoholism are very complex. You may be confronted with some difficult decisions resulting from peer pressure and problems of personal willpower. It is no longer true that Jews enjoy a much lower rate of alcoholism than the total population in this country. How do you feel about this problem? Is it because Jews have become farther removed from tradition? What should the legal drinking age be? Is alcohol usage, both religiously and politically, different from smoking marijuana?

2. Consider these two talmludic statements:

> "Rabbi Ishmael ben Elisha said, 'Since the day of the destruction of the Temple we should, by rights, bind ourselves not to eat meat nor drink wine, only we do not put a hardship on the community unless the majority can endure it.' "
>
> _____
>
> (*Baba Batra 60b*)

> "Rav Yehudah stated in the name of Samuel, 'He who has drunk a quarter of a *log* (549 cubic centimeters) must not give a legal decision!' ... Rabbah son of Rav Huna ruled, 'One who is under the influence of drink must not pray, but if he did pray, his prayer is regarded as a proper one. An intoxicated man must not pray, and if he did pray, his prayer is an abomination.' How are we to understand the expression 'one who is under the influence of drink' and 'an intoxicated man.' ... The former is one who is able to speak in the presence of a king; the latter is one who is unable to speak in the presence of a king."
>
> _____
>
> (*Eruvin 64a*)

3. What does the phrase "first among the holy festivals" say about the place of Shabbat in our tradition?

4. Why do we recall the Exodus from Egypt in the Kiddush, as we do in the morning and evening services every day?

5. Shabbat fantasy: Close your eyes and imagine yourself sometime in the future, in your own home. Who will be sitting at your Shabbat table? What will it look like? What kind of rituals will you perform? How important will Shabbat be to you? Imagine you could invite any five Jews from our entire history as guests to your future table. Whom would you invite?

6. In Judaism, happiness and celebration are an extremely important part of being alive. Too often, we tend to think only of the pragmatic issues in our lives, of our tensions and daily frustrations, without stopping to appreciate the happiness that all of us are privileged to experience at various times. Look through the Siddur for prayers reflecting joy, *Simhah*, and see if you can interpret the context of happiness, e.g., does it come from the observance of a particular commandment, the celebration of a holiday, being with other people, being alive, or receiving a gift from God? Start by looking at selections such as Kiddush; (Halleluyah) psalms; Adon Olam; Psalm 92; *Yismaḥ Mosheh* (in the Shabbat morning Amidah); and *Yism'ḥu* (in the Shabbat Musaf Amidah).

EXERCISE 1

List below ten important things which (will) make you happy. After listing the items, number them in rank order starting with the single item which gives you the most happiness or pleasure. Once you have numbered the items from 1 to 10, decide how much time, energy, or effort you invest in obtaining that particular event or item. Do you wait for it to happen by chance? Is there anything you can do to bring it about? What do the items say about you?

EREV SHABBAT HOME RITUALS בִּרְכַּת יְלָדִים, שָׁלוֹם עֲלֵיכֶם, אֵשֶׁת חַיִל

BACKGROUND:

The custom of blessing the children on Friday evening is linked to the Patriarchs, who repeatedly extended blessings to their children. Today, when returning home from the synagogue on Friday night (or as part of the Shabbat dinner in families attending t'fillot after the meal), the parents place their hands on their children's heads, reciting several verses for boys and girls, including the Priestly blessing. This custom was incorporated into the Siddur around the sixteenth century. The Talmud (Shabbat 119b) tells us that two angels, one good and one evil, follow a person home from the synagogue on Erev Shabbat. If the home is prepared and ready for Shabbat the good angel calls out, "May it be this way again next Shabbat," and the evil angel begrudgingly answers "Amen." But if the house is not prepared for Shabbat, the angels' exclamations are reversed. The hymn Shalom Alaychem, sung at this point, was written by the Kabbalists in the Middle Ages to welcome the angels of peace to a home of joy and peace.

In many homes, just before Kiddush, husbands turn to their wives and recite Ayshet Ḥayil, "A woman of valor" (Proverbs 31:10-31). This poem talks of the virtues of the ideal woman who is competent and strong, yet warm and loving. The woman was viewed as the mainstay of the family and its household, so Friday night became a time to honor her especially since she had worked so diligently to prepare Shabbat for the family.

Other aspects of making the meal special include singing Shabbat songs (Z'mirot) and studying or discussing together, as a family.

CONCEPTS:

1. Welcoming guests is central to the Friday night home ritual.

2. Shabbat can only exist if it is properly prepared for, in advance. Especially when we work hard in its preparation, we can enjoy its peacefulness and luxury.

3. The centrality of family structure in Judaism is eloquently reflected in the parents' blessing their children. For the children, the feeling of parental love and warmth is symbolized by the placement of their parents' hands on the children's heads during the blessing.

"Prayer Analysis"

1. Talk or write personally of Shabbat in your home. How do you feel about being in a place where Shabbat has been prepared for and anticipated?

2. Based on the model of Ayshet Ḥayil, write a poem of praise for any brothers or sisters you have.

3. Look at the "Blessings of Children." Do the blessings seem appropriate to you? Write your own "Blessing of Parents." As part of the process of adding to Shabbat observance at home, read or chant one of the poems you have written.

PASSAGES OF PRAISE FOR SHABBAT (AND FESTIVALS) פְּסוּקֵי דְזִמְרָה לְשַׁבָּת

BACKGROUND:

P'sukay D'zimrah for Shabbat and Festivals has the same structure as for weekdays, with a few additions and omissions. Since there were no Thanks-offerings in the Temple on Shabbat or holidays, Psalm 100, "A Psalm of Thanks," is omitted. In its place we recite nine psalms which have as their theme praise of God for His wondrous creations. One of those passages (Psalm 136) is called the "Great Hallel," parallel to the "Hallel (of Egypt)," Psalms 113-118, added just before the Torah reading on festivals and Rosh Ḥodesh.

Following the Song of the Sea an additional poem, *Nishmat*, "The breath of every living thing...," is added; it is also known as the "Blessing of Song." It is also recited as part of the Seder on Pesaḥ. Though there is some question of who wrote this prayer (which include the paragraphs שׁוֹכֵן עַד, וּבְמַקְהֲלוֹת, יִשְׁתַּבַּח) attempts at "discovering" the author's name from the initials of Hebrew words, have led to Yitzhak or Shimon (ben Shetah).

CONCEPTS:

1. According to tradition, on Shabbat, we receive a *N'shamah Y'tayrah*, an additional "Shabbat soul." Thus, the longer P'sukay D'zimrah reflects a more leisurely, devoted approach to prayer than is possible on the weekday.

2. Three basic notions are contained in the various psalms for Shabbat morning: remembrance of creation; remembrance of the Exodus; and forecast of the world to come.[13] Again we see the formula *creation, revelation,* and *redemption* in the liturgy.

3. Nishmat is a prayer of thanksgiving and blessing for the Song of the Sea, summarizing the themes of the psalms which precede it by declaring there are no words adequate to praise God, who is beyond all praise, song, and thanksgiving.

4. A passage near the end of Nishmat is the first prayer to be "officially" read by the shaliaḥ tzibbur, thus introducing the central part of the service beginning with Barechu. (The point the shaliah tzibbur begins is determined by the day, reciting the phrase appropriate to themes of the occasion: Ha'Ayl on Festivals; HaMelech on the High Holidays; Shochayn Ad on Shabbat.)

"Prayer Analysis"

1. When you are in a congregation which recites the complete P'sukay D'zimrah on Shabbat, and you are feeling overwhelmed, select one of the psalms and read it carefully. Compare the Hebrew and English; apply some of the analytical questions found at the beginning of this Section. If you do this each time you pray, over a period of months your understanding and competence will increase drastically.

2. There are some striking images in Nishmat. What do you think of them?

   a. "If our mouths were filled with song like the sea, and if our tongues (were filled with) singing like the multitudinous waves..."

   b. "If our hands were outstretched like eagles' wings..."

   c. "If our feet were swift as the wild deer."

MORNING SERVICE FOR SABBATH AND FESTIVALS שַׁחֲרִית לְשַׁבָּת וְלִרְגָלִים

BACKGROUND:

There are only three major differences in the b'rachot preceding the Shema for Shabbat and Festival mornings. On Shabbat, after Birkat HaYotzar, in place of the piyyut "You bring light to the earth," we substitute the poem "All shall acknowledge You...," because its theme complements the Shabbat theme of God as Creator of all. We also add the well-known hymn Aly Adon. This poem was probably composed by a group of mystics known as the *Yorday Merkavah,* "Searchers in the Chariot," also credited with a few other sections of the morning service. Ayl Adon is followed by a passage specially devoted to the theme of Shabbat and rest.

CONCEPTS:

1. God is remembered and thanked on Shabbat for having created everything.

2. The liturgy was a vehicle for individual poets to respond creatively to their experience of God and prayer.

3. Ayl Adon praises God for the creation of the heavenly spheres which are subject to His will. He is the God of nature which is subservient to Him.

4. God's rest on the seventh day serves as an example to us. If the King of kings can find time to rest, so must we.

"Prayer Analysis"

1. Compare the initial words in each line of Ayl Adon with the weekday morning poem L'ayl Baruch.

2. Could you write your own poem responding to the Yotzayr b'rachah ("...who creates light and forms darkness...")? Choose any word or idea in that b'rachah which seems important to you and expand upon it. In so doing you will be entering the same creative process which built the Siddur.

HALLEL (PSALMS OF PRAISE) הַלֵּל

BACKGROUND:

Recited on Rosh Ḥodesh, the Pilgrimage Festivals, and Ḥanukah, Hallel is composed of Psalms 113-118 surrounded by an opening and closing b'rachah. (On Rosh Ḥodesh and the latter days of Pesaḥ, Psalms 115 and 116 are recited only in part.) In ancient times, various forms of responsive and repetitive chanting were used by the leader of the congregation for those Psalms of Praise, which were always quite common during the Second Temple period. Hallel is usually recited standing.

During Sukkot, the *Arba'ah Minim* ("Four species," *Lulav* and *Etrog*) are held and waved in all the directions, symbolizing God's presence everywhere in the universe.

CONCEPTS:

1. Overall scheme of organization:

> Psalm 113: Overall directive to praise.
> Psalm 114: Divine revelation (*past*).
> Psalm 115: God's work in the *present*.
> Psalm 116: How God will be glorified in the *future*.
> Concluding Verses: reference to salvation and the Messiah (*End of Days*).

2. We fulfill a need to offer special passages of praise in addition to the regular liturgy, to highlight special occasions.

"Prayer Analysis"

1. Make a list of the things for which you are so grateful you would praise and thank God. What does your list tell you about your values and priorities?

2. Psalm 114 uses the poetic device of ellipsis (omitting words) to reflect its content by its form. Try to determine which words are left out and why.

Hint: The basic thrust is toward a return to the fountain (source) of water and life.

3. Do you agree with the verse in Psalm 118, "It is better to seek refuge in the Lord than to trust in men; it is better to seek refuge in the Lord than to trust in princes"?

PRAYERS FOR SCHOLARS AND COMMUNITY.   יְקוּם פֻּרְקָן

BLESSING THE NEW MONTH   בִּרְכַּת הַחֹדֶשׁ

BACKGROUND:

Following the Torah and Haftorah readings on Shabbat, prayers are recited for the welfare of scholars (in schools in Babylonia and Palestine), and for the welfare of the community and its institutions. The institutions of learning and prayer are thus singled out and highlighted immediately following the ritual study of Torah in the service. The first two paragraphs of this section are written in Aramaic, the language spoken by Babylonian Jews when it was composed.

It became customary (only about 100 years ago in the Ashkenazic liturgy) to announce the dates of Rosh Ḥodesh (the start of the New Month) on the preceding Shabbat, since people didn't have printed calendars of their own. This, too, is done following the Torah service in the hope that the new month will see us grow closer to God's law. In the opening paragraph of Birkat HaḤodesh, we ask for a long life of peace, well-being, and positive values. The sentence "to renew unto us this coming month for good and for blessing" was added to make the prayer more appropriate to the occasion. The following paragraph, "may He who worked miracles..." formally announces the date of the new month commences. The passage concludes with prayers hoping for a month of salvation and redemption.[14]

CONCEPTS:

1. Scholarship and Torah study are a central aspect of our continued survival and growth as a people.

2. The vernacular (the language spoken in a particular locale) has a definite place in our liturgy.

3. Those who maintain Jewish communal institutions are involved in an important mitzvah.

4. The monthly cycle of time is a reminder of our limited time on earth, and the need to take best advantage of the time allowed us.

5. Each new month is viewed as a new beginning for our physical and spiritual lives; we have renewed chances to change and grow.

"Prayer Analysis"

The regular return of the beginning of every new month, with its call to return to the path of proper living, raises an interesting question. What is a reasonable self-checking time span for setting personal growth goals?

Often we make a commitment to change something about ourselves, but give ourselves too little or too much time to reach the goal. What amount of time is good for you to fix as a stopping point for self-evaluation in pursuing a desired goal in your life? A day? A week? A month? A semester? A year? In the attempt to increase your involvement with t'fillah, what are reasonable periods to mark as self-evaluation points? Obviously, different goals will demand different time spans.

170

MEMORIAL SERVICE FOR DEPARTED (YIZKOR) יִזְכּוֹר

BACKGROUND:

The service for remembering our deceased relatives and friends, and all martyrs of Israel, stems from a midrashic interpretation of Deuteronomy 21:8, "Forgive Your people Israel, whom You have redeemed." This is interpreted to mean that the dead also need redemption, and the living must help redeem them.[15] The memorial service was said on Yom Kippur (when both the living and dead were believed to stand before God in judgment). In the Ashkenazic liturgy it was added to the three Pilgrimage Festivals in the eighteenth century, though some communities omit it on Shabbat.

The service consists of silent prayers in memory of loved ones; *Ayl Mahlay Raḥamim*, asking God to shelter the deceased in His protecting care; Psalm 23, "The Lord is my sheperd"; and other meditations. Customs relating to Yizkor include lighting a memorial candle which burns one full day, giving tzedakah, and reciting Kaddish, to make the memory of the deceased into a blessing for the living.

A superstitious custom has been for people with both parents alive to leave the synagogue during the recitation of Yizkor prayers, lest their remaining somehow lead to a premature demise of their parents. There is no basis for this custom in a service which recalls the memory of all departed among our people, including those Jews who died for the sanctification of God's name throughout our history. Yizkor helps us understand the cycle of life and death, of which we are all a part and must all accept.

CONCEPTS:

1. Recalling the dead helps the living by giving us models to follow, encouraging us to good deeds in their honor.

2. By linking ourselves with the past we gain a sense of identity and ties with our roots.

3. Remembering our dead sensitizes us to make better use of the time we spend with our loved ones while living.

4. Central to Yizkor (and the Martryology service on Yom Kippur) are the ideas of *Kiddush HaShaym*, "Sanctification of God's name," and *Ḥillul HaShaym*, "Profaning God's name."

5. Life is a cycle of birth, growth, and death. This is natural, to be expected and accepted, not feared.

6. "It is no challenge to die like a Jew, the real challenge is to live like a Jew" (Chafetz Chaim).

PRAYERS FOR RAIN AND DEW תְּפִלּוֹת גֶּשֶׁם וְטַל

BACKGROUND:

On the first day of Pesaḥ, we add a prayer for dew in the Musaf service; on Shemini Atzeret in Musaf we add a prayer for rain. Having little fresh water available from rivers or lakes, Israel is dependent on dew and rain. Almost a foot of dew is needed each year for successful summer crops; the rainy season, from Sukkot to Pesah, must be abundant, but not too heavy. However, since we hope the prayer for rain will be answered quickly, we do not recite it until the end of Sukkot, since we do not want to see the holiday "washed out," making it difficult to eat or sleep in the Sukkah.

CONCEPTS:

1. On Pesaḥ we combine the spiritual rebirth of our people with the Spring rebirth of nature. The soft, delicate dew is a beautiful symbol of these two realms of existence.

2. All people rely on nature and have a responsibility to care for and protect the natural world.

3. We dwell in the Sukkah at the time of most threatening weather, demonstrating that though material comforts are important, our ultimate protection and security come from God.

4. Nature responds to the actions of man insofar as we carry out God's will.

"Prayer Analysis"

1. Why were these prayers said by Jews long after they had left Israel and found themselves in totally different climatic regions?

2. The prayer for rain appeals to the merits of our forefathers in asking God to grant us rain. Each verse is written as a kind of "riddle" relating to one of our famous ancestors. Can you identify each one?

3. See the discussion of the second paragraph of the Shema, regarding responses of nature to the actions of mankind.

AYN KAYLOHAYNU אֵין כֵּאלֹהֵינוּ

BACKGROUND:

Originating in talmudic times, this hymn appears every day in the rituals of the Sephardic and Yemenite Jews, but only Shabbat and holidays in the Ashkenazic ritual. In some Siddurim it is followed by a passage describing the incense used in the Temple service. (Some object to this passage since it may date back to the days of epidemics when it was recited apparently in memory of Aaron, who offered incense in the Temple to stop a plague; Numbers 17:12.[16]) Some Siddurim add a passage from the end of *Masechet B'rachot* "Rabbi Elazar said..." with its well-known play on the words *banayich* (children) and *bonayich* (builders). These final passages are optional, the formal public service ending with the Mourner's Kaddish.

CONCEPTS:

1. The hymn begins as an acrostic, spelling out אָמֵן , a fitting end to the service.

2. In almost irreducible, staccato phrasing the entire essence of the service is summarized: God is one, unique; with no peer; we are grateful to Him; we praise Him and submit to His will; we acknowledge Him as Sovereign, Master, King and Savior.

3. The final passage from *B'rachot* explains that those who study Torah bring peace to the world and to themselves.

"Prayer Analysis"

1. Write a new melody for Ayn Kaylohaynu. Why did you choose the music you wrote?

2. The acrostic of Ayn Kaylohaynu may have been created by rearranging the order of the stanzas Which verse should, logically, be first?

3. How can Torah study bring peace to the world?

HAVDALAH הַבְדָּלָה

BACKGROUND:

The Havdalah service (literally, "separation") (from the Hebrew word לְהַבְדִּיל) separates the holiness and specialness of Shabbat from ordinary weekdays. Before Havdalah, we add a paragraph to the first petition of the Amidah, the blessing for discernment, in which we recognize the distinction and formally make the separation. (In order to light the Havdalah candle, Shabbat has to be over already!) We distinguish between the sacred and secular; between light and darkness; between Israel and other nations. Traditionally the men of the Great Assembly set the Havdalah prayers which consist of b'rachot over wine, light, spices, and separation of Shabbat from the weekdays. When recited at home, we add an introductory paragraph consisting of biblical verses. Preceding Havdalah, some Siddurim include paragraphs which reassure the people that God will indeed bless them and fulfill their hopes of deliverance, peace, comfort and protection in the coming week.

CONCEPTS:

1. God's abundant blessings are symbolized at the beginning and end of Shabbat by a cup of wine. It is hoped that the sweetness of Shabbat, symbolized by the wine, will pervade the weekdays.

2. Though our "extra soul" leaves us at Shabbat's end, the smell of the spices gives us extra spiritual strength to continue through the week. (In earlier times spices were used as incense to prevent various food odors, and so had to be rekindled at the end of Shabbat.)

3. The creative power of fire and the creation of light are reminders that Shabbat is a day of rest from our weekday creative energies. Since we recite a b'rachah over light, we are obliged to use it. Generally we cup the hands to see the shadow of our fingers in our palms, though some people use the light in other ways, such as looking at a watch. The candle is multi-wicked, complying with the blessing's phrase, "who creates *lights* of the fire," which is in the plural.

4. Sometimes wine is poured out to symbolize an over-abundance of blessings it is hoped will fall on the household. Ḥasidim wipe their eyes after dipping their fingers in wine, to bring the sweetness of the mitzvot closer to their consciousness.

5. The idea of holiness in time is emphasized in this ceremony.

6. The Jewish people are separate and distinct from others. People show their values by particular, detailed behaviors. Judaism maintains that human beings show their beliefs and values through specific, day to day actions, which need guidance and evaluation.

7. Both in the introduction to Havdalah and in "Eliyahu HaNavi" traditionally sung before the ceremony, we express our trust in God's power, and hope that peace, symbolized by Shabbat, will soon come to the world.

"Prayer Analysis"

1. Discuss the meaning of the phrase: "In joy you draw water from the fountains of salvation."

2. What do you do because you are Jewish, separating you from non-Jews? Consider all areas, including your food, clothes, name, education, leisure activities.

CHAPTER 8
THE MAHZOR AND HIGH HOLIDAY LITURGY
Introduction

When the Siddur became too big to contain the hundreds of piyyutim (creative poems) written by many worshippers over the centuries, the early Siddur calligraphers found it more convenient to print the prayers for the High Holidays in a separate special edition. We have already seen that from the second century on, even on Shabbat and weekdays, different liturgical poems were included to vary and enrich the service.

In the sixth century, the famous poet Yannai wrote many poems still included in the High Holiday Maḥzor (Prayer Cycle). At a time when talmudic study was forbidden, he added much teaching and study material through his poetry. The Payyetan Elazar ben Jacob Kallir also wrote many poems which were included in the rituals of Rumanian, Italian, and Ashkenazic Jewry. Other great poets later influenced by him (in the tenth century) were Meshullam ben Kalonymous, Yekutiel ben Moses, and Simeon ben Isaac ben Abun. In the following two centuries Hebrew poetry was profoundly influenced by Arabic poetry and took many of its forms, meters, and structure. Solomon ibn Gabirol, Moses ibn Ezra, Yehudah HaLevi, and Abraham ibn Ezra were all influenced by Arabic poetry in Spain. Continuing into the seventeenth century, piyyutim, *selihot* (penitential prayers) *kinot* (lamentations) and *hoshanot* (prayers for salvation) were composed and incorporated into the liturgy. The Maḥzor became filled with these creations, placed in the appropriate spots within the regular holiday prayer structures. Though many poems were carried along by force of tradition and became obscure in their meaning, others were beloved and became famous.

Look at the diagrams at the beginning of Section II once again to see the overall structures of Shabbat or Holiday prayer. Basically, the structure of the High Holiday t'fillot is the same as that for Shabbat and Holidays, with the addition of large numbers of piyyutim, the three-section Musaf Amidah on Rosh HaShannah, and Kol Nidray and Ne'ilah services on Yom Kippur. If you understand the basic structures we've examined so far, the organization of Mahzor should no longer be a mystery to you. By the way, the words לְעֵלָּא לְעֵלָּא , used in this volume's title, come from the Ashkenazic High Holiday Kaddish.[17]

Now we shall study some highlights of the High Holiday liturgy. They are offered merely as a brief introduction to some of the additions which make the High Holidays so special.

SOUNDING THE SHOFAR תְּקִיעַת שׁוֹפָר

BACKGROUND:

Sounding the shofar was originally mandated for all holidays and Rosh Hodesh while sacrifices were still in effect. However, after the destruction of the Temple, the Shofar was sounded only for the High Holidays and each morning (except Shabbat) in the month of Elul, as preparation for the High Holiday season. Usually a ram's horn is used as a reminder of the ram sacrificed in place of Isaac.

In the Ashkenazic ritual, Psalm 47 precedes the Shofar blowing. (It contains the word "Elohim" seven times and is recited seven times in some communities. Remember, seven is a mystical number: seven days of the week; seven weeks between Pesah and Shavuot; seven firmaments of heaven.) Traditionally there are two series of blowing the Shofar. The first set is sounded after the Torah reading; the second is part of the Musaf Amidah. Each consists of combinations of three "notes":

    a. *Teki'ah* -- a long sound.
    b. *Sh'evarim* -- three broken notes.
    c. *Teru'ah* -- nine short staccato notes.

CONCEPTS:

1. We proclaim the kingship of God.

2. The shofar motivates people to repent--to wake them up to critical introspection.

3. It reminds people of the revelation at Sinai, continued through subsequent Jewish history.

4. The shofar reminds us of Abaraham's willingness to sacrifice Isaac, out of his faith in God.

5. It reminds us of the Day of Judgment.

6. It reminds us of the messianic age.

"Prayer Analysis"

Write your own meditation before hearing (or sounding) the Shofar. Check it against the creative prayer guidelines in Section I.

ROSH HASHANAH MUSAF AMIDAH מוּסָף לְרֹאשׁ הַשָּׁנָה

BACKGROUND:

The Musaf (Additional) Amidah for Rosh HaShanah has a total of nine b'rachot instead of seven, usually recited on Festivals. The first three and last three are as usual. The middle three blessings are

1. *Malchuyot* (Kingship verses), including the K'dushat HaYom blessing, declaring the special nature of the day;

2. *Zichronot* (Remembrance verses);

3. *Shofarot* (Shofar or proclamation verses):

Each of the three sections has ten biblical verses: three from Torah (*Ḥumash*); three from *K'tuvim* (writings, specifically from Psalms); three from *N'vi'im* (Prophets); and one more from Torah. Each section has an introduction and conclusion, followed by blasts of the Shofar. The source of the well-known prayer concluding every service, Alaynu, is as an introduction to the Malchuyot section.

The general structure of this Amidah has its source as far back as the Mishnah *(Rosh HaShanah 4:5)*.

CONCEPTS:

1. Malchuyot proclaims the absolute kingship and majesty of the King of kings, before whom we stand in judgment. The entire liturgy of the High holidays is steeped in this royal imagery.

2. The Zichronot section remembers that God is just, rewarding and punishing human beings according to their deeds.

3. The Shofarot passages recall the revelation at Sinai and look to the coming of the Messiah. Our hopes of being judged worthy of the world to come lie in our observance of the Torah.

"Prayer Analysis"

1. Check each of the sources used in the Rosh HaShanah Amidah. Look up their original context in the Tanach to see why they were chosen.

2. Compare the Musaf service as it appears in the Rabbinical Assembly *Maḥzor for Rosh HaShanah and Yom Kippur* with older editions of the Maḥzor. See what has been added, and why.

U'N'TANEH TOKEF וּנְתַנֶּה תֹּקֶף

BACKGROUND:

This meditation was apparently written in the eleventh century. It describes God's judgment of every person, declaring that "some will live and some will die." After a detailed list of the life and death decrees, the poem affirms that "t'shuvah (repentance), t'fillah (prayer), and tzedakah (righteousness) will avert the severity of the decree."

CONCEPTS:

1. God is shepherd of His flock, Israel. He tends it, caring for and supporting it, rebuking and punishing when necessary.

2. We recount the uncertainties and travails of life as a way of sensitizing ourselves to use time wisely.

3. T'shuvah--true repentence; t'fillah--praying with kavanah; tzedakah--acts of righeousness on behalf of others, can enrich and ennoble our lives so as to save us from pain, humiliation, and anguish.

EXERCISE 1

Rosh HaShanah and Yom Kippur are traditionally a time of self-evaluation. We look at our lives and see what we are doing with them, and what we are becoming. In U'n'taneh Tokef, the poet lists many possibilities which might occur to individuals during the next year. Try the following exercise for a perspective on the years you have lived up to now and where you hope things will go in the future.

What have you done on the eve of Rosh HaShanah during the past years of your life? Briefly describe as many pre-holiday experiences as you can remember, in chronological order. What does this chronology say about you now and in the past, and what does it show about your developing values?

EXERCISE 2

On Rosh HaShanah and Yom Kippur the theme of God's sovereignty is combined with God as Father. God is at once our leader and our teacher. Whom do we set up in our own lives as our leaders and teachers? To whom do you look for direction, influencing your behavior, and a model on whom you will base some of your actions?

Who have been your important teachers--both in school, and out, young or old? In other words, who taught you that what you regarded, then or now, as valuable lessons in your life? List their names, and briefly describe what influence they had on your life or what they taught you, or what in them you seek to evaluate.

TASHLICH תַּשְׁלִיךְ

BACKGROUND:

Tashlich, originating in the Middle Ages, is a ceremony of repentance and symbolic self-purification. On the afternoon of the first day of Rosh HaShanah (the second day, if the first is Shabbat), worshippers gather at a body of running water. They recite several biblical verses including Micah 7:19, which declares God's commitment to "cast all their sins into the depths of the sea." At that time the participants toss crumbs from their pockets into the water as a *symbolic* way of casting away sins of the past year.

CONCEPTS:

1. We symbolize self-purification, new beginnings and a yearly rebirth of the spirit.

2. Man's link with nature is recalled by the ritual.

3. We show communal support for those admitting transgressions, and the need to support one another in the process of repentance.

4. There is an optimistic hope that God does forgive, and we can begin anew.

EXERCISE 1

This custom is being increasingly observed. Discuss with your rabbi the possibility of observing it as a group. Try to find a lake or creek in walking distance of the synagogue. Return to the synagogue after Tashlich for some singing and dancing before the Ma'ariv service for the second night of Rosh HaShanah.

KOL NIDRAY (EREV YOM KIPPUR) כָּל נִדְרֵי

BACKGROUND:

The custom of vowing to do things or not to do them is very old, and the Bible and Talmud reflect that Jews did not take vows lightly. We are obliged to keep our vows, and only if circumstances prevented their fulfillment could they be renounced. Kol Nidray was designed as an absolution only of unkept vows made to God. On Yom Kippur we can ask forgiveness only for wrongs against God; wrongs against other human beings must be rectified with them.

There was some debate in our tradition whether reciting Kol Nidray was a good idea or whether it would minimize the value of one's promises. Popular opinion prevailed, and it was retained. Although the "prayer" already existed in Rav Amram's time, it was changed to the future tense by Rabbi Jacob Tam in the Middle Ages; our version is a strange mixture of past and future. A passage attributed to Rabbi Meir of Rothenberg, introducing Kol Nidray, asks that we be permitted to worship with "sinners." It supposedly referred to Marrano Jews forced to convert to Christianity during the Spanish Inquisition. They would secretly gather in cellars to recite Kol Nidray, as a way of renouncing their vows to the Church.

An Ashkenazic Ḥazzan, in the year 1500, sympathizing with the plight of his fellow Jews in Spain, probably composed the haunting melody we still sing today. Traditionally, Kol Nidray is repeated three times (since it is a legal formula), from soft to loud. The Torah scrolls are taken from the Ark making the proceeding very dramatic and moving.

CONCEPTS:

1. He who truly wishes to repent is always accepted by the people of Israel.

2. Our words are sacred and should be taken seriously.

3. We ask to be released from vows to God unkept due to circumstances beyond our control, so we can begin the process of true repentance, culminating on Yom Kippur.

4. This is a legal formula and, therefore, since Jewish courts do not transact business on holidays, the ceremony takes place before the onset of night and the Yom Kippur holiday.

"Prayer Analysis"

1. List some of the promises, vows, and commitments you make to yourself, God, family, and friends. Do you keep them? Take them seriously? Does your word mean something to people?

2. Study about the Marranos and write a page from a diary about "your" experience in a cellar on Yom Kippur night. Use this in your service next Erev Yom Kippur.

THE "CONFESSIONAL." ASHAMNU; AL ḤAYT   וִדּוּי אָשַׁמְנוּ עַל חֵטְא

BACKGROUND:

Said numerous times on Yom Kippur, the confessional developed over many centuries. The alphabetic acrostic, Ashamnu, is found in Rav Amram's Siddur. The longer confessional, Al Ḥayt, is an acrostic which developed after the Talmud. In our version there are two lines for each Hebrew letter, preceded by the words Al Ḥayt, "For the sin..." After every few verses we recite a refrain, "For all these ... forgive us." It is a tradition to beat the breast with the right hand upon reciting each transgression in both of the confessionals. We recite the Viddui publicly as a way of sharing mutual responsibility for human actions; as a way of comforting one another, none of us being free from sin; and as a way of giving us the moral support to change and grow.

CONCEPTS:

1. The passage reflects communal responsibility, support, and nurturing.

2. The word חֵטְא , or "sin," connotes having "missed the mark." We can, and should, try to aim at the target of the good life, again and again.

3. The sins enumerated do not deal with ritual transgressions, but rather with the denial of God in our midst, and interpersonal relations.

4. Wrongs committed with the tongue are stressed.

5. Wrongs stemming from pride, arrogance, and contempt of others are emphasized.

EXERCISE 1

Ashamnu lists a large number of transgressions which seem to cover the range of possible wrongdoings by all people. Not all of us are guilty of all of the sins, but since they are recited in community, we help each other have the courage to face our misdoings. To help appreciate this self-analysis, look at the following life inventory list as a way of personalizing Ashamnu.

1. What was the happiest year or period of your life?

2. What things do you do well?

3. Tell about a turning point in your life.

4. What has been the lowest point in your life?

5. Was there an event in which you demonstrated great courage?

6. Was there a time of heavy grief? More than one?

7. Tell about some things you do poorly, which you have to continue doing anyway.

8. What are some things you would like to stop doing?

9. What are some things you would really like to do better?

10. Tell about some peak experiences you have had.

11. Tell about some peak experiences you would like to have.

12. Are there some values you are struggling to establish?

13. Tell about one missed opportunity in your life.

14. What are some things you want to start doing now, right at this point in your life?

EXERCISE 2

Make a contract with yourself about some change you would like to make in your life. It can involve starting something new, changing something old, adding something Jewish or relating differently to people. Be very specific about exactly what you plan to do, e.g., you will make Kiddush on Friday night or you will say "hello" first to friends when you meet them on the street. List some target dates in which you hope to achieve certain of your goals. Look at this sheet on those dates to see if you have lived up to your self-contract.

EXERCISE 3

Many verses in the Al Ḥayt listing refer to responsibilities we have towards others and as youth, in particular, towards adults. Often there is great tension between what youth wishes and what adults demand. Consider the following questions, as you think about Al Ḥayt:

What bothers you most about adults? Why?

When you become an adult how do you want to be similar to, or different from, adults you know?

If you were an adult looking at you, a teenager, what would your reaction to "you" be?

How might "you" as an adult try to change or influence "you" a teenager?

NE'ILAH; CLOSING SERVICE FOR YOM KIPPUR נְעִילָה

BACKGROUND:

The central image of Ne'ilah (literally, "locking") is the closing of the gates of heaven at the end of the Day of Judgment. (Historically, this may have referred to locking the Temple gates at the end of the day, as well.) For the previous ten days, yes, even the last forty days, Jews have stood in fervent prayer, and now, one last pleading time, standing before God before He symbolically seals the books of life and death. We ask Him to accept our prayer. In this final hour, the congregation--having prayed and fasted for more than twenty-four hours--finds renewed strength and determination and remains standing for much of the service.

The service begins much like a Shabbat Minhah service, with Ashray and "A redeemer shall come to Zion." It continues with an abridged Amidah, in which the language "inscribe us" in the book of life is changed to "seal us." Among meditations and poems, we read a beautiful piyyut, "Open the gate to us at this time of the closing." The payyetan begs that our prayers be acceptable, and forgiveness be granted. Only a Jew who has spent much of the entire day of Yom Kippur in fasting and prayer can fully appreciate the spiritual strength of this moment.

CONCEPTS:

1. Even at the very moment of decision, God is subject to our influence; He cares for His people and wants to forgive them.

2. The sense of awe and majesty associated with the High Holidays is climaxed in the imagery surrounding the final moments of judgment.

3. Everything the congregation has prayed and atoned for is summarized in the closing lines: The first line of the Shema is said once; "Blessed is the name of his Glorious Kingdom" is said three times; "Adonai is God" is said seven times, followed by *teki'ah g'dolah*, a very long shofar blast.

4. The day of fasting, self-denial, and self-analysis ends in joy and exaltation that life can be, and is, renewed.

"Prayer Analysis"

1. Why is it probable that the profound emotional high experienced at Ne'ilah only occurs for one who has been in the synagogue most of Yom Kippur?

2. Make a list of the poetic images in the Ne'ilah service, such as the "open gates," and see how they relate to the other High Holiday themes.

3. Write your own final prayer for the end of the High Holiday Season. Recite it at the end of next Yom Kippur.

CHAPTER 9
SPECIAL PRAYERS

We shall examine a few "special" prayers in this Chapter. As in all parts of Section III, many more prayers can be studied and added to this looseleaf source book.

BEDTIME SHEMA קְרִיאַת שְׁמַע עַל הַמִּטָּה

BACKGROUND:

At night, as in the morning, we relate to our personal physical and mental needs. The b'rachah "...who closes my eyes in sleep" is recited at night (cited in *B'rachot 60b*) and is parallel to the morning b'rachah... "who removes sleep from my eyes." It is also written in the first person singular. We recite the bedtime Shema in fulfillment of the commandment "When you lie down and when you rise up."

This nighttime ritual includes passages (Psalms 91:3) with the theme of God's protecting us from evil and hurt. Other passages from the evening service are recited without their blessings, followed by selections called "Verses of Divine Mercy." The bedtime prayer concludes with Psalm 128 (which looks to God's protection and remembers Jerusalem) and Adon Olam.

CONCEPTS:

1. Sleep is a great benefit to our physical and psychological well-being, and should not be taken for granted.

2. Night can be a threatening time; pain is more easily sensed. We turn to God for solace and support.

3. In the last act of the day we set forth what we ultimately believe, identifying who we are, and to Whom we belong.

4. Sleep is the closest we come in life to death, and so it is natural to pray for renewed life in the morning.

"Prayer Analysis"

1. Compare your childhood prayers with *Kriyat Shema Al HaMitah*. What similarities and differences did you find?

2. Have you ever had "sleep paralysis" where you are conscious and awake, but unable to move a muscle because your body was not yet fully awake? How did you feel?

PRAYER FOR A JOURNEY תְּפִלַת הַדֶּרֶךְ

BACKGROUND:

The origin of this beautiful prayer is in the Talmud (*B'rachot 29b*); several biblical verses are also included (Genesis 32:2; 35:5; 48:16; 49:18; Exodus 23:20; Numbers 6:24; Psalms 91 and 121). Today, only the first paragraph is usually recited.

Some alternate versions were discussed by the Rabbis (*Tosefta B'rachot 6:16*):

> Upon entering a town, one recites... "May it by Your will, our Lord my God, that I enter in security." If one entered safely, he said, "I thank You,.O Lord my God, that You have enabled me to enter in safety. May it be Your will that You allow me to leave in safety." After leaving, one was to recite, "I thank You, O Lord my God, that You have led me out safely; may it be Your will that I reach my home destination in peace."

CONCEPTS:

1. Judaism embodies every aspect of life, so even going on a trip is viewed in religious terms.

2. Making a brachah changes the nature of the experience.

3. This prayer voices the normal worries and concerns a person feels when leaving home.

4. Reciting T'fillat HaDerech at the beginning of journey may remind one of the religious obligations and duties which may require advance preparation on the trip, such as kashrut, Shabbat or prayer.

"Prayer Analysis"

1. In our age of fast, high-technology travel do you still feel there is need for a prayer obviously written at a time when travel was more physically and emotionally trying?

2. Explain the reasoning behind the selection of the various biblical verses. You might have to read them in their original context.

PERSONAL PRAYER
A Physician's Prayer תְּפִלַת הָרוֹפֵא

According to tradition, Maimonides (twelfth century) composed the following prayer. He was not only a great Jewish law codifier, but also a renowned physician.

> God on high! Before I begin my holy work--that of healing Your own creatures, I stand and plead before Your throne of glory, that You give me a courageous spirit and much energy to faithfully perform my work. Prevent any desire to acquire fortune or fame to blind my eyes from clear vision; may You enable me to look upon every suffering individual who comes to ask my advice as a human being, regardless of his wealth or poverty, regardless of whether he be friend or foe, a good man or bad. When an individual is in trouble, let me see only the person.
>
> When doctors greater than I wish to teach me wisdom, grant me the will to learn from them, because there is no limit to the study of medicine; but when fools seek to mislead me, save me. Strengthen my love for the spirit of my profession

and let me pay no heed to those who show scorn. Let only truth light my path, and may I never waiver from that truth, lest I bring sadness and disaster upon one of your creatures.

Please, dear merciful and compassionate God, strengthen me and give me courage in both body and mind; implant in me a fulfilled spirit.

"Prayer Analysis"

1. This is just one example of a special prayer. How does it fuse religious beliefs with medical practice?

2. Write a prayer of your own, either a "Student's Prayer," or a prayer relating to an occupation you have or plan to have.

MODERN PRAYERS

In modern times many Jews have felt the need to create new prayers which respond to our particular time and place. Since 1948, for instance, prayers have been written for the State of Israel. We have learned that in our own Movement, new prayers, new translations and interpretations, and new meditations have been included in the liturgy. As just one example from among many, we cite the following prayer,[19] composed by Morris Silverman:

Lord, God of our fathers, as we gather to pay homage to the founders and builders of this, our country, we ask Thy blessing. With courage and vision, they made of these United States a land of freedom and opportunity. For all that they have so firmly established, we render thanks unto Thee. "Our lines are fallen in pleasant places; yea, we have a goodly heritage."

We are grateful for the faith that made fearless, and the courage that kept firm these valiant men and women. Above all, we are grateful that the spirit of Israel's Prophets so lived in their hearts that they knew all men are created equal in Thy sight, by Thee endowed with the imperishable right to life, liberty and the pursuit of happiness.

In tribute to the Founding Fathers of this blessed Republic, may we strive to keep these United States forever righteous and just. May ours be a land where none shall prey upon or exploit his fellowman, where bigotry and violence shall not be tolerated, where poverty shall be abolished, and all men live amicably as brothers.

Vouchsafe unto us, O Lord, wisdom equal to our strength and courage equal to our responsibilities, to the end that our nation may lead the world in the advancement and fulfillment of human welfare.

May all nations become aware of their common unity and all the peoples of the world be united in the bonds of brotherhood before Thee, the Father of all. Amen.

Now that you are completing this initial phase of your study of the Siddur, you are able to apply the guidelines for creative prayer (Section I) and analysis questions (Section III) to prayers in the Siddur and Maḥzor, prayers which have been part of our tradition for centuries and prayers which are added to our tradition today.

We pray that as you learn to interpret these prayers on your own, your love for our precious possessions--the Siddur and our prayer tradition--will grow and enrich your life. We hope that upon completing this source book you will, indeed, have come higher and higher towards making Jewish prayer part of you.

FOOTNOTES

SECTION I

1. E.A. Speiser, "The Stem *PLL* in Hebrew," *Journal of Biblical Literature,* Vol. 82, No. 3 (September, 1963), 301-306.

2. Abraham Joshua Heschel, *Man's Quest for God* (New York: Charles Scribner's Sons, Publishers, 1954), 36-37.

3. Max Wohlberg, "Shiru Lo: Aspects of Congregational Song," *Conservative Judaism,* Vol. XXIII, No. 1 (Fall, 1968), 58.

4. For further explanation about the minyan, see Isaac Klein, *A Guide to Jewish Religious Practice* (New York: The Jewish Theological Seminary of America, 1979), 14-15, 21.

5. Burt Jacobsen, *The Teaching of the Traditional Liturgy* (New York: Melton Research Center, 1971), 48-51, modified.

6. *See Newsweek*, Vol. XCIII, No. 11 (March 12, 1979), on the one hundredth anniversary of Einstein's birth.

7. Abraham Joshua Heschel, *Man Is Not Alone* (New York: Farrar, Straus & Giroux, Inc., 1951), 37.

8. John Ciardi, *How Does A Poem Mean?* (Boston: Houghton Mifflin Company, 1959).

9. *Ibid.,* 669.

10. *Ibid.,* 763-764.

11. See Max Kadushin, *The Rabbinic Mind* (New York: The Jewish Theological Seminary of America, 1952); and *Worship and Ethics* (Northwestern University Press, 1964).

12. Ciardi, *Poem,* 710.

13. The criteria are selected from those suggested by Ciardi.

14. Nahum N. Glatzer, *Franz Rosenzweig: His Life and Thought* (New York: Schocken Books, 1953), 352.

15. Seymour Rosenbloom, *T'fillah: Considerations for Dialogue with Ramah Counselors* (New York: National Ramah Commission, 1972), 13-14.

16. Yosef Heinemann, *T'fillot Yisrael V'toldotayhen* (Jerusalem: The Hebrew University, 1968), 2.

17. Elie Munk, *The World of Prayer,* translated by Henry Biberfeld (New York: Philipp Feldheim Publisher, 1954), Vol. I, 19-20.

18. These objects are described in depth in Klein, *Guide,* 3-9, 51-52.

SECTION II

1. For details, see Evelyn Garfiel, *The Service of the Heart* (Cranbury, New Jersey: Thomas Yoseloff Publisher, 1958), 42.

2. *Sabbath and Festival Prayer Book* (New York: The Rabbinical Assembly and The United Synagogue of America, 1946), vi.

3. Based on Heinemann, *T'fillot,* 4.

4. Based on materials of Leaders Training Fellowship; see bibliography.

5. Cited in *Kallah Readings: Keva and Kavanah in Jewish Prayer* (New York: Leaders Training Fellowship, n.d.), 2.

6. Munk, *Prayer,* I, 108.

7. *Ibid.*, 117.

8. *Ibid.*, 119.

9. From Rosenbloom, *T'fillah: Considerations.*

10. For details, see A.Z. Idelsohn, *Jewish Liturgy and Its Development* (New York: Schocken Books, 1967), 120.

11. Max Arzt, *Justice and Mercy* (New York: The Burning Bush Press, 1963), 72.

12. Based on Heinemann, *T'fillot*, 4.

13. Munk, *Prayer*, I, 152; see Kadushin, *The Rabbinic Mind*, 152-167.

14. This concept was related by me by Professor Aaron Demsky.

15. Translation based on *Sabbath and Festival Prayer Book*, 26.

16. *Ibid.*, ix-x

17. Based on Klein, *Guide*, 35.

SECTION III

1. See *Sabbath and Festival Prayer Book*, x; and Robert Gordis, "A Jewish Prayer Book for the Modern Age," *Conservative Judaism*, Vol. II, No. 1 (October, 1945), 16-17.

2. Idelsohn, *Liturgy*, 83.

3. *Ibid.*, 83-84.

4. Munk, *Prayer*, I, 79.

5. *Ibid.*, 83-84.

6. *Ibid.*, 90.

7. Idelsohn, *Liturgy*, 110.

8. Munk, *Prayer*, I, 192.

9. Idelsohn, *Liturgy*, 74.

10. Abraham Millgram, *Jewish Worship* (Philadelphia: The Jewish Publication Society of America, 1971), 422-423.

11. Idelsohn, *Liturgy*, 74; Munk, *Prayer*, 17.

12. Cited in Idelsohn, *Liturgy*, 134.

13. Munk, *Prayer*, II, 22.

14. Idelsohn, *Liturgy*, 141.

15. *Ibid.*, 230.

16. Munk, *Prayer*, I, 193.

17. It is used all year in the Yemenite ritual.

18. See Herman Kieval, "The Paradox of *Kol Nidre*," Philip Goodman, *The Yom Kippur Anthology* (Philadelphia: The Jewish Publication Society of America, 1971), 84-98.

19. *Sabbath and Festival Prayer Book*, 355.

BIBLIOGRAPHY
FOR FURTHER STUDY AND REFERENCE

ABUDRAHAM, DAVID. *Abudraham HaShalaym* (Hebrew.) Jerusalem: Usha Press, 1963.

ADAR, ZVI. *The Biblical Narrative.* Translated by Misha Louvish. Jerusalem: Publishing Department, Jewish Agency for Israel at Goldberg's Press, 1959.

_____ *Humanistic Values in the Bible.* Translated by Mrs. Victor Tcherikover. New Yor' Reconstructionist Press, 1967.

AGNON, S.Y. *Days of Awe.* New York: Schocken Books, 1965.

ARIAN, PHILIP and EISENBERG, AZRIEL. *The Story of the Prayer Book.* Hartford: Pray Book Press, 1968.

ARIEL, Z., ed. *Sefer HeḤag V'HaMoed* (Hebrew, "The Book of Holidays and Festivals.") Tel Aviv Am Oved, 1964.

ARZT, MAX. *Justice and Mercy.* New York: The Burning Bush Press, 1963.

BAMBERGER, DAVID. *A Functional Teacher's Guide for "When a Jew Prays."* New York· Behrman House, Inc., 1973.

BIRNBAUM, PHILIP. *Daily Prayer Book.* New York: Hebrew Publishing Co., 1949.

_____ *High Holy Day Prayer Book.* New York: Hebrew Publishing Co., 1951.

_____ *A Book of Jewish Concepts.* New York: Hebrew Publishing Co., 1964.

BROWN, STEVEN M. *Media, Materials and Instruction in Jewish Religious Education.* Unpublished Doctoral dissertation, Teachers College, Columbia University, New York, 1975.

BRUNER, JEROME. *The Process of Education.* Cambridge, Mass.: Harvard University Press, 1960.

BUBER, MARTIN. *Darcho Shel Mikra, Iyyunim B'dfusay Signon BaTanach.* (Hebrew, "The Biblical Way: Studies in Biblical Style.") Jerusalem: Bialik Institute, 1964.

CHANOVER, HYMAN. *Teaching the Haggadah.* New York, Jewish Education Press, 1955.

CIARDI, JOHN. *How Does a Poem Mean?* Boston: Houghton Mifflin Co., 1959.

COHEN, GERSON D. "The Talmudic Age." *Great Ages and Ideas of the Jewish People.* Edited by Leo Schwartz. New York: The Modern Library, 1956.

DECECCO, JOHN R. *Educational Technology: Reading in Programmed Instruction.* New York: Holt, Rinehart and Winston, 1964.

DRESNER, SAMUEL and SIEGEL, SEYMOUR. *The Jewish Dietary Laws.* New York: Burning Bush Press, 1959.

EISENBERG, YEHUDAH. *Iyyun T'fillah* (Hebrew). New York: Jewish Education Press, 1975.

——— *A Curriculum in Tefillah for Yeshiva Day School.* New York: Torah Education Department, World Zionist Organization, 1976.

EISENSTEIN, JUDITH KAPLAN. *Heritage of Music.* New York: Union of American Hebrew Congregations, 1972.

ELKINS, DOV PERETZ. *Clarifying Jewish Values.* Bala Cynwyd, Pa.: Growth Associates, 1976.

EPSTEIN, BARUKH HALEVI. *Baruch Sheamar* (Hebrew.) Tel Aviv: Am Olam Press, 1968.

FIELDS, HARVEY J. *Bechol Levavcha: With All Your Heart.* New York: Union of American Hebrew Congregations, 1976.

FINKELSTEIN, LOUIS ed. *The Jews.* Philadelphia: The Jewish Publication Society of America, 1949.

GARFIEL, EVELYN. *The Service of the Heart.* New York: The Burning Bush Press, 1958.

GASTER, THEODOR H. *Festivals of the Jewish Year.* New York: William Sloane Associates, 1952.

GERSH, HARRY. *When A Jew Celebrates.* New York: Behrman House, 1971.

GLATZER, NAHUM N. *Franz Rosenzweig: His Life and Thought.* New York: Schocken Books, Inc., 1953.

GOMBRICH, E.H. "Visual Metaphors of Value in Art." *Symbols and Values: An Initial Study.* Edited by Lyman Bysom, et. al. New York: Harper Bros., 1954.

GORDIS, ROBERT. *The Ladder of Prayer.* New York: National Academy for Adult Jewish Studies, United Synagogue of America.

GREENBERG, SIMON. *The Jewish Prayer Book: Its Ideals and Values.* New York: National Academy for Adult Jewish Studies, United Synagogue of America, 1942.

——— *Foundations of a Faith.* New York: The Burning Bush Press, 1967.

HERTZ, JOSEPH H. *The Authorized Daily Prayer Book.* New York: Bloch Publishing Co., 1948.

HESCHEL, ABRAHAM JOSHUA. *God in Search of Man.* New York: Farrar, Straus, and Co., Inc., 1955.

——— *Man Is Not Alone.* New York: Harper & Row, 1951.

——— *The Sabbath.* New York: Farrar, Straus, and Young, 1951.

——— *Man's Quest for God.* New York: Charles Scribner's Sons, 1954.

HEINEMANN, YOSEF. *T'fillot Yisrael V'toldotayhen: Leket M'korot* (Hebrew.) Jerusalem: The Hebrew University, 1968.

——— *HaT'fillah Beet'kufat HaTanna'im V'ha'Amora'im* (Hebrew.) Jerusalem: Hebrew University, The Magnes Press, 1964.

HEINEMANN, JOSEPH and PETUCHOWSKI, JAKOB. *Jewish Literature of the Synagogue.* New York: Behrman House, Inc., 1975.

HOWE, LELAND W. and HOWE, MARY M. *Personalizing Education: Values Clarification and Beyond.* New York: Hart Publishing Co., 1975.

IDELSOHN, ABRAHAM Z. *Jewish Liturgy and its Development.* New York: Schocken Books, 1967.

JACOBSON, BURT. *The Teaching of the Traditional Liturgy.* New York: Melton Research Center, 1971.

JAMES, WILLIAM. *The Varieties of Religious Experience.* New York: Longmans, Green and Co., 1902.

KAPLAN, MORDECAI M. *Judaism as a Civilization.* New York: Reconstructionist Press, 1957.

_____ *The Meaning of God in Modern Jewish Religion.* New York: Reconstructionist Press, 1962.

KADUSHIN, MAX. *The Rabbinic Mind.* New York: The Jewish Theological Seminary of America, 1952.

_____ *Worship and Ethics.* Chicago: Northwestern University Press, 1964.

KAUFMANN, YEHEZKEL. *The Religion of Israel.* Translated and abridged by Moshe Greenberg. Chicago: The University of Chicago Press, 1960.

KITOV, ELIYAHU. *The Book of Our Heritage.* Translated by Nathan Bulman. New York: Philipp Feldheim Publishers, 1970.

_____ *The Jew and his Home.* 5th ed. Translated by Nathan Bulman. New York: Shengold Publishers, 1963.

KLEIN, ISAAC, *A Guide to Jewish Religious Practice.* New York: The Jewish Theological Seminary of America, 1979.

KLEIN, MAX D., editor and translator, *Seder Avodah.* Philadelphia: 1951.

LEADERS TRAINING FELLOWSHIP OF THE JEWISH THEOLOGICAL SEMINARY OF AMERICA, New York:

An Approach to Tefillah	The B'rakhah
B'rakhot, Building Blocks of Jewish Prayer	The Rabbi Chaim Potok "Ethics" Series
Creation-Revelation-Redemption	Ultimate Concern: Imitatio Dei
Keva and Kavana in Jewish Prayer	What Happens When You Die?
Ritual	What Makes Shabbat "Shabbat"?

LEVINSKY, YOM TOV. *Sefer HaMo'adim.* (Hebrew, "The Festivals Book.") Tel Aviv: Dvir Co., Ltd., 1955.

MAIMONIDES. *Mishnah Torah.*

MARCUS, AUDREY FRIEDMAN, ed. *A Family Unit on Bar and Bat Mitzvah.* (Mini-Course.) Denver: Alternatives in Religious Education, Inc. 1975.

————, ed. *The Jewish Calendar.* (Mini-Course.) Denver: Alternatives in Religious Education, Inc. 1975.

MARCUS, AUDREY FRIEDMAN; BISSELL, SHERRY; and LIPSCHUTZ, KAREN S. *Death, Burial and Mourning in the Jewish Tradition.* Denver: Alternatives in Religious Education, Inc., 1976.

MARKLE, SUSAN MEYER. *Good Frames and Bad: A Grammar of Frame Writing.* 2nd Ed. New York: John Wiley & Sons, Inc., (1964), 1969.

MILLGRAM, ABRAHAM. *Jewish Worship.* Philadelphia: The Jewish Publication Society of America, 1971.

MOSKOWITZ, GERTRUDE. *Caring and Sharing in the Foreign Language Class: A Source Book on Humanistic Techniques.* Rowley, Mass.: Newbury House Publishing Co., 1977.

ROSELL, SEYMOUR. *When A Jew Prays.* New York: Behrman House, Inc., 1973.

ROSENBAUM, SAMUEL. *To Live as a Jew.* Edited by Abraham Karp. New York: Ktav Publishing Co., 1969.

————— *A Guide to Haftarah Chanting.* New York: Ktav Publishing Co., 1973.

ROSENBLOOM, SEYMOUR. *T'fillah: Considerations for Dialogue with Ramah Counselors.* New York: National Ramah Commission, 1972.

ROTHSCHILD, FRITZ A. *Between God and Man.* New York: The Free Press, 1965.

————— *The Shema.* New York; The Burning Bush Press, 1964.

SARNA, NAHUM M. *Understanding Genesis.* New York: Jewish Theological Seminary of America, 1966.

SCHAUSS, HAYYIM. *The Lifetime of a Jew.* New York: Union of American Hebrew Congregations, 1950.

SCHWAB, JOSEPH J. "The Religiously Oriented School in the United States: A Memorandum." *Conservative Judaism*, VIII. No. 3.

SEGAL, M.D. *Mavo LaMikra.* (Hebrew, "Introduction to the Bible.") Jerusalem: Kiryat Sefer, Ltd. 1967.

SIEGEL, SEYMOUR. *A Conceptual Teacher's Guide to "When a Jew Prays."* New York: Behrman House, Inc. 1973.

SIEGEL, RICHARD; STRASSFELD, MICHAEL; and STRASSFELD, SHARON. *The Jewish Catalog.* (Vol. I.) Philadelphia: The Jewish Publication Society of America, 1974.

SILVERMAN, ISRAEL. *Birkat HaMazon with Introduction and Commentary.* New York: National Youth Commission, United Synagogue of America, 1973.

SIMON, SIDNEY B.; HOWE, LELAND W.; and KIRSCHENBAUM, HOWARD. *Values Clarification.* New York: Hart Publishing Co., 1972.

SPIRO, PINCHAS. *Haftarah Chanting.* New York: Jewish Education Press, 1964.

STEINBERG, MILTON. *Basic Judaism.* New York: Harcourt Brace and World, Inc., 1947.

STERN, JAY. ed., *A Curriculum for the Afternoon Jewish School.* New York: United Synagogue Commission on Jewish Education, 1978.

STRASSFELD, MICHAEL, and STRASSFELD, SHARON. *The Jewish Catalog, Vol. 2.* Philadelphia: The Jewish Publication Society of America, 1976.

STRAUSS, ARYEH. *B'Darchey Hasifrut.* ("In the Paths of Literature.") Jerusalem: Mosad Bialik, 1965.

VANSTEIN, YAKOV. *The Cycle of the Jewish Year.* Jerusalem: The World Zionist Organization, 1953.

WACHS, SAUL P. "Discovering the Siddur: Overview of the Literature." *The Synagogue School,* XXXIII, No. 3-4.

———— "A Review of Materials for the Teaching of Prayer and the Siddur." *The Synagogue School,* XXXIV, No. 1-2.

———— *"An Application of Inquiry - Teaching to the Seedur."* Unpublished Doctoral dissertation, The Ohio State University, 1970.

WASSERMAN, HOWARD; KING, DIANE; CHARRY, ELLEN Z.; and RUDERMAN, JEROME. *The Board of Jewish Education Idea Cookbook.* Philadelphia: United Synagogue of America, Philadelphia Branch, Division of Community Services, Gratz College, 1976.

WAXMAN, MORDECAI, ed. *Tradition and Change.* New York: The Burning Bush Press, 1958.

WIESS, MEIR. *HaMikra Kid'muto.* (Hebrew, "The Bible and Modern Literary Theory.") Jerusalem: Bialik Institute, 1967.

YAKOBSON, ISSACHAR. *Netiv Binah* (Hebrew.) Tel Aviv: Sinai Publishing Co., 1964, 1968, 1973.

ABOUT THE AUTHOR.

STEVEN M. BROWN is currently Director of Religious Education at Congregation Adath Jeshurun, Elkins Park, Pennsylvania and Visiting Lecturer in Education at Gratz College, Philadelphia. He is a member of the Jewish Educators Assembly, the Education Committee of the Solomon Schechter Day Schools, and many other educational boards and associations.

Dr. Brown received his B.A. and B.H.L. from the Combined Program of the Jewish Theological Seminary of America and Columbia College; his M.A. from Teachers College, Columbia University; and his Ed.D. in Instructional Materials and Curriculum Development from Teachers College, Columbia University in 1975. In addition to his academic credentials, the author has vast experience in Jewish youth work and education. He has served as National Director of Leaders Training Fellowship, Division Head and Teacher at Camp Ramah, and Principal of the Central Hebrew High School, Oceanside, New York.

Steven Brown and his wife Michele (Leimberg) have one child, Dory Adam. Dr. Brown has long been active in youth activities of the Conservative Movement.

NOTES:

NOTES: